***Godfolks*MediaGroup.com**

## CONTENTS

Dedication, *7*

Acknowledgments, *8*

### Part One
1. Denisha is Way Too Trusting, *11*
2. Hope, *24*
3. Lisa Needs to Edit Her Mouth, *49*
4. Billy Helps Cathy, *77*
5. Denisha is Framed, *96*
6. Lisa and Lucille Confront Cathy, *114*

### Part Two
7. Denisha Flees, *127*
8. Roy Counsels, *133*
9. Hope Arrives, *158*
10. Everyone Meets at Faith & Fitzroy's, *174*
11. Walking While Black, *200*
12. Hawaii Ain't the Virgin Islands, *207*

### Part Three
13. A Celebration For Hope, *227*
14. Kamari Won't Go Into The House, *241*
15. Faith Explains, *264*

### Part Four
16. Dreams Do Come True, *279*
17. Who Said It Can't Be Done? *316*
18. Dot's Family, *328*
19. Life Has Its Challenges, *347*
20. Healing, *377*
21. Closing Ceremony Hits A Snag, *389*
22. It's Hard Saying Good-Bye, *423*

ALSO BY AISHA BANKS

**Novels**
*Under Caribbean Skies*

*Moonlight Over Caribbean Skies*

**Screenplays**
*Under Caribbean Skies*

**Teleplays**
*#Forever Family*

**Film Shorts**
*A Career, Not a Job*

*Cry Blood, South Africa*

**Stage Plays**
*Family Affair*

*Herod is After Your Child*

*Just Let Me Live Before I Die*

*The Office*

# *Wings Over the Virgin Islands*

A Novel

by

Aisha Banks

Copyright© 2016 by Aisha Banks

All rights reserved. No part of this book shall be reproduced or transmitted in any form or by any means, electronic, mechanical, magnetic, photographic including photocopying, recording or by any information storage and retrieval system, without prior written permission of the publisher. No patent liability is assumed with respect to the use of the information contained herein. Although every precaution has been taken in the preparation of this book, the publisher and author assume no responsibility for errors or omissions. Neither is any responsibility assumed for damages resulting from the use of the information contained herein.

This is a work of fiction. Names, characters, places, and incidents are either the product of the author's imagination or are used fictitiously. Any resemblance to actual events or locales or persons, living or dead is coincidental.

᪣

# DEDICATON

This book is dedicated to the memory of
two important women in my life:
my mother, Willi Lou Bradley Cheatham,
who gave me wings to fly;
and my mother-in-law, Vivian Elmolene Simpson Banks,
who modeled the quiet dignity of a godly woman.

☙

## ACKNOWLEDGMENTS

I am eternally grateful to my Lord and Savior, Jesus Christ who is the strength of my life, the author of my faith, and the center of my joy. Thanks to my readers whose encouragement continues to inspire me. Finally, thanks to my husband, John, for his partnership in making this book a reality.

# PART ONE

# Chapter 1
## Denisha Is Way Too Trusting

Denisha Liburd, receptionist at the St. Thomas Police Department, is on the phone, talking to her best friend, Camille. Denisha's weave repeatedly falls into her face. With her extremely long fake fingernails, she pushes it back.

"Me ain't no puppy! How him tink he gon pat me on de head and tell me to stay like a friggin' dog while him go out and do all he business and den come home! No sa, me ain't taking dat no more. Yeah, he say him gon take me ta St. Lucia ta meet he family, but him been saying dat for two years now. I tired, girl! Me can't take it no more, yah 'ear! Da man got ta go soon as him pay me back me money I give he fa he mudder surgery."

Detective Fitzroy Brown enters the police station and notices Denisha on the phone. He stops to pick up his messages from his mailbox on the wall while zeroing in on Denisha's conversation. He confirms it's a personal conversation.

Denisha waves at him. Fitzroy gives her a stare that says "get off the phone now!"

"Camille, dis man standing 'ere all in me conversation. Me gon have to get off de phone. Me go to lunch in ten minutes. Nah, me ain't drivin'. De man take me car last night, and me ain't see he since. For true! Meet me by de Green House in fifteen minutes. One Love."

She hangs up the phone and glares at Fitzroy. "Wa you all in me conversation fa, Detective Brown?"

"Me in your conversation? You better be concerned with answering that telephone and leaving all the drama in your life for the *Jerry Springer* show!" Fitzroy says as he reads a few of his messages. "Denisha, who is Hope? You didn't get her last name?"

"The woman call an' say she want ta get in touch wit' your wife. She say she coming ta St. Thomas. Me tink she say she ha sister." Denisha busies herself with brushing her hair and getting ready to meet her friend for lunch.

"My wife is an only child, and please don't comb your hair at your desk. You know that hair sheds all over the office," Fitzroy says.

"Dis 'ere is one hundred percent Philippine hair; me pay tree hundred dollars for it!"

"And why do you think I need to know that?" Fitzroy asks sarcastically.

"Maybe you might want to get some of dis 'ere hair fa Mrs. Faith?"

"No! Mrs. Brown has all the hair she needs. Now what about this message? My wife doesn't have any sisters."

"Well, den maybe she ha cuzzin! You can call she fa youself and find out wa family she is ta Mrs. Faith. In me mind, I hear the gil say she ha sister." Denisha stands firm with her statement.

"I would call her back, but you only wrote down six numbers and no area code," Fitzroy points out.

"Lord Jesus." Denisha looks at the message Fitzroy hands her. "Well sa! You does know de area code for de state Mrs. Faith from? Den put dat in front of de number den fa the missing last number try all de numbers on de phone pad starting wit one through zero, and you gon get de gil on de phone." Denisha picks up her purse to leave for lunch.

Fitzroy stops her. "And why would I want to do that? You're the one who messed up the number; you fix it! Start out by looking online and finding out the area codes for Atlanta, Georgia. There are several. Go from there. When I come out of my meeting, I'll be expecting a proper message with the complete and correct phone number." Fitzroy turns to leave and catch the elevator.

"How me gon meet Camille fa lunch and do dat, too?"

Fitzroy ignores her, shakes his head and steps onto the elevator.

In a small conference room inside police headquarters, fifteen police officers are sandwiched into the room. Half the officers are seated at the table and the other half slouch around the wall or sit on the window ledge. The chief of police, Hubert Leonard, age fifty-five, handsome and graying at the temples, is sitting at the head of the table. The air conditioning is not working, and everyone is sweating like pigs.

"Man, open de window! It blazin' hot in 'ere!" one of the officers screams.

"We gon make dis meetin' quick. Now I need all you attention, 'cause dis 'ere is some serious business. De United States Government is pissed dat we ain't solving dees crimes more quickly. The people dem does say we loosing too much money because of dis. The tourist dem scared to come to we island because of de crimes," the chief explains.

A smart-mouth officer speaks out. "Den let dem go somewhere else. Dey can take dem Yankee backsides to St. Martin and get robbed! Dem boys der got bigger guns!"

Roaring laughter fills the room from the other officers except Fitzroy, who shakes his head in disbelief.

The chief is angry and yells, "You does tink dat shit funny? Let me see how funny you does tink dis is when you ain't got no job! Detective Fitzroy 'ere has been appointed to help solve dees murders, and the governor has given dis man authority ta get rid of all of you who ain't doing nut-ting to help wit de crime."

A dead silence falls across the room.

"Wat, ain't nobody got jokes now?" The chief glares at each of his offices in turn with disgust as if daring them to respond.

Fitzroy cuts in and says, "What I need from all of you is to be my ears and eyes these next few months as me and my team of agents aggressively do everything in our power to eradicate the crime that's suffocating our island."

A beautiful Spanish police officer, Olga Hernandez, speaks out. "You sure you need our help? I hear you're the man. You got mirrors in de back of ya head; dey does say your ears can hear a pin drop under de water on de bottom of de sea. You're the real Superman!"

Fitzroy laughs. "I'm flattered, but that sounds like something out of a Sci-Fi movie. These are some real down to earth problems we're dealing with here, so let's not get it twisted that I'm some super hero. I'm a man who's serious about cleaning up crime, and I welcome all of you in this room to join me. If you don't want to do your job then… we'll have a healthy chat about your unemployment benefits."

Mumbling fills the room.

The chief takes over the conversation. "With that said, you better get you shit straight! If you taking bribes, you better stop that shit. If you pimping Santa Domingo whores out of Garden Street, you best send dem on vacation, and if any of you running business out of Wally's Supper Club, den I suggest you turn in your badges right now 'cause dat's gonna be de furst place dat get a shake down!"

"Wally's?" one of the officers cuts in. "Me thought dem close Wally's and he son run to de States owing people money?"

Another officer interjects, "Da boy been back now tree good months, and he fadder let he run de business again. The boy tell he fadder he gon do de right ting."

"Well, I ain't sure 'bout dat. All me know is dat you best not find your backside up in dere for your own good. Now like me already don said, many of you does know Detective Fitzroy here and him don clean up a lot of mess around 'ere already and him gon need we to help, too!"

A few officers nod their heads in agreement.

"Now I don't know 'bout you, but me need me job! I does have six month before me retire, and I ain't gon let none of you mess dat up. So like me say, check you self before you wreck you self. Dismissed!"

A few of the officers pat Fitzroy on the back while others ignore him and walk away quickly. As Fitzroy turns to leave, the chief calls out, "I need a moment of you time."

Fitzroy settles back down in his seat. Chief Leonard waits until he is sure all eyes and ears are out of hearing and seeing range before he engages Fitzroy in conversation.

"Now me know you done got promoted to FBI Agent but me invite you 'ere to dis meeting ta put fear in dees boys' hearts. I want dem to know you's a bad mudder! Now you's me boy and me want to asks if you would be so kind ta keep me informed as tings progress wit de investigations round 'ere... De more me does know, de more me chance of getting a little raise before me retire wit me pension money. You does understand, right?"

Fitzroy pats him on his back and replies, "Yeah, mon, I understand!"

Fitzroy leaves the meeting room and steps down the hall to his office where he has a bird's eye view that stretches from the parking lot to the beautiful Caribbean Sea just across the street. He picks up the telephone to make a few calls. His first call is to Wally, owner of the supper club.

Lucille, Faith's aunt and Wally's wife, answers the phone in a cheerful voice. "Hey, sweetie! No, Wally's gone to the government office to pay the taxes on the club. I'll have him call you later or, better yet, we're spending the night in St. John at one of you guys' house. The ladies are getting together to have a heart to heart talk with Lisa. Maybe you, Roy and Wally can hang out while we hens do our pecking?" Lucille laughs.

"Sounds like a plan. Let him know I'll catch up with him tonight. Oh, Lucille, before you hang up, the receptionist here at the station had a message for me from someone looking for Faith. She swears the woman said she was her sister, but I told her Faith is an only child. Then she said it might be her cousin. Is everything okay in Atlanta?" Fitzroy inquires.

"As far as I know. I spoke to Debbie, Faith's only girl cousin, last week and like you said, Faith is an only child. Did you try calling the person back?" Lucille asks.

"Now that's another story I'll save for tonight so I can give you a good laugh. Be blessed, and I'll see you soon," Fitzroy says as he hangs up.

* * *

Out in the reception area, Denisha is about to leave for lunch as Wally Jr. enters the police station carrying a small box.

"Denisha, I need to leave dis 'ere box for Officer Olga Hernandez."

"Dem in a meeting," Denisha says as she grabs her purse. "I thought you was living up in de States? I does 'ear you left town real quick, me son! Wa you doing back 'ere? Me hope you ain't giving ya fadder no grief."

"Girl, me ain't come up in 'ere for you ta be all in me business. Listen, can you call she and let she know de box 'ere?"

"Look, man, me already late for lunch. Just rest de box down dere and when me come back from lunch me gon call she to come for de box."

Wally Jr. seems nervous and doesn't want to leave the box. "Can't you put it in she office?"

"You tink me de mail carrier now? I's de receptionist, not FedEx! Me son boy, rest de box down. I tell ya me gon make sure she get de box. You actin' like it got gold inside! Cheese-n-bread!"

Wally Jr. pushes the box under Denisha's desk then turns to leave.

"Boy, you know you crazy!"

"Just make sure she gets the box, girl!" he hollers.

"You better mind de company ya keepin' or ya gon be running out of town again! 'Ear what me say, Wally Jr."

He brushes her off with a wave as she takes a compact out of her purse and refreshes her lipstick, ready to leave, placing an *Out to Lunch* sign on her desk.

"I need a raise for dis!" she says as she places the corrected message in Fitzroy's inbox.

\* \* \*

Holding his cellphone in his hand, Shakoi, Denisha's man, is shirtless with dreadlocks hanging below his waist, sitting on a crate outside an old one-room tin shack, in the bush. Sitting next to him on an old discarded car seat used for furniture is thirty-year-old police officer Sydney Huggins, smoking a joint and coaching Shakoi on what to say to Denisha on the phone.

"Call the gil now, mon, before Officer Olga come out of de meeting an get de box," Officer Huggins says as he takes a deep hit on a fat joint rolled with a banana leaf.

"Ya sure we can't call somebody else to do it? Dis 'ere woman gon harass me head! Danesha ain't nothing but a first-class nag. An me know she vexed 'cause me ain't return she car!"

"Boy, it ain't nothing but a ting! Just tell she ya comin' wit Officer Olga ta pick up de box and ya bringin' she car back. Ain't nothing but a ting, I telling ya!"

"De gil troubling me head bout money me does owe she! Now dat you gon pay me, I gon give she her money plus double and drop she big behind! I sick of she, ya 'ear!" Shakoi reluctantly pulls out his cellphone and calls Denisha.

* * *

As Denisha turns to leave for lunch, the phone rings. She notices the number on the Caller ID display and stops to answer the call quickly.

"Shakoi! Where dee hell are you wit me car? Boy, you best bring me car now!"

"Rest you self now! Me calling wit great news but ya got ta listen good."

"The only damn good news you does have fa me is dat ya lying ass is outside dis door wit me car!"

"Denisha, girl, shut up now, mon, and let me get a word in. Now me got a way ta pay ya back de money me owe you just now. But wa me need ya ta do is tell me if der is a box in ya office addressed to Officer Olga?"

Denisha looks under her desk at the box addressed to Officer Olga that Wally Jr. just dropped off.

"Wa you meddling in police business fa? Me already leave a message for Officer Olga ta come fa de box but she no answer de phone."

Shakoi jumps up, happy. "Dat's 'cause she 'ere wit me. De box still dere? Listen ta me, my sweetie. Me does need ya ta meet me in de back of de police station car park in five minutes wit de box. Don't let no one see yah leave wit de box."

"Shakoi, what shit ya smokin'? Ya must be out of ya crazy ass head if you does tink me gon steal police mail for ya ass. I hanging up dis 'ere phone and if ya ain't 'ere in fifteen minutes wit me car, I gone send police fa ya!"

"Denisha, fa once can ya just listen and do what me say! Trust me, gil, I finally gon make tings right but I does need ya ta listen like a woman spose ta listen ta she man. Give me a chance now, mon? I telling ya I gon do right by you; now me and Officer Olga getting in de car right now so make ya way down ta de car park wit de box." Shakoi talks real sweet to Denisha, who is savoring every word.

"But, Shakoi, how Officer Olga gon be wit you and she 'ere in a meetin'?" Denisha spews roughly.

"Who tell you she was in dat meeting? Why you tink she not answer she phone? Gil, how you gon wok der an don't know who in de meeting? Wa you tink ya boss gon say if him does know you don't even know wa going on in de office?" Shakoi tries to make Denisha feel inadequate as he and Officer Huggins walk toward their cars. Officer Huggins gets into his sports car that has dark tinted windows, and Shakoi jumps into Denisha's hooptie. He speeds off toward the police station with a big joint in his mouth, grinning like he just won the lottery.

* * *

Denisha is standing in a corner of the police station parking lot. A shawl covers the small box she is holding. Shakoi pulls up in her car, grinning.

Denisha is not happy. "Boy, come fa ya box and get the hell out of me car. Shakoi, I telling ya straight, me ain't want to 'ear me name in nothing dat has to do wit dis 'ere box! Ya 'ear?"

Shakoi gets out of the car and tries to kiss Denisha, who pulls back as she walks to her car.

"Denisha, me ride supposed ta be following me! Me ain't seeing dem! I know you're gonna give me a lift!"

"You don got all de rides you gon ever get from me! Me and you is finished. So just give me me money like you say and keep moving."

"Damn, girl, you ain't easy! One minute. I soon come back."

Shakoi takes the box with the shawl wrapped around it, throws the shawl at Denisha and goes inside a closed ticket booth. Denisha is impatient. Her mouth is pushed out, and she taps the steering wheel with her long fake fingernails while she waits. Shakoi appears and throws a wad of cash into her car.

"Wha dis is, Shakoi? Me ain't want no shit! If dis 'ere is drug money, me ain't want it!"

"Ain't no pleasing yo ass, is it? Dat's the money me owe you plus a little extra something! Now we even! Move from 'ere… me does see me ride! And, Denisha, I done wit you fat ass! So don't ring me phone again and come fa all dem big ass clothes ya leave at me house or me gon use dem ta light me stove wit!"

The same sports car with tinted windows pulls up next to Denisha's car. The dark windows prevent her from seeing who is in the car. Shakoi jumps inside, giving Denisha the finger. Denisha blows her horn for him to come and take the money as the black car with tinted windows pulls off burning rubber.

* * *

Fitzroy, smiling from his conversation with Lucille, becomes concerned as he watches what's going on between Denisha and Shakoi in the parking lot from his office window. Fitzroy turns from the window as he sees Shakoi jump into a black sports car and pull off. Puzzled, Fitzroy heads downstairs to the receptionist area to retrieve the corrected message that he asked Denisha to fix.

Hope picks up on the second ring. Fitzroy identifies himself as Faith's husband. Hope sounds very pleasant and lets Fitzroy know that she Googled him and that's how she got his contact information.

Fitzroy pauses.

"I found your wife Faith on Facebook, and I've been trying to friend her for some time, to no avail."

"Well, now that you have found me, how can I help you?"

"I'm Faith's half-sister," Hope says after another pause. "I would like to meet her. I'll be coming to St. Thomas in a few days, and it would mean the world to me if we can finally meet each other."

"Ms. Hope, are you sure you have the right Faith Davis Brown? You see, my wife is an only child," Fitzroy explains.

"Mr. Brown, I know this comes as a surprise to you, as I'm sure it will be to her and especially to Mrs. Davis, but my father, the late Reverend Brown, asked me not to contact Faith until he was deceased. I recently lost my mother to cancer and now I have no family but Faith. I felt like now is a good time for me to meet my sister." Hope's voice cracks as if she wants to cry.

"Have you contacted anyone else in the family about this?" Fitzroy inquires.

"Of course not, it's only proper I speak with my sister first and you, of course, since you're officially my brother-in-law."

# Chapter 2
# Hope

Hope and her deceased mother's best friend of over thirty-five years, Mabel Jordan, are having a yard sale. Mabel is helping Hope sell everything out of her mother's Section 8 townhouse. The ladies are sitting behind a long table that blocks the entrance into the house. They are only letting select people, escorted by either Mabel or Hope, inside to purchase items that are for sale. Some of the neighborhood kids and adults stop by just to wish Hope a safe trip to the islands, a place they can only imagine in their dreams, but will never experience.

"So what did the man say when you spoke to him?" Mabel asks, hanging on to Hope's every word.

"Of course he was skeptical when I told him I was Faith's sister, but I think he believed me. I told him I was coming to the islands to meet her. He asked that I allow him a day or two to talk to the family so they would be prepared to meet me, especially my father's wife, Mrs. Gloria, which is understandable, given the situation."

"Ooooh, child, if I could be a fly in the corner when he tells her about you. I'd give everything I have just to see the expression on her face. You don't know how many times I told your momma, 'Let's just go over there and introduce ourselves to *Mrs. High and Mighty First Lady!*'"

"And my daddy would have killed both of you and asked his Lord for forgiveness immediately after you took your last breath," Hope says, shaking her head.

"You know that's right!" Mabel says, letting out a bellowing laugh. "It's funny how even though he had his family across town, you had to respect him because he always made it clear he came over here to see his daughter and nothing else. Most men would have fled the scene and acted like they didn't know the child or the mother; but no, Rev took care of his responsibility. I can say, without a doubt, that other child of his didn't get any more from your daddy than he gave you."

"Well, that's not exactly true. She had him there when she went to sleep and when she woke up. Faith had a twenty-four/seven daddy. I had a drop in on Monday, Wednesday, and Friday daddy!" Hope says with a sad look on her face.

"Child, you ain't got nothin' to be sad about. Some of these daddies are in the house all day and every day and don't give their children the attention your father gave you! It's the quality of time you spend together, not the quantity of time. Every year, when Rev went to his Baptist conventions, he reserved a few extra days so the two of you could have a vacation together. You are the only child in these projects who's been to Hawaii, Nova Scotia, Israel, California, London, Disney World at least five times that I remember, and a whole bunch of other places I can't even spell; not to mention the cruises he paid for your momma to take you on. Honey, the way I look at it, you had the best daddy a girl could ever imagine."

"You're right, Mabel. My daddy was good to me. I only wish he had been just as good to my mother. Do you think he ever loved her?" Hope asks with regret in her voice.

"Now see, that's where children mess up, when they try and get in grown folks' business. I can only give you my opinion of the situation, since neither one of them is here to dispute it. And even if your mother were here, we wouldn't get anything out of her. Barbara did not discuss her business or nobody else's; she didn't get in other peoples' business, which made it easy for her to live in these projects in peace. Can't a damn soul say anything bad about your mother. She was a lady!"

Hope nods her agreement.

"Now, the way I see it... no, he didn't love your mother," Mabel continues. "I don't think she loved him or was looking for love either, but they were kind and respectful to one another. Wasn't no cussing and fussing going on.

"In my honest opinion, I don't think Reverend had any business having sex with her, he was a married man, but that was their business and nobody dared to say a word about it. There was a respect for them, even given the situation. Girl, the whole damn thing was strange, but you know what? We minded our business!

"At your daddy's church, your mother was the President of the Altar Guild. Oh, how that woman lived to dress that altar. If it was Easter, she had the finest lilies money could buy on that pulpit. Same with Christmas; I don't know where Barbara found those giant, strong, long-lasting poinsettias. She made sure the cloths that draped over the podium matched the little doilies that rested on the back of the pastor's and deacons' chairs with the flowers. The water pitchers, I swear, might have been made from real gold. Barbara didn't play when it came to making sure that pulpit shined every Sunday when the doors of Solid Rock Baptist Church opened, and the Reverend appreciated it."

Hope is transfixed as Mabel discloses intimate details her mother never shared with her.

"The church was her life, God rest her soul, but that wasn't enough. She wanted a baby, and that's all she talked about! Barbara was determined to get one by hook or crook. She was not concerned with a husband like most of us desperate chicks; she wanted a child to make her whole and preferably a baby girl. Sure she was happy that your daddy came around and spent time with you, but to tell you the truth, she was not interested in him one bit. It was like he was just the way to get her little girl. I never saw a yearning or heard a jealous word come out of her mouth toward your father or his family. Barbara was happy; she finally had what she called family, you and her.

"You know she was an only child. Her father died when she was just a teenager, got run over by a moving van one day when he was crossing Flat Shoals Road, leaving work. Your grandmother was a wreck. The poor woman ended up in the crazy house, and your mother's only living relative was a very wealthy doctor and his half-white wife who took her in. They had a son who was around Barbara's age. What was that boy's name? Bedford, Bedford Jennings. He became a doctor like his daddy and inherited all that money. Mrs. Jennings didn't care too much for your mother because she didn't have the complexion for protection."

"What in the world is the complexion for protection?" Hope interrupts.

"It's when you're light, bright and almost white! These were some high-class Negro folks your momma was living with. If your skin color was any darker than the color of their coffee with plenty of cream and sugar in it, then you did not have the complexion for protection from being looked at as just an ordinary Negro. And you know your momma was just a few shades lighter than midnight!" Mabel says, laughing.

"You need to stop lying on my mother. She had a beautiful complexion and skin," Hope says.

"No doubt! Beautiful *black* skin! Mrs. Jennings didn't want your mother to go to the debutante ball because all her friends' daughters looked so beautiful, and she thought Barbara would stand out like an ink spot on a white dress. The Nadinola bleaching cream she made your mother rub on her face twice a day that was supposed to lighten her skin was not working fast enough.

"Bedford, Jr., her cousin, insisted she go and he was her date. Now when *Webster's Dictionary* came up with the word, "Debonair" they was talking about him. Every eye at the ball was on your mother and Bedford. Mrs. Jennings was not happy and, to add insult to injury, your mother refused to press her hair! Miss Barbara walked into that hoity-toity ball wearing the world's biggest afro! She may have given them the Black Power fist as she walked down the marble grand staircase. Barbara said Mrs. Jennings almost choked on her dentures when she saw her. But Bedford, Jr. was a real gentleman; he escorted her like she was a Nubian Queen."

"I saw those pictures in my mother's photo album when I was deciding what to keep and what to toss. So that's who that man was in the picture. I thought it was a prom date. Whatever happened to him? Sounds like he's my only relative, other than my sister Faith."

"You can count him out. The man died! I heard he was engaged to marry a lovely woman from right here in Atlanta and the night of his bachelor party a lap dancer came in and killed him. She said he was supposed to marry her. The woman was insane. Months earlier, she tried to break into Neverland, swearing she was supposed to marry Michael Jackson. Even though Bedford and Barbara went their separate ways when he went to Yale and your mother went to Spellman, they would always send Christmas cards and try and have lunch at least once a year, since it was only the two of them left in the family. His death hit your mother like a brick! Thank God she had you or I'm sure she would have lost her mind just like her mother."

"Wow! I'm so glad she had a friend like you, Miss Mabel." Hope pulls a ripped picture out of her jeans pocket. "I found this picture of my mother in a locked box along with my first report card, award ribbons I won running track, and from my piano recitals. She does look like a queen, but you can see she cut the person standing next to her out. Part of his hand is holding her hand. He has a large diamond ring on his finger, and she has a beautiful engagement or wedding ring on her finger," Hope tells Mabel, like she's been doing some investigative research.

"Lord, would you look at your momma! This picture looks like it might have been taken in Africa. That house in the background looks like somewhere foreign. Now I know she went to Africa when she was in college and got involved in some radical Black Power movement. Barbara used to have the Red, Black and Green flag hanging in the house with a glow-in-the-dark poster of people with big afros and their fists raised giving the Black Power sign. But all that radical stuff faded away after she got back into the church."

"Did she ever talk about Africa? Did she say anything about a man over there? She looked kind of sad in this picture. I just wondered if this man broke my mother's heart and that's why she cut him out of the picture. Suppose he's really my father!" Hope cries.

"What? Honey, the Rev spit you out! You look just like that man! Now I don't know what this picture is about, but I do know your mother planned to have you. You were not a mistake, and she raised you so that you would be a blessing in a lot of folks' lives. And from the day you were born, the first person you blessed was her, then me, and all these crazy-ass people in these projects.

"There hasn't been a time that you refused to help somebody in need around here. And don't think God didn't have a purpose for your life; why you think He had you studying Social Work and Psychology at the university? So you can help these ignorant folks in these projects! Look at Day-Day; remember when Rufus shot him in the foot? You was the one who took him to the hospital. Foot bleeding all up in your car, but you didn't care. I told you to call 911 and mind your damn business, but you knew the boy would bleed to death waiting for them to get here," Mabel says, laughing.

"You would have done the same for him," Hope modestly says.

"Look in my face, Hope... Hell no! My boy would have bled to death waiting for the ambulance or hopped his broke ass to the hospital on his good foot. Well, maybe I would have given him cab fare; but he would have to pay me back with interest!"

Hope and Mabel laugh.

"And what about the time Kesha's boyfriend beat the mess out of her and she ran over to your house? You let her in and went out on the porch and talked to that fool. I can't believe the respect he showed you 'cause that was one rude man. He didn't think twice about cussing his own momma out. I thought about coming over as backup, but I knew I would have had to shoot him. What did you say to him to calm him down?" Mabel asks.

"I told him he was a good person and reminded him that he already had two strikes, was on probation and if Kesha called the police he would not be getting out of jail any time soon. I told him I would go in the house and deal with Kesha for him and the next time he sees her, she would be a better person. He hugged me and left."

"Kesha's a sweet girl; her only problem is she's stupid for being with his ass. And the boy still ended up in jail for riding in the car with some fools that stopped to rob the grocery store before they dropped him off for a job interview at Jiffy Lube. I hear he's facing twenty years for armed robbery. It's a damn shame how much time they give a black man for doing stupid petty crimes and them big-time, rip-off business men be getting like two years' community service for stealing millions of taxpayers' money! The shit just ain't right. And now Kesha got to raise that boy by herself because her man got in the car with a bunch of thugs. That boy was beginning to turn his life around. I know it was because you was counseling him. I watched out my window him coming out of your house smiling, walking like he had a little more pep in his step. I don't know what you were telling him, but you was filling that boy with hope… Hope!" Mabel screams.

"My daddy told me in order for people to hear what you're saying, you have to give them words of encouragement first," Hope says.

"I'll have to remember that one. Now I know you had to dig down real deep to find something about him that would make you say he was a good person or you just lied; 'cause ain't nothing good about that child. From the time he was born, he was a miserable little cuss just like his daddy who's doing life in the pen. Let's pray that little boy of theirs will have sweet Kesha's genes and be the one to break the generational curse."

"You go right ahead and pray. What Kesha needs to do is move her child from around here and expose him to some positive male role models like you find in Big Brothers and Boy Scouts," Hope says.

"Long as she do a background check on them men 'cause some of them is sexual perverts looking for young boys, pretending to be mentors!"

Hope shakes her head.

"And where you think Kesha gon move to? With her Section 8, Kesha probably pays zero in rent, gets three hundred a month on her EBT Card, which is enough to buy food for the first week of the month, and four-fifty a month from welfare. She don't drive and the bus stops right on the corner, the Weave Café is in walking distance and the nail shop and Family Dollar is next door to that. Most of her clothes are hand-me-downs from the church when they have their seasonal giveaways. What more could she possibly want? By ghetto standards, the girl is living large!"

"How about a better life! My professor once said, 'If you associate with four broke people, you are going to be the fifth broke one!' If you don't change your location, how are you going to know anything else?" Hope asks.

"You have a point, Hope. And because of the way you feel about leaving here, especially after your momma died, I can see why you are moving. What I just don't understand is why you would rent an apartment before you leave to go to the islands. Suppose you decide to stay, what you gon do with your apartment?"

"It's not an apartment. It's a house, and I'm going to move you into it. Why you think I got four bedrooms and three-and-a-half bathrooms?" Hope shares with a smile on her face.

Mabel is shocked. "Say what? Girl, you must be crazy! I've been living in these projects for forty years; where you think I'm gon go? I don't know nowhere but here!"

"And forty years is long enough. Momma made me promise not to leave you here if I move, and I'm going to do just what she told me to do; buy a house and put you in it!"

"How you gon move me out of the projects, drop me in some strange neighborhood, leave me and go to the islands? Have you lost your mind? Child, did you say you bought a house! Oh my God! How could you afford something like that?"

"My mother must have saved every dime she made working as a manager at Denny's for thirty years and put it in a trust for me," Hope says.

"Lord have mercy! I feel like I just won the lottery! But, honey, I can't live alone. Why you think I let that trifling son of mine and his son live here with me? I might act big, bad and tough but there's something about being alone that I just can't stomach. I think I just need someone to fuss with, yell at, and cuss out! Sick huh?"

"No, not at all. That's why we have an extra room for Mookie. He's a good kid, and there are some great schools in the area that will offer him a better education and a better chance at life."

"You ain't never lied about that, girl. Dem damn bullies at that ghetto-behind school been picking on him 'cause he made the honor roll. Now he scared to make good grades. I told him he better be scared of me, and what I'm going to do to him if he lets his grades slip. Honey, I had to go down to that school three times last week and threaten to open up a can of whoop-ass on some boys that was messing with him.

"One thing my momma told me, God rest her soul, was never to look a gift horse in the mouth. So, I'm going to think about your offer, Hope, 'cause it might be the only way I can save my next generation. Now the boy will come with me, but his drunk-ass daddy can stay here until the government figures out I ain't living there anymore and kick his trifling butt out on the street. Hope, you are God-sent."

"What about Mookie's mother?" Hope quietly asks, knowing Mabel gets upset at the mention of her name.

"What about her ass?" Mabel retorts.

"Will we need to let her know where the child is? I know I see her coming around from time to time to visit Mookie," Hope ventures, knowing Mabel never lets the woman in the house.

"And every time she comes I cuss her ass out and tell her to go climb back into the crack pipe she just climbed out of," Mabel boldly says.

"I heard she's been clean for over a year now, got a job as a secretary with Creflo Dollar Ministries. They say she got a car, an apartment, going to night school and everything," Hope gingerly says, being careful not to upset her friend.

"Who the hell is "they?" They… don't know Charlotte like I do! The woman was a crackhead, she sold all her momma's shit out her house when the woman was in the hospital dying from HIV. What kind of person would do something like that?"

"A sick drug addict! That crack is no joke. And she must be a really strong woman to have overcome it," Hope says, hoping Mabel will give Charlotte some credit.

"Joke is the key word! She's a joke, especially if she thinks she can fool me with the "I've found Jesus and I'm a new person now" line! Hell no! I'm from the Show Me State!" Mabel hollers.

"Well, what will it take for you believe she has changed?" Hope inquires.

"Have you been counseling Charlotte? 'Cause it sound like you trying to mediate some shit!" Mabel has her lip turned up.

Hope is laughing. "You know you're crazy, don't you? It's a new day, Miss Mabel, a new house for you and Mookie, a new school and all I'm asking is that you give the woman a chance. If she's full of it, your B.S. radar will detect it immediately! So start packing, 'cause you are moving and I will not take no for an answer!"

"Packing? I ain't taking nothing from this roach-infested place! These are some angry ghetto roaches, can't nothing kill them. I might go butt naked to make sure ain't nothing hiding in the lining of my clothes."

Hope and Mabel roll with laughter. Mabel suddenly stops laughing and has a serious look on her face.

"What?" Hope asks.

"I hear you, girl. I know that boy misses his mother. Mookie's still at the age where he don't see no wrong in her. The child sleeps with a picture of her. I'm going to meet with Charlotte and feel her ass out. Like you said, I do have B.S. radar and if she is who she says she is, then I'm going to let her visit the boy. Hope, this might sound selfish, but I don't want you to go to the islands. I want us to both start our next chapter together in this new house you just bought," Mabel says sadly.

"And we will. I am not going to the islands to stay and if I'm there too long, you better be working on your fear of flying 'cause I'm coming to get you and bring your behind down there, too!"

Mabel is overwhelmed and looks like she wants to cry. "I don't know what to say, honey. Ain't nobody ever done nothing for me before."

"Well, get used to it, 'cause we are going to spend my mother's money, and I can't think of a better person to do it with than her best friend. I only wish she had spent some of it on herself before she died," Hope says sadly.

"Us moving is coming at a good time because you heard the Tenant Association finally lost their case, right? These "Bricks" are coming down, you know, so staying here isn't really an option anymore! The last of the public housing projects will be demolished three months from now," Hope reminds Mabel.

"What? Damn! Well, them fools fought a good fight. What's it been, ten years trying to keep us in here? Did anybody say just where all these people gonna go? 'Cause don't nobody want to take Section 8 from a bunch of ghetto Negros. Hell, white people and working folks got Section 8, and we gon have to fight them to see who will get a place to live first? You know the poor person gon lose!" Mabel screams.

"I hope they will take their vouchers and spread out all over Atlanta and meet new people with goals and ambition," Hope says.

"It will snow in Jamaica first. Why you think everybody was fighting so hard to keep the government from tearing down these projects? This is home for them, as horrible as it is." Mabel laughs.

"I don't believe that. We might live in the projects, but we are not the projects! Look at how that billionaire Tom Cousins came in and tore down East Lake Meadows AKA Little Vietnam. He built beautiful housing, bought the golf club nearby, gave people jobs, charter schools and job training. What that man did for people in the projects has become a model others are using all over the country. Expose black folks to more than poverty and we will latch on and run with it!" Hope says with passion in her heart.

"I hear you, and trust me, my big behind will be running out of here never to be seen again! And if I run into any of these people from the "Bricks" after I move, I'm going to act like I never knew them; I'll tell them I'm suffering from Alzheimer's!" Mabel lets out a hearty laugh, then changes her tone to a serious one. "Hope, have you thought any about how these people in the islands are going to accept you? There might be a lot of anger and resentment."

"Yeah. I've rehearsed over and over again in my mind what I'm going to say when I meet my sister and it changes every time. I've never been so nervous in my life, but I know it's something I have to do and, most importantly, it was my daddy's wish for us to meet after his death." Hope smiles.

"Well, at least he left you an introduction letter to give to the daughter and First Lady Gloria. The letter will do a lot of the talking for you." Mabel tries to calm Hope's nervousness.

"I'm sure the letter Daddy wrote will do a lot of explaining, but in the end, folks will not be happy and feel deceived by him. And having to look at me, looking like him and my sister, could add insult to injury."

"You have a point there. There's no denying he's your daddy! And the pictures you've shown me on that Facebook of Faith... damn you guys almost look like twins!" Mabel shouts.

"Well, in case you forgot, we were almost twins! Faith was born September 15 and I was born September 18, three days later, the same year! Poppa was truly a rolling stone!"

"You ain't never lied! Now that was one close call for the Reverend. The day your momma arrived at the hospital to deliver you was the day Gloria was checking out to go home with Faith. Girl, I just sat back and said, 'I can't wait to see how this man is going to handle this!' Watching him operate was better than watching *Scandal*. He must have gotten Gloria and her baby home in neck-breaking speed so he could make it back to the hospital to help deliver you and that was one time he had to lie. He told the doctors he was standing in for his brother, helping with the delivery because he was out of the country," Mabel tells Hope.

"How is it that a man of God can lead a double life like that, step into his pulpit every Sunday and talk to his congregation about sin? It's so hypocritical! Don't get me wrong, I loved my daddy and I knew he was a good man, but I am having the hardest time stepping into a church without wondering if every pastor is leading a secret life as well."

"Did you ever talk to your daddy about how you felt?" Mabel asks.

"Actually, he brought it up when we were in Israel, the summer before he died. Daddy wanted us to go to a Jewish church service and I told him I would be at the hotel when he got back, that it wasn't something I was interested in. Actually, I really didn't want to go to Israel at all; it was something he wanted to do, being into the holy thing and all. Looking back on things, I'm glad I got to do it with him for his sake before he passed away." Hope takes a moment to reflect.

"You still ain't told me what he said about the hypocritical thing," Mabel presses excitedly.

"Oh! When he came back from the Jewish service all excited like they asked him to preach or something, he could sense that I really didn't share his jubilance because I paid more attention to the room service menu than him. So, out of the blue, he asked me what I thought about God."

"Just like that? I know he caught you off guard! What did you say?" Mabel anxiously awaits Hope's answer.

"I told him I didn't think about God at all. Of course you know that shocked him. He took the restaurant menu out of my hand, moved me over to the sofa and said we needed to talk. Daddy recited scriptures to me, he prayed, anointed my head with oil, served me communion and we talked late into the night about God. Then he finally asked me if he was the reason I didn't feel close to God. It was as if he was reading my mind."

"Child, what did you say?" Mabel asks.

"You mean after I stopped crying? I told him yes and it cut through him like a knife. I never saw my daddy so sad before. I shared with him how I find it hard to sit in church and listen to preachers talk about God and not wonder if they are living a double life like him," Hope says sadly.

"Ooo, child! Now if that were my daddy, he would have smacked the taste out of my mouth and had my head spinning around like that *Exorcist* child; instead of that green shit flying out of my mouth like in the movie, it would be my teeth and snot!"

Hope cracks up at Mabel, who is pretending she is the possessed child.

"Miss Mabel, you are crazy!" Hope says, barely able to compose herself.

"And so was my daddy!" Mabel says.

"Well, my daddy never lifted his hand to hit me. He said hands were for healing not hitting," Hope proudly says.

"Yeah, right! I sure could have used "Mr. Holy" to talk to my daddy and all my exes, 'cause them was some angry hitting fools. Anyway, finish the story!"

"He told me he was not Jesus. That Jesus was the only person free from sin. He said not to look on him or other people who are human and make mistakes, but to find God and have a personal relationship with Him. He asked me if I thought he should have demanded that my mother have an abortion. I told him no! He agreed and asked me to forgive him for anything I may have thought he did wrong and one day I would understand, and to promise not to judge all pastors. He held my hand and looked me in the eye and said he unequivocally loved the Lord and believed what he preaches."

"My, my my, I think there is nothing else to say, honey. Your daddy explained it to you straight from the heart!"

Hope and Mabel are quiet for a second.

Mabel finally breaks the silence. "Is that Kesha and her son? Look like they are coming this way. Did we just talk them up or what? Wonder how much she paid for the weave hair; that thing looks better than Rapunzel's."

Hope bursts out laughing. "Now you know you ain't right talking about that girl!"

Mabel whispers, "She probably used all of her welfare check to pay for that hair! And don't let her talk you into giving her nothing for free!" She raises her voice. "Hey, Kesha, how your daddy doing? I heard he on dialysis now."

"Yeah, Miss Mabel; he having a hard time with that shunt dey put in his shoulder. Other than that, he okay," Kesha says.

Her little boy cuts in the conversation. "Miss Hope, why you going way down there to them islands? You not scared the plane might fall out of the sky like them other planes did?"

"Boy, shut your ignorant mouth!" Kesha pops him upside the head, being careful not to break her long, designer-sculptured fingernails.

"Sean, there are more car accidents and bike accidents than there are plane accidents. I'll be fine," Hope says with a smile on her face.

"I know that's right!" Mabel chimes in.

"Dey ain't got no buses or trains going over there? I'm scared to death of flying. If God wanted me to fly, he would have given me wings!" Kesha says, laughing.

Mabel pounces on her words. "Now that's the dumbest shit I've heard all day! God didn't stick wheels on your ass and you ride the bus!"

"Miss Mabel, you are too funny! Y'all got any blenders in there for sale? I think I'm going to do a liquid diet and try and lose fifty pounds. My doctor says I'm pre-diabetic and if I don't get this weight off, he gon put me on insulin. Girl, I'm scared of needles."

"Yes, we have a blender," Hope says.

"How much it going for?" Kesha asks as she pulls money out of her bra.

"It's almost new, so I can sell it to you for ten dollars."

"Can you take five dollars?"

"Hell no, didn't you hear the girl say it's a new blender? The thrift store selling them for fifteen dollars and they got all kinds of crap stuck up under dem blades!" Mabel hollers.

"Hope, I only got seven dollars. Will you take that?" Kesha says, sucking her teeth, hoping Mabel will butt out.

"Sure." Hope takes the seven dollars.

"Go on inside, and you'll find it on the counter in the kitchen. And make sure that's all you take out of there! You hear?" Mabel hollers as Kesha enters the house with her son following behind.

"Naw, little man, you wait out here. Your momma don't need any help carrying that blender."

Hope shakes her head at Mabel, smiling. "You know you missed your calling as a drill sergeant or prison guard!"

"Living in these projects will make you hard! Child, I done seen every game these fools got."

Kesha comes out of the apartment with her new blender, smiling. "Thank you so much, Hope. This is a real nice blender. I gon keep you in my prayers while you down there in those islands."

"Yeah, thanks," Hope says, cutting her off quickly as she holds her head down and busies herself counting the money.

Mabel stares at her but doesn't speak until everyone is gone. "So you still blaming God for your momma and daddy's death?"

"Miss Mabel, today is a good day and I don't want to start with you talking about God. Now as far as I'm concerned, God is dead! I've chosen to be an atheist: so can we just leave it at that?"

"Hell to the no! Your momma would climb out of her grave and beat the crap out of me if I let you believe some mess like that. You are the last person who need to let the word atheist come out of your mouth. Your daddy was a pastor and your mother love the Lord like he was her husband," Mabel says.

"And look where it got them... dead!" Hope cries.

"Well, baby, we all gonna die one day, and God just don't let you pick the date; it don't work like that. When He calls you home, it's not open for discussion or debate, you take your ass, excuse me Lord, "behind" home to the Father. Your momma loved you so much, child, that there is no room in there for you to hate God. You had some beautiful years with her. Now granted your daddy wasn't always there and lived a double life, but he loved you and provided for your every need, both spiritually and financially. I still don't understand to this day why your momma never moved y'all out of these projects especially after the Rev offered to put y'all in a house."

"What would she do without you, Miss Mabel? You were her rock and the sister she never had. My mother had everything she needed right here in this hood, you and me," Hope proudly states.

"I just wondered how she could go all those years without getting some! I mean us girls got needs!" Mabel says, shaking her head.

"Hello, Miss Mabel, TMI! I don't want to hear that about my momma!"

"Sorry, dear, it's just that I always wondered how she managed all those years. I know, I know, TMI – too much information," Mabel says, flapping her arms.
"Now they say the seed don't fall too far from the tree, so I'm going to give you a bit of wisdom and you'd better listen."

"What's that, Miss Mabel?" Hope asks with a sarcastic look on her face.

"Now when you get down there in them islands, you get yourself some of that Mandingo stuff and ride it like a cowgirl on a horse—"

Hope cuts her off. "Miss Mabel!"

"Sorry, I was just going to say, ride that thing into the sunset! Now, I said it!"

"You are the nastiest grown woman I have ever met! I can't believe you and Momma were best friends!" Hope says, laughing.

"Opposites do attract! Oh Lord, here comes that no-good, thieving Day-Day! I can't stand his behind!" Mabel says with a sour look on her face.

"Yo, Hope! I hear you having a moving sale. You got any flat screen TVs in there?"

Hope says, "Yes," at the same time Mabel says, "Hell no!"

"Miss Mabel, you need to stop acting so mean! This here is Hope's sale, not yours."

"So? And you need to keep moving!"

Day-Day ignores her. "Hope, how much you selling the flat screen for?"

"Two hundred dollars," Hope says.

"Cash! And we need to see the money before we even think about continuing this conversation with you," Mable asserts.

Day-Day pulls a wad of money out of his pocket and flashes it in front of Mabel. "So, can I go in and check it out?"

"When bears stop shitting in the woods! Wait right here."

Hope laughs as Mabel quickly gets up and enters the house, leaving Day-Day standing there.

"Girl, you know you don't need to be going to dem islands. They got some big-ass sharks down there and a whole lot of hurricanes that be blowing peoples' roofs off and shit. You can just stay right here and be my woman," Day-Day says as he gets real close in Hope's face, grinning and showing his row of gold slip-on teeth.

Mabel comes back with her cellphone in her hand.
"Man, get out of that girl's face! You are way out of your league! Now here is a picture of the television."

Day-Day reaches for the cellphone to get a better look at the picture.

"You must be crazy if you think I'm going to let you touch my phone! This is the closest you are going to get to this TV and my cellphone. Look but don't touch!" Mabel says with her hand on her hip.

"Ain't nobody trying to steal nothing around here!" Day-Day says, hurt and trying to defend his character in front of Hope.

"Mmm-hmm, so you say. I know you're the Negro who stole my TV when I went to New York for my sister's funeral."

Day-Day laughs at Mabel and this makes her even angrier. "What I gon do with that K-Mart brand TV? Don't nobody want to buy that."

"That's why you should have left it right in my living room! Now what you gon do, boy? Like Hope said, the television is two hundred dollars!" Mabel takes a seat at the yard sale table.

"Say, Hope, I see there's a DVD player, too. Can you throw it in as part of the deal?"

"No!" Mabel hollers.

"Man, Miss Mabel, why don't you go home and check on your drunk-ass son! He probably pissing the bed right now!"

Mabel jumps up to confront Day-Day.

"Hey, hey! Bring it down a notch," Hope intercedes. "Day-Day you can have both the television and DVD player for two hundred dollars."

"Thank you, Hope. You know I always used to tell your mother you are the sweetest girl around here and she needed to take you from here because you deserved better. You ain't nothing like these stank women sitting around here waiting for the first of the month for a government check. Your momma raised you to be a real lady! I'm kind of glad you leaving, because if you stayed you might become a bitter old lady like Miss Mabel's ass."

"You must be talking about your one-legged momma! The woman still hookin' from her wheelchair!" Mabel screams at Day-Day.

"Miss Mabel, you got one more time to disrespect my momma and it's going to get ugly round here!" Day-Day angrily retorts.

Day-Day pulls up his shirt and brandishes a weapon.

Mabel swings her leg up on the tabletop and pulls up her pants leg, exposing a gun strapped to her leg. "Mine's bigger than yours! Let's see who will go down first."

"Enough! Day-Day, calm down and, Miss Mabel, this is not the way my momma would expect you to be acting."

Mabel hollers over to her porch for her grandson. "Mookie, I need you to help me with the flat screen TV and DVD player for this fool."

The young boy obliges his grandmother, and they both go inside and quickly return with the items for Day-Day.

"Hope, you stand strong and never forget where you came from. I'm going to be here rooting for you to make it big down there in them islands."

Hope smiles and waves goodbye to Day-Day as he walks off with his goods.

Mabel, with squinting eyes and a menacing look on her face, watches Day-Day closely as he carries the just-bought items into his apartment, smiling.

"Mookie, go in the house and wake your daddy up and tell him as soon as Day-Day leaves his house to go in there and get the television and DVD player. Tell your daddy to take it across town to Uncle BoBo's house to let it cool off."

Hope's mouth widens in disbelief. She tries to speak but no words will come out.

"Close your mouth, child! An eye for an eye and a TV for a TV. Day-Day is getting just what his thieving behind deserves. And, Mookie, tell your daddy if he sees my TV in there, take that, too!"

# *Chapter* 3
## Lisa Needs to Edit Her Mouth

*"Do not let any unwholesome talk come out of your mouths, but only what is helpful for building others up according to their needs, that it may benefit those who listen."*
*- Ephesians 4:29*

"There is no damn excuse. Today is his daughter's birthday, and he needs to have his ass here!" Lisa whispers into her best friend Faith's ear.

Standing next to them is Lisa's golden, afro-headed, five-year-old birthday girl Kamari, wearing a princess dress and a tiara.

She overhears their conversation, as she picks up a cupcake from the dessert table. "Aunt Faith, are "damn" and "ass" bad words?"

Lisa and Faith look at each other, embarrassed.

As Faith struggles for an answer, Lisa cuts in. "Dam is a place where a lot of water is being held and ass is another word for a donkey. Now go over there and play with your friends. The magician is about to do his magic show for you, birthday girl!"

"So if dam is a place where water is held and ass is a donkey then does that mean my daddy has turned into a donkey and he's being held under a lot of water and that's why he's not at my party? Maybe the magician can turn him back into my daddy and get him out of the water so he can come to my party," Kamari conjectures with the sincerest look on her face.

"Sweetie, your daddy is at work, and he loves you very much. Now go and gather Poppa, Grammy, Aunt Dot and Uncle Marlin. Tell them it's magic time!"

Kamari runs off in the direction of her adopted family, skipping and smiling.

"Sounds like someone needs to edit their conversations. Big ears are always listening!" Faith admonishes Lisa.

"The girl is too damn... I mean too smart! This child doesn't miss a thing! Last night, she asked me if I was lonely and needed her daddy home to sleep with me in my bed." Lisa shakes her head.

"And just what has she been watching on television?" Faith asks.

"I only let her watch PBS kids and videos I purchased for her and Sarafina." Lisa has a puzzled look on her face.

"It's the commercials! Even the most innocent ones have sexual overtones," Faith asserts. "Listen, Lisa, you knew the first couple of years were going to be hard on the family when Billy started El Shaddai Airlines. You need to suck it up and stop complaining. The man is living his dream and needs your support more than ever now."

"Hell, what about my dreams? I'm stuck home with a five-year-old who will be smarter than me by her next birthday and a one-year-old who won't suck nothing but my breast! I can't fart without Sarafina looking for her tits! My damn breasts don't even belong to me anymore; she has 'the girls' on lockdown! I've lost my identity! I have nothing! Oh, and did I tell you I haven't had sex in three weeks and the last one was a quickie in the cockpit before takeoff!" Lisa throws her hands up in frustration.

Faith laughs.

"Oh, you think that shit is funny?"

"Edit your words, Miss Caca Mouth!" Faith teases.

"Girl, I am so frustrated, you better let me cuss or I might bite you! I feel like a crazy animal trapped in a cage," Lisa says.

"You mean that million-dollar cage Billy bought you on Beef Island? Nice cage," Faith points out.

"Yeah, right next to the airport so we can see his plane land and quickly take off. Now how's that for torture?"

Gloria Davis, Faith's mother, is walking toward Lisa and Faith, carrying Lisa's little girl Sarafina, who is crying.

"Mother cow, looks like you're being summoned!" Faith teases.

Lisa punches Faith in the arm.

"You know I can have my husband arrest you for that!" Faith admonishes her best friend as she rubs her arm.

"And I wouldn't do a day in jail as crazy as I am right now. Take your backside over there and get your niece's party started while I feed the little vulture!"

Faith gives Lisa a cross look for calling Sarafina a little vulture.

"Lisa, are you sure Sarafina won't take a bottle? The child is a year old. It's time to start weaning her," Gloria encourages.

"Well, Mother Gloria, I'm open for suggestions. I've tried everything short of starving her," Lisa sadly reports.

"Are you staying at the Chocolate Hole house tonight or are you taking the ferry back over to Tortola?" Gloria asks as she passes the crying baby to Lisa.

"We're going to stay over here for the next couple of weeks. Kamari is out of school and Billy is working around the clock, so it doesn't make sense to sit up in that big-ass house alone. At least I have you guys here in St. John," Lisa cries.

Gloria glares at Lisa with a stern look on her face. "Did you just say "big-ass" house? Lisa, I hope you haven't been cussing around Kamari. You know the child is like a sponge. She picks up on everything that comes out of our mouths, good and bad."

Lisa lowers her head. "I'm sorry, Mother Gloria. It's just that I've been under a lot of stress lately. Please pray for me."

"I will, but God will hear your prayers just as much as He will mine. I think staying over here makes sense and will sure make Roy happy. He misses Kamari so much. That man was ready to swim over to Tortola from East End if you didn't bring her here to have her party at Faith and Fitzroy's home. I hope you know what a blessing those babies are in our lives, especially since it don't look like Faith and Fitzroy are trying to do nothing in the way of making babies. Listen, why don't you let me keep Sarafina and Kamari tonight at my house?

Sarafina might take the bottle if she doesn't smell your milk," Gloria suggests.

"Smell my milk? You make it sound like she's a baby goat!" Lisa laughs as she covers her breast with a cloth diaper and starts to feed the cranky baby.

"Oh my God!" Lisa screams a few moments later.

"Did the baby bite you?" Gloria asks with concern.

"No, would you look at who just walked in? Fitzroy, Billy and Cathy!"

Kamari runs across the backyard and leaps into her daddy's arms. "I just asked the magician to change you from a 'damn ass' back to my daddy, and it worked! Mommy, my daddy is not a 'damn ass' anymore! I told you the magician could do it!"

Lisa is mortified! Gloria's mouth is wide open and she cuts her eyes at Lisa.

Everyone, including Kamari, bursts into laughter.

"Hey, Cathy. Hey, Fitzroy," Lisa says, ignoring Billy.

"And where did you find this missing-in-action pilot, Detective Brown?" Faith asks her husband as she embraces him with a warm kiss.

"I retrieved him and his faithful attendant Cathy from the St. Thomas airport, after he made a special landing so he could say happy birthday to his little girl. I'm just the chauffeur!" Fitzroy proudly says as Kamari gives her daddy a big smile and a kiss.

"Happy Birthday, Kamari. I brought you a little gift from the beautiful island of Dominica," Cathy says as she passes a wrapped present to the beaming child.

"Thank you, Miss Cathy! Daddy, can I open it now?" Kamari asks with anticipation.

"Sure, sweetie, it's your birthday."

Kamari gets out of Billy's arms and rips the wrapping off the gift, finding a beautiful baby doll dressed in Dominica's traditional festive clothing.

"Wow! She is beautiful! Thank you, Miss Cathy!" Kamari hugs her.

"That's so thoughtful of you, Cathy," Lisa says, smiling.

"Kamari, why don't you let me put it with the rest of your gifts?" Faith asks.

Kamari reluctantly hands the doll to Auntie Faith.

Lisa, still nursing the baby, walks over closer to Billy. "Fitzroy, you saved his Puerto Rican ass!" Lisa says with a smile.

"What happened to us editing our caca mouth, Miss Mother-of-two?" Faith whispers.

Fitzroy laughs as he walks off to greet his dad, Roy, who is helping the children get seated for the magic performance.

Billy kisses Lisa. "I thought I was wearing my invisible suit."

"You are!" Lisa says angrily.

Faith gives him a thumbs up as she walks away to help her father-in-law with the children.

Cathy smiles awkwardly.

"Hi, Billy!" Gloria gives him a peck on the cheek. "I haven't seen you since Skippy was a pup."

Billy laughs. "Mother Gloria, I'd like to introduce you to Cathy, my flight attendant."

"What a beautiful lady! Flight attendants these days are not required to be pretty anymore. When we flew here the last time, I know several of the flight attendants must have been old enough to apply for their Social Security benefits. Billy, you might have to hire an air marshal to protect this lady from crazy men trying to hit on her."

Cathy laughs, reaching out to shake Gloria's hand.

Gloria greets her with a hug. "Girl, we hug in Atlanta where I'm from."

Cathy smiles, enjoying the affection.

Billy puts down Kamari, who has found her way back up in his arms, and takes nursing Sarafina away from her mother.

"Birthday girl, come with me. Your daddy isn't going anywhere until after the big show. Let's go and get this party started!" Gloria encourages. "Cathy, come on with us. Maybe we can put you to work before you guys have to take off to the friendly skies."

Gloria, holding Kamari's hand, walks toward the little stage area where the show is about to start. Smiling, Cathy follows. Kamari's eyes are on her dad, looking for reassurance that he's not leaving.

"I'll be right there, sweetie," Billy assures her.

Kamari gives him the biggest grin and continues being led by Gloria to the magic show.

Sarafina is fussy. Billy plays Peek-a-Boo with her, and she starts to laugh.

"You know this shit is getting old, Billy!" Lisa immediately attacks him.

"I don't remember you cussing so much, Lisa. It's certainly not becoming."

Lisa stares at him with a look of disgust. "Maybe if you brought your behind home more often and didn't leave me stuck on Little Mountain with two very demanding kids, I might have better words coming out of my mouth."

"Listen, sweetie, today is all about Kamari. Why don't we join our daughter and family and table this conversation until…" Billy pauses.

"Until when, Billy? How about two weeks from Sunday? No, three weeks from next Friday!" Lisa storms off, leaving Billy standing there holding the baby.

"Well, Sarafina, I'd say that didn't go well at all."

Sarafina laughs as Billy tickles her. With the baby in his arms, Billy steps quickly to keep up with angry Lisa as she takes a seat for the magic show.

Cathy picks up on Lisa's anger toward Billy as she gently removes a little boy's hands from rubbing her long, straight red tresses. Clearly the little man is enamored with her beauty.

\* \* \*

Faith's Aunt Dot and her husband Marlin have been watching the whole scene between Billy and Lisa from a distance. They are sitting in a pair of lawn chairs under a tree, where Marlin has a baby goat tied and Dot is bottle-feeding the animal.

"Dem don't look happy, me darling," Marlin says.

"Yeah, looks like trouble in paradise," Dot sadly observes.

"Me gon have a talk wit Billy," Marlin says.

"I don't know, Marlin. Maybe we should just stay out of it. These young people need to go through a few things; it might make their marriage stronger," Dot says, unsure of her words.

"Dem might not survive the test and me don't want to see dem beautiful chilren without dey daddy," Marlin asserts.

"Lord, please don't let that happen," Dot prays aloud. "Kamari just lost her biological daddy last year and only God knows where her birth mother is. Since the woman left the islands what... three years ago, vowing to come back for her and never returned." Dot shakes her head in revulsion.

"The woman did de right ting letting Lisa adopt she. And look at how dat child look like Billy. Dat's Billy's child, ya 'ear! Me ain't care what nobody say… dat's he child!"

"Marlin, you are so crazy! Billy was nowhere around when that little girl was conceived! Now what's the big surprise is that little Sarafina is Billy's child! Especially when the two of them supposedly swore off sex until marriage!"

"Me could of tell dem dat not gon wok. God ain't make man not to get none, 'specially when dere's a beautiful woman in he face all de time. Man wood ain't bent dat way!"

"What? So what you do with your 'wood' while you was waiting for me to say yes?" Dot asks with a serious look on her face, needing reassurance that Marlin was not like her unfaithful ex-husband George.

Marlin quickly changes the subject. "An me can't believe Lisa leave Billy an go back to dat no good Trevor, too. You know how we all tink he were Sarafina's fadder. Lawd forgive me fa talking 'bout de dead. Me ain't sure if him up dere wit You but me hope so fa he sake, 'cause him was one lying, cheating man." Marlin looks up toward the heavens as he speaks.

"Why don't I invite the ladies over to the house tonight and we have a talk with Lisa and you get the men together and you guys talk with Billy?" Dot suggests. "I'm not sure how long he'll be on the ground, honey, so you might want to go over there and ask."

Dot gives Marlin a peck on the cheek as he beams like a schoolboy getting his first kiss.

"Certainly, me darling, I gon go ask he and me come back and let ya know wat him say."

As Marlin walks off, Dot quietly calls out to him. "And, Marlin, when you get back, I want you to tell me what you did with *your* 'wood' during our waiting period before we got married."

Dot smirks as Marlin picks up his steps, praying Dot will drop the conversation.

* * *

The magic show is in full swing and the children are loving it. Billy and Lisa clap after each trick while watching beaming-with-joy Kamari as she enjoys the magician and having both her parents sitting with her.

Wally enters the yard with a worried look on his face. Fitzroy and his dad, Roy, cross to meet him, wondering why his wife Lucille isn't with him.

Before they can ask where Lucille is, Wally blurts out, "They are holding Lucille at the police station."

"What station and why?" Fitzroy immediately asks.

"Right here in St. John," Wally replies with sadness in his voice.

"Well, we need to go and get her, right, son?" Roy directs his question to Fitzroy.

"Yes, of course, dad. Why is she being held, Wally?"

From across the yard, Gloria zeros in on the men talking and can tell right away something is wrong; she steps quickly and joins them.

"What's the matter, is everything all right? Where's Lucille? Why isn't Lucille with you, Wally?"

"Gloria, why don't you give the man a chance to answer you before you throw another question at him?" Roy begs.

"Lord Jesus, something terrible has happened to my baby sister! I can feel it! Please don't tell me she's… she's dead! I just can't handle that." Gloria feels faint.

"No, Mother Gloria, she's just in jail," Fitzroy calmly states.

"In jail! What in the Sam hell is she doing in jail! Wally, how could you let my sister go to jail?"

"Now, Gloria, you know how pig-headed Lucille is, so please don't blame me!" Wally yells.

"Well, I thought you wore the pants in the family!" Gloria screams back at him.

"Hold up! Gloria, attacking Wally isn't helping," Roy reprimands her.

Gloria calms down. "I'm sorry, Wally. Why are they holding her at the jail?"

"Wally was just about to tell us, Mother, before you started with the interrogation," Fitzroy calmly states.

"Well, get to the point! Lord, I hope she didn't shoot anybody!" Gloria nervously exclaims. "You know how crazy she gets."

Everyone stops and looks at Gloria.

"Okay, okay, I'm shutting up. Talk, Wally!"

"On our way here to the party, Lucille had it in her head that she wanted to get Kamari this Addy book to go with the Addy doll she ordered for her last month, so we stopped by the bookstore just down the road. They had the book, and it cost fifteen ninety-nine. When Lucille went to pay for the book with her MasterCard, the man told her she had to charge at least twenty-five dollars in order to use her credit card. Lucille told him he was out of his mind and she would report him to the credit card agency and sue him if he didn't ring up her purchase at the listed price. The man tried to explain that he had to pay six percent on the purchase, which made no sense to Lucille. She said he has pays the six percent regardless of whether the purchase is fifteen ninety-nine or twenty five dollars, so why is twenty-five the magic number? 'Hell,' she said 'since you're gouging your customers, why not make the minimum one hundred dollars?'"

"The owner of the store got belligerent and told her to put his damn book back on the shelf and remove her Yankee ass from his store! I swear I tried to get to the man and shield him before Lucille snatched him from behind the counter by his collar, knocking all the man's displays to the floor. One of the customers ran out of the store to the market across the way and got the security guard, who helped me break Lucille's grip off the man's neck. Look, mon, we need to get down to the police station before any more damage is done," Wally cries.

"Don't worry, nobody at the police station is going to hurt Lucille," Fitzroy assures Wally.

"Hurt Lucille? It ain't she I'm worried about! Lucille has threatened everyone down there, including the man's wife if they don't release her now!"

Wally, Fitzroy and Roy quickly leave the party and jump into Wally's car, speeding toward the jail.

* * *

Later that evening, after Kamari's birthday party, the ladies assemble at Dot's house.

Since moving to St. John from Atlanta, Gloria, Faith's mother and Dot, her aunt, decided to purchase houses from Faith and Lisa, in a section of St. John called Bordeaux Mountain. Faith and Lisa were originally building them for themselves, before the two of them became enamored with the island men they married who had their own homes already.

Faith's Aunt Lucille, one of the three investigators who left Atlanta for a visit to the Virgin Islands to see why Faith quit her dream job, has also gotten married to an island man and lives on St. Thomas in a beautiful home.

Even though Gloria's two sisters have gotten married, she refuses to let any man come close to her heart after having enjoyed over thirty-five years of marital bliss with her recently-deceased husband, Reverend Davis. She has made it clear to everyone that no man can fill that void. She had the 'perfect marriage' and her husband's memories will live forever in her heart.

Gloria and Dot's two beautiful properties border each other with spectacular views. They spared no expense in having a professional decorator put their personal stamp on the interior and exterior design.

Gloria lives alone, and Dot, who recently married Marlin, lives next door, when they are not staying on Marlin's pig farm a few miles down the mountain.

Faith, Gloria, Lucille, Lisa and Dot are all assembled in the living room of Dot's house, watching a chick flick on the television.

"Now as soon as they start cussing in this movie, I'm turning to something else!" Gloria says.

"No, Miss Holiness! What you are going to do is march your behind next door to your house if you don't like what's on my television!" Dot exclaims.

"Hey, just being around adults is a treat for me, forget the movie!" Lisa exclaims. "The kids are sleeping, and I'm just enjoying time with my family. It's amazing, the little things we take for granted that mean so much. You just don't know how much I miss you guys."

"We miss you, too, sweetie. I'm just praying Billy will agree to move you guys back over to the US Virgin Islands. What's a grandmother supposed to do without her grandbabies?" Gloria laments.

"You could move your behind over to Tortola and help Lisa out with the kids. It isn't like you're doing a whole lot over here in St. John other than sitting out on that veranda and looking at that awesome view. I'm sure you must have studied every nook and cranny out there by now and probably know each little island and mountain by name," Lucille sarcastically says.

"Lucille, you don't know what I do all day!"

"Sounds like the pot calling the kettle black to me!" Dot says, laughing.

"I beg your pardon, Mrs. Farmer and the Dot!" Lucille teases.

"You do the same thing, Lucille. Sit out on your terrace looking down the mountain, counting how many cruise ships arrive in the St. Thomas Harbor for the day! Who would have ever thought Miss Business Woman of Atlanta would end up on an island sitting on the veranda in her rocking chair? Looks like the both of you are leading the old boring life I used to lead in Atlanta. Thank God I have been delivered and live life with a purpose!" Dot raises her hands in the air, giving God praises.

"And just who do you think wants to spend their day on a stinking pig farm? I'm sure the highlight of your day is watching all the male sheep line up to see who's going to get their turn next to gang rape the ewe that's in heat! The animal police need to come in and arrest all of the horny bastards!" Lucille says with disgust.

"You are so nasty, Lucille! That's life for these animals. The ewe is built to sustain the pressure. Besides, the ram will refuse to mate if he hasn't been fed enough," Dot informs them.

"Sounds like most men! But Home Girl Sheep is probably too stupid to kick the hell out of them humpers. You know they say sheep are humble, little stupid, dumb animals!" Lisa interjects.

"Stupid? Dumb? You must be joking. There's a gang of three that can open any gate on the farm if they work together. They stick their tongues through the holes of the gate's latches; if a bolt is stiff, one will lean against the gate to ease the pressure while another slides the bolt back with his mouth and the third kicks it open," Dot proudly says like she's talking about some mischievous children.

"Sounds like the Gang of Three might be regular little convicts, escaping from prison life on the farm," Lucille says playfully.

"You'd be surprised at how much sheep are like us. They have best friends, Lisa and Faith; they seek out a boyfriend ram that they like the most. However, after they mate, they tend to forget which one it was," Dot sadly says.

"Sounds like some of my old girlfriends," Lisa says, laughing.

"Sounds like you," Faith whispers to Lisa, who hits her.

"I've been delivered from the lust of the flesh, for your information," Lisa whispers back, grinning.

"Everything you need to know about life you can learn on the farm. Those animals are amazing, and I have a relationship with each one of them. Now take Gertrude the goat. She and Gloria are best friends.
They sit around on the old concrete cistern, watching everything. Gertrude is such a gossiper, and Gloria just hangs on to her every word. Lucy tries to hang with them but Gertrude always snubs her. Three is a crowd; and she hates the fact that Lucy, who is a goat, hangs out with Diane the sheep. I think there is a rule that goats and sheep don't hang out together."

"Naw!" Lucille sarcastically shouts.

"It's true. Now a male sheep will never mate with a female goat. They tend to be a little racist. However, a male goat will cross the line and mate with a female sheep. And the little lambs and sheep will play together so well until they grow up and realize they are different. Then they go their separate ways and only hang with their own kind."

"Oh no! There goes everything I believed about *Animal Farm* and *Charlotte's Web*," Faith cries.

"Lord, Dot, you're harboring racist animals on your farm. I say we go and slaughter them and sell all their asses to Starfish Market!" Lucille angrily says.

"You are not going to kill my friends! I've got this under control. Gertrude's behind is locked up in the barn with Chester, the horny ram, so Lucy and Gloria can hang out together. They look so happy. And the baby lambs and the little kids I make sure they sleep together every night, sucking from each other's mother," Dot says, smiling as if she just helped save the world.

"Okay, that's it, Dr. Doolittle, your ass is coming off that farm for a while. You done lost your mind, talking to the animals and all up in their business," Lucille yells.

Faith and Lisa are dying laughing, rolling on the couch.

"Wait, wait, I got to go pee! This is too funny!" Lisa runs to the bathroom.

"I'm happy, Lucille, for the first time in my life. If you know what's good for you and Gloria, the both of you need to find out your purposes at this stage in your life because we are not getting any younger!" Dot says.

"I might be sitting on the veranda rocking this week, but as soon as Wally comes to his senses and realizes that son of his is still up to no good and needs to get his behind out of my club, I'll be running the best jazz supper club the Caribbean has ever witnessed! I'm just stacking my chips and waiting this thing out." Lucille proudly asserts.

"Good for you, Auntie!" Faith says, giving Lucille a high five.

Lisa runs back in the room. "Did I miss anything?" she asks, still laughing and zipping up her jeans.

"No, and did you wash your hands?" Lucille questions pointedly.

Everyone looks at Lisa, who smiles sheepishly. "I didn't want to miss anything!"

"Now that's just nasty!" Lucille chastises. "Girl, take your pee-pee hands back in the bathroom and wash them! Sounds like you don't have the sense of a goat!"

Everyone falls out laughing!

Lisa walks toward the kitchen sink.

"Don't even think about it!" Dot yells.

Lisa runs back into the bathroom to wash her hands.

Dot continues her conversation. "And just what do you plan to do with the rest of your life, Mrs. Former First Lady?"

"I already told you what she could do. Go over to Tortola and help Lisa with the babies. She can be like those Asian grandmothers. Their whole purpose after age forty is to never get anymore sex and carry the grandbabies around on their backs all humped over!" Lucille says, laughing.

Gloria throws a couch pillow at Lucille.

"Momma might not be the First Lady at Solid Rock in Atlanta anymore but she is doing a great job at Cruz Bay Baptist Church here in St. John," Faith boasts of her mother.

"Please! Gloria is just holding down the front row until one of those lonely ladies in the church gets Roy's attention and marries him. How long you think this brother-sister relationship Roy and Gloria got is going to last? As fine as Roy is, I know it's just a matter of time before one of them hot mollies moves in on that," Lucille says, snapping her fingers.

"Then I pray it's the right woman that God sends his way," Gloria says.

"Yeah, right! You better step back and take a better look at that man. Rev's been gone three years now, and it might be time to rethink this lonely, matronly-until-you-die role, 'cause I know you miss getting some," Lucille yells.

"You need to hush your mouth, Lucille, in front of these children!" Gloria admonishes.

"What children? Ain't no children in this room. Every one of these ladies are grown and getting some except you!" Lucille says with a serious look on her face.

"I say we change the subject and move on to other pressing business. Momma had a stellar marriage with my father, one that most women can only dream of. And I know when the time comes, she and only she will know when that is, and will either make a decision to remarry or stay a widow," Faith interjects.

"I second that!" Dot yells.

"Okay, back to why we're here. You need to stop beating around the bush and just tell Lisa to sit her wide behind down, now that she's washed her hands, so we can tell her a thing or two about her funky attitude before she loses that fine Spanish man!" Lucille says.

"When the Lord was giving out the gift of finesse, He just skipped all over your soul," Gloria says, shaking her head in disbelief.

"What the Lord gave me was the gift to eliminate B.S.!" Lucille rejoins.

"Praise the Lord, and thank you for that bit of information… moving on!" Faith interjects.

"This is a set up!" Lisa laughs.

"Yeah!" Faith says. "Now as your best friend ever, I feel it's only fitting for me to open this therapy session."

"I hope you start with prayer first," Gloria admonishes.

"Gloria, do we look like we're in church? Next you're going to want to read the damn bulletin and take up a collection!" Lucille screams.

"There is nothing wrong with a little prayer. I think it's important to invite the Lord into our conversation. Don't you agree, Lisa?" Gloria matter-of-factly asks.

Caught off guard, Lisa stammers, "Of course, Mother Gloria."

"Aunt Lucille, would you do us the honors of opening us up in prayer?" Faith invites.

Everyone is surprised.

"Oh, ya'll think I can't pray?" Lucille smoothes out her clothes, clears her voice and prays, "Lord, thank you for everything seen and unseen, heard and unheard and most of all, Lord, thank you for allowing me to be me, in Jesus' name and everyone says…AMEN!"

Lucille does a proud strut and snaps her fingers in her sister Gloria's face. "How you like that, Miss Holy Roller?"

Faith cuts in. "As I was saying, I will start the conversation. Lisa, your foul mouth is out of control and I propose that we fine you fifty dollars for every cuss word that comes out of it, including words like ass, pissed, hell, damn and punk, just to name a few."

Faith takes a seat on the couch, as if resting her case.

"Well, hell, ya'll not going to let the girl speak at all! Why don't you just cut her tongue out of her mouth?" Lucille throws her hands up in exasperation.

"Aunt Lucille, you're not helping," Faith whispers.

"No, no, let her say what's on her mind! I can handle it. Who's next?" Lisa asks, as if in a challenging match.

"Well, I'm concerned that you're all alone over there in Tortola with no help with the kids and it might be too much for you. I think you should talk with Billy about selling the house and moving back to St. John," Gloria proposes.

"Gloria, women have been raising children on their own for years! If Lisa's husband wants her on Tortola, then I think we should mind our business and let them work out their issues," Dot says under her breath.

"You can't even say that foolishness that just came out of your mouth loud enough for us to hear because it sounds dumb! Why should this woman live a life of misery like you did for over thirty years with your ex-husband George? Women just ain't taking that mess anymore, Dot! The days of girdles and corsets are over! We are free to choose where we want to live, when we want to have babies and whom we sleep with! You need to turn on *Oprah*, 'cause you are stuck in the sixties and life on the farm with Marlin is like the time machine captured your brain and took both of you back to post-slavery times," Lucille says.

"Thank you, Aunt Lucille," Lisa says.

"Just so you know, a lot of the past was good! At least women knew their places and men were men!" Dot says, her feelings hurt.

"You have a good point, Aunt Dot. I met a girl while I was waiting for the seaplane the other day to take me over to visit Chloe and Nyla in St. Croix at the Atkins' place. This young lady was dressed just like a teenage boy; basketball shorts that hang below the knees, Miami Heat tank top jersey, boys' high-top sneakers and a sports cap turned backward. Very nice young lady who shared with me her plans to finish school at University of the Virgin Islands and transfer to the University of Oxford. Then she asked me if I had a tampon," Faith shares.

"And your point is what? Lesbians get their periods, too!" Lucille snaps.

"I think Faith is just trying to say that God made a woman in that body, not a woman dressing up like boy. And no matter how much you try to act like the opposite sex, your womanly organs are still there and telling you that you're a woman not a man!" Gloria calmly says.

"Oh, please! Give me a break. With a little bit of money, that child can get that period stopped and a penal implant in that same little coochie area. Cher's son who was a daughter had it done! The man looks and talks like a man. He swears that's what God intended him to be!"

"A lot of people lie on God! Believe me, He didn't make any mistakes!" Gloria counters.

"Excuse me! But we are not here to talk about people's genitals and sexual preferences. That's a conversation for another day, and trust me, it won't be solved overnight! Let's stay on point. The last thing that was said that related to our topic was that Lisa and Billy would have to decide if moving back to St. John is a good idea," Faith says, as if running a boardroom meeting.

"Of course, it's up to Billy and Lisa to decide if selling the house and her moving back to St. John is the right thing for their family. We're just tossing out ideas for her to present to him for discussion. Faith, I think the fifty dollar fine per cuss word should be more like one hundred dollars per curse word. Lisa really needs to clean up her act quickly. Kamari is repeating everything she hears, and I swear I heard Sarafina say damn when I was bathing her," Gloria worries aloud.

"Mother Gloria, you are exaggerating! You know Sarafina did not say damn!" Lisa hollers.

"Well, when I told her it was time to get out of the tub, either she said damn or ham! Even Kamari was caught off guard and looked at me with a puzzled look on her face. We both shrugged our shoulders and the baby laughed!" Gloria shares. "However, on a more positive note, Kamari and I did get her to eat!"

"You got her to eat?" Lisa is surprised.

"Well, actually it was her big sister Kamari who shared her food with her. She pretended the spoon was an airplane like their daddy flies, and she made the sound and everything. Sarafina was laughing, opened her mouth and ate the food. Every time that airplane spoon passed her mouth, she opened up and ate," Gloria explains.

"Well, I'll be… darn!" Everyone looks at Lisa, who quickly uses a better choice of words.

"Mmm, looks like that one hundred dollar fine might be working sooner than we think," Faith says.

Laughter fills the room.

"Okay, okay, I'm in with the one hundred dollar fine, but I think it's only fair that all of us be censored, since each of us talk and share conversation around the children," Lisa says with a smile on her face.

"That's fair! I don't have a problem with that," Gloria agrees.

"I guess you wouldn't, Miss Polly Purebred! When was the last time you cussed?" Lucille wants to know.

"That's not the point. The point is we all need to be held accountable," Gloria says.

Lucille reaches for her purse and takes out a checkbook and pen.

"What are you doing, crazy lady?" Dot asks.

Lucille continues writing. "I'm writing a check for one thousand dollars! That should cover me for at least a month, 'cause I know I'm going to mess up!"

Everyone shakes their head and laughs.

"We might need to get one of those five-gallon water jugs to hold the money we rake in from Auntie!" Faith says.

"And what exactly do you ladies plan to do with this money? Both the kids have a college fund already," Dot points out.

"I think we should donate it to Rosalinda's charity in St. Croix," Faith excitedly says.

"Rosalinda raises a boatload of money every year already. This little chump change won't mean a thing," Lucille says.

"Why don't we take the money and use it to teach children about farm life and agriculture? Marlin has been dying to teach classes on the farm to local school children. He says if we don't raise up another generation of farmers, we are going to continue be an island of importers paying high prices for what we can grow here on our own," Dot expresses with concern.

"Now that's the most intelligent thing that has come out of your mouth all night, Dot! Hell, I might even throw in a few extra cuss words every month just to help the cause!" Lucille teases in response and pats her sister on the back.

Dot playfully hits her and all the ladies shake their heads in agreement at the idea, just as Wally, Roy and Fitzroy enter the house.

"Hey, what are you guys doing here? This is a pecking party! No roosters, only hens!" Lucille declares.

"I'm hungry, baby, and all the food at Fitzroy and Faith's house is frozen. I volunteered to cook, but it might be tomorrow before that goat defrosts, and Fitzroy insisted on us coming here because he needed to talk to Gloria about something," Wally cries as he moves toward the kitchen, where there are platters of food on the counter.

"Looks like all the food is up here, Wally! These ladies have a real smorgasbord going on. I think I'll grab a plate and do something about the rumble in my tummy!" Roy says with a big smile on his face.

"Excuse me, but the carnival village is open, and you guys have a choice of a wide selection of food," Lisa interjects.

"Are you crazy? That's Sodom City down there! And nothing but fried food! You can smell the grease all the way up Jacob's Ladder. No thank you, my dear," Roy exclaims.

"Oh, Roy, stop acting like a prude! Go on down to the village and get your swerve on! I'm sure most of your church members are down there winding up their backsides and chugging Heinekens and Guinnesses!" Lucille says.

"Hush that wicked mouth, Lucille! He who is without sin let them cast the first stone!" Roy says as he loads food onto a plate while talking with a piece of bread in his mouth. "Besides, I'm sure on Sunday morning there will be a lot of repenting souls at the altar and the Lord, in all His mercy, will be forgiving."

Everyone laughs.

"Mother Gloria, can I talk to you in private?" Fitzroy asks.

Nervous, Gloria follows Fitzroy into an adjoining bedroom.

Everyone in the room is wondering if something is wrong. After a minute of silence, except for the men fixing their plates, they all hear Gloria scream from the bedroom.

"That's a damn lie!"

"Ooo! Sounds like more money for the cuss jar!" Lisa hollers.

"And who would have ever thought it would come from Miss Polly Purebred!" Lucille says, chuckling.

# Chapter 4
## Billy Helps Cathy

"Thank you for flying El Shaddai Airlines," Cathy, the beautiful West Indian flight attendant says to each one of the thirty passengers as they deplane.

Captain Billy, standing at her side with a big smile on his face, gives a pleasant nod to his customers.

As the last person descends the staircase, Cathy greets the cleaning crew as they board. She finishes restocking the galley with wine and cordials then says goodnight to Billy, who remains on the plane with the cleaning crew in his pilot chair, making entries into his flight logs and making sure all systems are turned off.

After double-checking everything, he grabs his briefcase filled with travel logs and exits the plane. All passengers have cleared customs and disappeared from the airport, almost like magic. Once inside the lonely Beef Island terminal, Billy exits to his car that sits alone in the barely lit parking lot. He waves to Cathy, who stands at curbside, waiting for her ride to pick her up. As he exits the parking lot, he pulls up to the curb to make sure Cathy's ride is coming.

"You okay?" Billy asks, concerned.

"Justin was supposed to pick me up. I've been ringing his phone since we left St. Lucia and he's not answering," Cathy says in a defeated voice.

"Well, all the taxis are gone for the evening, so unless you plan on walking or sleeping here at the airport, I suggest you get in and let me drop you home." Billy reaches over and opens the door from inside for Cathy to get in.

"No! No! I can't ask you to drop me all the way west to Sea Cows Bay when you live right over there!" Cathy points to Little Mountain Estates, in the near distance.

"I'd be a terrible pilot if I left my flight attendant stranded at an empty airport in the middle of the night. Get in, Cathy!" Billy insists.

Cathy reluctantly climbs into the front seat with a smile of appreciation on her face. As they pass the turnoff for Billy's development, Cathy cries, "Lisa is going to kill me for taking you so far out of the way."

"Lisa and the girls are over in St. John while Kamari is on break from school," Billy reveals.

"Oh, then I don't feel too bad, other than the fact that your first flight departs tomorrow in five hours." Cathy laughs.

"Don't laugh too loud. Aren't you my flight attendant tomorrow?" Billy chuckles.

"Nope! Jessica is on for tomorrow! I get to sleep in until my back hurts!" Cathy says with anticipation.

"I'm jealous. I can't remember the last time I got to sleep like that. But, I knew what I was getting into when I started El Shaddai Airlines, and I'm in it for the long haul," Billy says with passion in his voice.

"It must be putting a strain on the family with you being in the air all the time." Cathy wants to take back her statement when she sees the smile on Billy's face drop. "I'm sorry, Captain, I wasn't trying to be in your business. Please forgive me, I was out of place."

"No, it's okay. And yes, it has been hard on Lisa and my little ladies, but I'm praying God's strength will carry us through for one more year. Then I'll be able to purchase another plane and hire a few good pilots so I can spend more time with my family." Billy smiles as he shares his short-term plan.

"Why don't you take out a loan and buy your next plane now? Why put off what you can do today for tomorrow? Life is way too short; make things easier on yourself and your family," Cathy matter-of-factly says.

"Well, because taking out a loan is called debt. I had the hardest time starting El Shaddai Airlines. The British government wasn't exactly thrilled with an outsider coming in and starting a business, no matter how much the people needed it. I had to put a British Virgin Islander on my trade license in order to be able to operate my airlines! A person who has no interest in flying whatsoever! I pay him a thousand dollars a month so I can operate without any hassles. The man can't spell El Shaddai and had the nerve to call me last week saying he wanted a raise because one thousand a month was not enough."

"So what are you going to do?" Cathy pries.

"I'm still praying about that. You know the saying; if you give a mouse a cookie!" Billy says, laughing.

"You better give that fool a cookie and some milk if you want to realize your dream, or move your business to the US Virgin Islands and just pay landing and departure fees to use the Beef Island Airport," Cathy suggests.

"It just might come down to that because I'm not going to let this man hold me hostage because his name is on my trade license," Billy says, very frustrated.

"Did you list him on the trade license as the majority shareholder?"

"Yes, but that was just so we could speed up the trade licensing process," Billy explains.

"Oh, you think so? Captain, that man owns the majority shares of your business and he can do whatever he wants to do with El Shaddai Airlines even if he has the sense of an imbecile."

Billy pauses and thinks about what Cathy just said. "I'm not worried about that. I'm going to run my race and move forward with my plans."

Cathy and Billy are both quiet as they continue the drive west. When they pull up to Cathy's apartment unit, Justin is hugged up on the porch with a very young woman on his lap. He rushes her into the apartment as if hiding her. Large-sized trash bags are filled and piled up at the foot of the stairs.

"What the hell?" Cathy screams as she jumps out of the car before Billy can come to a complete stop.

Justin meets Cathy at the stairs before she can put a foot on the first step. "All of you shit is here in dees plastic bags. You can take dem now or you got till noon when dem start burning trash at Pockwood Pond tomorrow."

"Have you lost your mind, Justin?"

"No, but you must have lost yours if you think I gon keep jerking me wood all de time while you fly around the

Caribbean. You ain't handling the business around here, girl, and so you been replaced. Now you can have your Captain boy drop you at your momma's or to a hotel but you ain't coming up here and get me girl upset." Justin stands with his hands on his hips like Superman.

"Justin, you know I can't go to Momma's house. She told me there was no coming back when I moved in with you," Cathy cries.

"Den looks like you got a problem. Dem might have a room at Village Cay or Maria's by the Sea."

"Justin, you know the front desk at all them places are closed!" Cathy continues.

Billy gets out of the car and walks toward Justin and Cathy. "Is everything okay?" he asks, knowing it isn't.

"Cool as a pig in sunshine far as I'm concerned but your girl here done messed up and find she self homeless. Maybe she can sleep on your plane." Justin belts out a big insensitive laugh.

Cathy is so upset she punches him a good one in his face, and blood spews out of his nose, dripping onto his white T-shirt.

Shocked, Justin grabs Cathy's neck and chokes her as she kicks him in his private area. Justin's young girlfriend has been looking out the window the whole time. She runs out on the porch and down the stairs to help Justin fight Cathy, ripping her uniform shirt open. Billy manages to break them apart and orders Cathy back into the car. Cathy gets a good look at Billy's girlfriend and she is surprised.

"Sariah! What the hell are you doing here with Justin?" Cathy yells at the young girl.

"What you think?" the young lady flippantly answers.

'So what you running up in that apartment, Justin, a daycare? Sariah's still in high school!" Cathy screams at him.

"Go on back in the house, Sariah! I told you to stay in dere." Justin is nervous.

"How you think I gon stay in there and watch she fight you?" Sariah cries.

"Just go on inside, baby!"

Sariah stomps up the stairs mad and runs into the apartment.

"You going to jail, Justin! That's my cousin Claude's child, and she ain't even sixteen yet! Claude is going to kill you when he finds out! Oh my God!"

Justin lunges toward Cathy to hit her. Billy jumps in between them, blocking Justin's punch and orders Cathy back in to the car. Cathy refuses to leave without her belongings. She and Billy load the plastic bags containing everything she owns into the trunk of his jeep and drive off with Cathy cussing Justin and condemning him to hell.

"I'm so sorry I got you into this mess, Billy! My girlfriend Yvonne lives just beyond the round-about by Virgin Queen. You can drop me off there," Cathy desperately says.

"Do you want to give her a call and let her know you're coming?" Billy suggests.

Cathy dials her number but there is no answer. "Yvonne turns her phone off at night and lets it charge. I'm sure she's home," Cathy declares as they continue driving.

Cathy stares out the window, biting her fingernails, reflecting on what just happened. "Can you believe that man is doing my underage little cousin? I need to call my cousin Claude right now to deal with that!" Cathy punches Claude's number into her cellphone.

He picks up on the first ring, recognizing her number. "Cathy, why the hell are you calling me so late? Somebody better be dead or something, 'cause you gon wake up Cynthia. She just got home from working twelve hours at the hospital," Claude whispers while walking into the kitchen with his cellphone.

"Claude, you need to go by my place and get Sariah. She's all locked up in there with Justin. He threw my stuff out the house in garbage bags and told me he got a new woman now. We got into a fight and here come your child out the apartment to help him fight me! She's wearing her big woman panties."

Cathy and Billy can hear Claude cussing into the phone then a click; he hangs up the phone on Cathy.

"He's on his way over there!" Cathy smiles as Billy pulls up in front of her friend Yvonne's place, which is accessed through an alley between two businesses.

"It's just back there." Cathy points out.

"You mean down that dark alley?" Billy clarifies.

"Yeah, it's late. I'm sure all the robbers are asleep by now," Cathy teases.

Billy gets out and opens Cathy's door. "Let me walk you to her door."

"You have done enough, Captain. I'll be alright. This is my old neighborhood. If anyone tries to hurt me, they are probably my family," Cathy tries to persuade Billy.

"Well, we all have crazy family members, so let's not take any chances." Billy and Cathy enter the dark alley together. Once at Yvonne's door, they hear her screaming at the top of her voice.

"Yeah, baby, get it! You know how momma likes it! Oh my goodness! Don't stop, please don't stop, dis ting good! Ooo, baby, don't stop! Yeah, big daddy! Oh my, you hitting my spot!"

Cathy is so embarrassed.

"Well, I guess that might be why she didn't answer her phone," Billy says.

Cathy starts to cry as they make their way back down the alley to Billy's jeep.

"Listen, Cathy, you can bunk out in our pool guesthouse until you find a place. I'll call Lisa in the morning and let her know the situation, but right now, I need to end this night and get some sleep."

Once at the Beef Island house, Billy and Cathy carry her plastic bags down the stairs to the guest cottage, a beautiful, open-concept one bedroom with a kitchen and spa bathroom, adjacent to a beautiful infinity pool and flagstone patio deck. There is an unobstructed view of Marina Cay, Little and Big

Camino and Virgin Gorda, as well as other neighboring islands.

Before saying goodnight, Billy prays with Cathy, who is surprised and feeling loved because of this. Cathy has never had any man pray with her before. Her parents are very strict Pentecostal Christians, who don't believe women should wear pants or date men unless it's with the intention of marriage. Cathy has never been able to find any men on the island who share their belief, even young men in their own church. She's gone out on dates with them, only to find out they are just horny and want to taste her cookie like every other man, Christian or not.

Cathy fell in love with Justin the first time she saw him in primary school but would never let him or anyone else know it for fear her parents might find out and shun her from the church and the family. After finishing school at the University of the Virgin Islands in St. Thomas, Cathy returned to Tortola and found herself living with her parents, who still wanted to treat her like a "good Christian" child. Cathy had to lie in order to go out, praying no one would report back to her parents if they saw her at a bar, party or any place where Jesus was not the center of attention.

Hanging out one night with her wild best friend, Yvonne, who encouraged her to go to a pajama party at the Bat Cave, Cathy spotted Justin from across the club, wearing pajama bottoms and no shirt. She, who was wearing a floor-length white gown with feathered high-heel slippers, was the belle of the ball. Despite her best friend's prodding to wear a sexy teddy, Cathy refused to go to the party looking like a hooker. Cathy's nightwear was so elegant it almost looked like a wedding gown. Justin made his way across the club with drink in hand and swooped Cathy off her feet. They drank and talked all night in a private corner of the club, stopping to dance every now and then, but for the most part they seemed as if they were the only two people in the world. It was only when Yvonne appeared in front of them saying it was time to go home that Cathy remembered she came with her. Justin promised to take her home and told Yvonne she could leave. Grinning, Cathy nodded her head in agreement.

That night, Cathy lost her virginity to Justin with the promise that there would be a June wedding forthcoming. Three Junes have passed and still no wedding in spite of Cathy's nagging and questioning Justin's intentions. Justin, a man with an insatiable appetite for sex, was a bit too much to handle for Cathy. Some nights, after flying all day, all she wanted to do was take a hot shower and sleep. Justin would meet her at the door, stripping her clothes off, ready to pounce. There were times when she would pretend to be asleep, hoping he would turn over and do the same; not a chance. Justin's sexual needs being met by her were more important than feeding him. For the most part, Cathy did fulfill her womanly duties, however, there was the one thing she refused to agree to and that was allowing Justin to put his private in her mouth. No matter how he tried to sugar coat it, put tasty food on it, Cathy just could not fathom something like that going into her mouth. The last time, after being pressured to no end, she tried to oblige Justin, but he pushed it so far down her throat she vomited all over him and the bed. Angry, he got up and jumped in the shower, not even bothering to help her change the sheets.

For some time now, Cathy had come to the realization that Justin probably would never marry her and was just hoping things would get better because she had no Plan B. Going back to her parents' house was out of the question. They refused to even speak to her after she moved into Justin's den of fornication. She had only been working at El Shaddai Airlines for six months, since its inception, for a whopping starting salary of thirty thousand dollars per year, which was barely enough to pay off the credit card debt she foolishly acquired while in college, and to help Justin with the rent and the exorbitantly-high BVI Electricity bill.

Justin was a brick mason, working on building the new hospital, but was recently laid off because the project got stalled until after the upcoming election. Depressed, he spends his days drinking Guinness beer and his nights at the local bar doing only God-knows-what. Lately, Justin has become resentful of Cathy being the breadwinner and having to ask her for money. Last week, Justin's dad offered him a job cleaning septic tanks with him. Justin told him, "Hell no," but quickly recanted when the bank called and said they were going to come and take his truck if he didn't catch up on his delinquent payment immediately. As horrible as the job is, it has restored some of his confidence as a man; at least he can buy his own beer, put gas in his truck and flash a few dollars to impress his new underage girlfriend.

After Billy prayed with Cathy and showed her around the guest house, checking to make sure everything she might need was in order, including a refrigerator with at least a few days of food, big screen television, clean linen, towels and a spa tub to die for, he said good night, walked up to the main house and climbed into his bed, falling fast asleep as soon as his head hit the pillow.

It was a while before Cathy was able to drift off to sleep. For the first time in years, she got on her knees and cried out to God for direction, feeling guilty because she did not heed her over-religious parents' words regarding the price you pay for disobedience.

Cathy was awakened by her cellphone ringing the tune of "That's What Friends Are For," a tune reserved for her best friend Yvonne. Barely able to see because of the bright sun beaming into the guest cottage, she stumbles to find her cellphone buried deep down in her purse.

"This better be good 'cause you woke me up out of a good dream. I was just about to be rescued by a hot handsome knight from some thieves who wanted all my gold."

"Mmm! Well, maybe you better go back to sleep, because I got a nightmare to share with you! Justin is in the hospital under police guard and your cousin Claude is in jail!" Yvonne cries.

Cathy's phone beeps, signaling she has a low battery.

"What the hell happened?" Cathy is coming out of her sleep-induced stupor.

"Claude's wife Cynthia called me a few minutes ago, screaming in the phone, looking for you. She said something about you calling her house late last night and Claude running out the house with his machete. Girl, that woman was so upset I couldn't understand most of what she was saying. I think you need to call her… or not!" Yvonne reports.

"She must be the missed call showing up on my phone. Yvonne, last night was the night from hell! My boss Billy drove me home 'cause Justin didn't come to pick me up. When I got there, Justin had put all my stuff on the street! But worse than that, he had my little cousin Sariah up in there! I called her daddy and told him. Oh my God, what have I done?"

"Sariah? Little Sariah who's barely in high school? Why didn't you call me last night?"

Cathy's battery signal peeps again.

"Billy drove me to your house because I needed my best friend and a place to stay! When we reached your door, all we could hear were you hollering, 'Ride it, daddy!'"

"Ooo, I'm so embarrassed!" Yvonne says, laughing.

"Look, if we get cut off, I'll have to go to the main house and call you back. I don't know where the hell my cellphone charger is."

"The main house? Where are you, Cathy?" Yvonne asks just as Cathy's phone cuts off.

Upset, Cathy decides not to go back to sleep but to sort through the plastic bags for something to wear, then jump in the shower, and call Yvonne back after she's had time to think. Overwhelmed with curiosity, Cathy turns on the television to the local news station, hoping there will be details of what happened to land her cousin in jail. As expected, Cathy finds two local reporters sitting at the news desk, reporting the twelve o'clock news.

"Thank you for joining us. Our headline story today at noon is, Sea Cow's Bay man chops off the fingers of a man with his machete after finding him in bed with his underage daughter!" the woman reporter says.

"That's right. Justin Deplantis is in the hospital, where it is reported all ten of his fingers have been severed. Mr. Deplantis is said to be in fair condition, heavily sedated and under police watch. Once the doctor feels he is in stable condition, he will be moved to Her Majesty's Prison to await his hearing for child molestation. The child's father, Claude Prentiss, is being held for malicious wounding. Mr. Prentiss is scheduled to be released sometime today once his surety is posted.

"In other news, the National Democratic Party has assured the people of the BVI that the new hospital will be completed sometime during next year once the funds are identified."

Cathy clicks off the television. With tears in her eyes, she quickly jumps into the shower and dresses in record time. Once out of the shower, she notices several keys, all labeled, hanging on the wall next to the refrigerator. Cathy picks up the key marked *main house front door*. Great! Lisa or Billy must have a phone charger.

Cathy is in awe at the beauty of Lisa and Billy's home. Everything is so well appointed and decorated with high-end quality furniture and appliances. Their home looks like it jumped out of the pages of a decorating magazine.

Cathy takes a peek into the one of the girls' bedrooms that's decorated like the bedroom of a real princess. This must be their daughter Kamari's room. Cathy picks up a picture off the dresser of Billy, Lisa, Kamari and Sarafina at the birthday party that Billy took her to a few days ago. The princess is wearing her tiara with a big grin on her face. Oh, how blessed Lisa is to have a godly man like Billy! Cathy gently places the picture frame back down on the dresser, feeling a bit jealous.

She moves on to another room where a baby-to-teen crib draped with a mosquito net that hangs from the ceiling over the bed dominates the room. A mural of farm animals is painted on one of the walls and bright and colorful ABC letters are on the other. A shelf filled with books and teddy bears is positioned in the corner along with a toddler-sized reading table.

"They're starting her off reading at a very young age; the child just started walking. These Yankee parents can really take things too far. The child will be sick of learning by the time she reaches primary school!" Cathy says out loud as she walks down a long hallway that leads to Billy and Lisa's bedroom.

"OMG! Would you look at that king-sized bed! Who sleeps here, Prince Phillip and Lady Katherine? Sister is living large up in this castle!" Cathy spots a phone on the nightstand, makes herself comfortable on the bed and calls her friend Yvonne back. Her call goes straight to voicemail.

Cathy leaves a message. "Yvonne, call me right back and don't give this number to anyone. I still haven't been able to charge my phone. Call me right back. I need you to help me come up with a plan!"
Cathy hangs up the phone and ventures into Billy and Lisa's walk-in closet. Dang! This closet is bigger than her whole apartment. You can open up a boutique with all the stuff she has in here!

Lisa's clothes are arranged by color and type. Cathy notices a section of nightgowns, long and short, hanging in a group. A long white nightgown catches her attention.

"Oh, my goodness, this is just like the one I wore when I ran into Justin that night at the Bat Cave." Cathy holds it up against her body and decides to try it on. Wearing it brings her to tears.

The telephone rings, and Cathy runs to answer it, making herself comfortable on the bed, ready for a long conversation with Yvonne.

"Okay, sweetie, tell me everything!" Cathy says, falling back on the bed.

It's Lisa on the other end of the phone, not Yvonne. Lisa has her phone video system monitor turned on; she can see everything going on in her house via her cellphone.

"Cathy! Why are you lying on my bed wearing my nightgown?" Lisa screams into the phone.

Dot comes running from the kitchen to see what's got Lisa so upset; they both watch Cathy as she sits up in the bed, surprised.

"Lisa, I thought you were someone else calling. I'm so sorry." Cathy is so nervous.

"Bitch, you still haven't said why you're sitting on my bed wearing my nightgown!" Lisa is boiling mad.

"Lisa, trust me, it's not the way it looks," Cathy manages to say.

"So you're saying what I'm looking at on my phone is not what I'm really seeing!" Lisa screams into the phone. "Where the hell is my husband?"

"He's flying. Please give me a chance to explain," Cathy responds.

"You don't have shit to say to me!" Lisa hangs up the phone.

Lucille and Wally walk into Dot's house having just come from Gloria's house next door, looking tired and sad.

Lisa walks right past Lucille and Wally, heading for the bedroom, as if she didn't see a soul. She slams the door very loudly. Lucille shrugs her shoulders, looking at her sister Dot for an explanation.

"Hey, Dot," Wally says in a very tired voice.

"You sound tired, Wally," Dot says.

"Yeah, it's been a long night, trying to get Gloria to find a little bit of peace, given the situation." Lucille sadly announces to the family members who are present. "She won't talk to nobody except Kamari and Sarafina. It's like those children are her new comforter. Wally and I think we should call a doctor to come up and give her a shot.

Wally nods in agreement. "You mind if I go out on the veranda and close my eyes?"

"Of course, Wally! If you like, you can go in one of the bedrooms and take a nap." Dot points to one of the rooms.

"Thanks, Dot, the veranda will be fine." Wally exits.

"Excuse me, but am I wearing my invisible suit, because I don't think Lisa saw me standing here. What's going on, Dot?" Lucille asks.

"Before I forget, remind me that Lisa needs to deposit two hundred dollars into the cuss bucket," Dot says before answering Lucille's question.

"They say when it rains, it pours. I just hope we're not expecting a hurricane 'cause this old lady can't take too much more drama," Dot rambles.

"Dot, what the hell are you talking about?"

"I'll deduct that "hell" from the running tab you have in the cuss bucket." Dot goes to the kitchen and takes out a small notebook.

"Dot, don't make me hurt you! Put that friggin' pad down and tell me what in the world is going on!"

"One minute, Lucille; I need to record "friggin'" as well." Dot jots down the two offensive words then heads to the living room where Lucille is about to lose her composure.

"Just before you and Wally walked in, Lisa made a phone call to her house in Tortola with one of those video phones where you can see what's going on in your house. That really, really cute airline stewardess Billy brought to Kamari's party was sitting on her bed, wearing one of Lisa's beautiful nightgowns," Dot sadly says.

"Oh heck no! Billy wasn't in the room, was he?" Lucille anxiously asks.

"No, thank God! The woman said Billy was in the air. She wanted to explain herself but Lisa cussed her and hung up," Dot says.

"I mean, what could she possibly say?" Lucille says in exasperation.

"Maybe there was an honest explanation. Who knows? I would have listened to what she had to say before I hung up the phone," Dot says.

"You are so damn gullible! That's why Sadie was with your husband all those years and you didn't have a clue! Sometimes I can't believe you are my sister!" Lucille screams.

"I am not gullible! For your information, I knew George was seeing Sadie!" Dot retaliates.

"And you did nothing about it! Now that's some sick mess!" Lucille attacks.

"Sick to you! All I wanted George to do was pay the bills and provide for the kids. After that, I didn't care who he was with, as long as it wasn't me! Now, I said it! And I hope he is happy with Zipporah living in Nevis because you want to know something... I'm happier than I've ever been in my life with my mango man!"

Dot walks back in the kitchen and angrily records Lucille's cuss word.

"Lisa... Lisa! Bring your behind out of that room. We need to talk. This is not the time to retreat! This is the time to go for the jugular!" Lucille screams as Wally looks in from the veranda door. Realizing more drama is on the horizon, he shakes his head, walks back to his easy chair and closes his eyes, tuning out everything except the Caribbean breeze wrapping him in its beautiful arms. It feels so good; sleep will soon come and who knows, maybe he will get to talk to Esther, his deceased wife, in his dreams.

## Chapter 5
## Denisha is Framed

Denisha and her girlfriend Camille Smith, a big-mouthed girl with weave hair, long fingernails, extremely high-heeled shoes and tight jeans, are in the car going to give the money back to Shakoi. Denisha pulls her car into a small quaint bed and breakfast hotel parking lot across the street from the bush where Shakoi lives. West Indian music plays in the car as the ladies talk

"You know I can lose me job over dis 'ere ting," Denisha cries.

"Denisha, gil, why de hell you give him de box? Me can't understand dat for de life of me."

"Camille, de lying man does say Officer Olga was wit he and dey was coming fa de box and fa me ta meet he in de car park and him would give me me car, and she de package."

"Me girl, something just ain't making sense 'ere. Shakoi have got your big ass whooped! You will do just about any ting dat man tell yata do! Honey, you stuck on stupid!"

"Maybe before, but dem days is over! Me gon take dis 'ere money back to he, grab my little bit of clothes from he place and take me behind back to me housing project and lock me door from all he shit! Look at me, Camille… Me finished!"

"Okay, girl. For de first time, me believe ya. Now go on down in dem thick ass bushes and get your tings. One question before ya go… Can't we just keep de money?"

"Hell to da no! Me ain't want dis money to come back and bite me. Dis 'ere ain't nothing but trouble! Now me done a few tings wrong in life but me mudder teach me never to take people's money dat don't belong ta ya."

"Wit all due respect ta ya mudder, Denisha, der is ten thousand dollars 'ere. Now me sure your mudder wouldn't mine if we took a little some ting, some ting as a finders' fee. Wha ya say?"

Denisha reaches in the glove compartment and takes the money out, gives Camille a disgusted look, then opens the door to leave.

"Me guess dat's a no! I gon be right 'ere when ya get back. Tell Shakoi ta send me a splif."

"Hell no! If you does want a joint den ya better bring your backside with me and ask for ya self. I tell you me finished! Me don't want a damn ting from de man!"

"You tink me gon walk in dat bush wit me new heels on? No sa! I parking me ass right 'ere till ya get back. Me ain't know why Shakoi ain't cut a proper road yet. The first time me walk down der I swear me never do it again! He house far down in dem bushes!"

"Camille, wha ya come fa? Ya supposed ta be me back up, girl!"

"Me got ya back. I gon be watching it the whole time while ya walk down der to get ya shit and give Shakoi *all* de damn money back. Denisha, you know I can barely walk on flat ground wit dees shoes. Gon, gil! I 'ere wit you."

Denisha sucks her teeth, crosses the road and disappears into the thick bush. Camille turns the music up in the car and lights a joint. A few minutes pass, and she notices a police car pull up alongside the road. She frantically turns down the music and closes the window so the scent of marijuana does not draw their attention. Two police officers, a woman and a man, get out of the car and head into the bush. Camille quickly texts Denisha to hide from the police coming down the trail.

Denisha pulls her cellphone out of her pants pocket and quickly reads the text. She lies flat in the bush, unknowingly on top of a red ant nest. Denisha can hear the two officers talking as they approach Shakoi's shanty, and she switches her phone to camera mode, videotaping them and their conversation.

"Oh shit! Somebody beat us here and shot him!" Officer Olga screams.

"What's that box next to his body?" Officer Sydney inquires as he walks over to examine the box.

"Damn! This box has your name on it, Olga! Fuck, this is the box the money was in. Someone shot him and took all our money!" Officer Sydney says as Olga is walking around in a panic.

"Half that money didn't belong to us! The Chief is going to be looking for his cut! Man, what are we going to do?" Olga cries.

"Let's go find his girl. I bet that bitch has the money!" Officer Sydney plants in Olga's head.

"When I find that project jungle bunny, I'm going to break this gun off in she fat ass!"

Officer Olga grabs the empty box with her name on it and quickly heads back up the path to their police vehicle, with Officer Sydney behind her.

The red ants are biting Denisha all over her body. She strips out of her clothes down to her shoes, moaning in discomfort, being extra careful not to scream out in pain. As soon as she hears the police car take off, she heads to the top of the road, making sure no cars are in sight. She darts across the dark empty road, butt naked, patting her body in pain, with nothing but her cellphone and the money in her hand, running to her car.

Camille has her face pressed to the glass, when she sees naked Denisha run across the road and jump in the car.

"What the fuck happened down dere! And where your clothes! Gil, you blowing me high!"

Denisha breaks out in tears. "I lay down on de grown when me 'ear de police come. Me gil, I lay right on top of a red ant nest! Lord Jesus, me whole body all bite up and me in pain! Camille… Shakoi dead! Dem find he dead and dey coming ta kill me next!"

"Who say Shakoi dead?" Camille wants to know.

"Da man body down dere all shot up. Camille, dem police officers does tink I kill he and take de money! What I gon do?"

Denisha cries on Camille's shoulders. Mucous is coming out of her nose.

"Look, Denisha; you my gil and all dat, but me ain't comfortable with dis 'ere naked shit and ya snotting all over me shirt. Now ya say you does have some clothes down dere in Shakoi's place?" she calmly asks.

"Sorry, girl. Sorry. Yeah, me does have clothes dere but me ain't going down dere! Did ya 'ear me say da man down dere dead!"

"Den drive you naked ass home and get some clothes. Shit!"

"Camille, you ain't listening! Dem police officers on day way ta me house ta kill me! Wha I gon go dere fa… ta die?"

"You got a point. Okay, let's tink. Soon as you put on some clothes, we can get de boat over ta St. John Carnival Village. Dem won't be able to find we dere wit all dem people. But we got ta get ya some clothes first."

Denisha stares at her best friend with a nervous smile on her face.

"Wa you looking at me like dat for, gil? Me know ya ain't gay! Oh, hell no, me ain't going down dere in dat dead man's house!"

A car pulls into the parking lot of the bed and breakfast. Denisha slides down on the floor, hiding until the couple enters the hotel.

"Camille, you does remember dat time you got busted fa weed and dey locked your ass up? Tell me who it was dat destroyed de evidence? Case never made it ta court."

Camille nods. "And me will never forget what ya did fa me."

"Camille, you does remember da time you get all dem parking tickets and parking enforcement put de boot on ya car?"

"Gil, you come to the rescue. Who would ever tink ta pay somebody in de parking enforcement ta burn all dem tickets?" Camille says.

"Me. I paid Ira $500. Couldn't pay me light bill, water bill or cable after dat. Sat up in de dark for two weeks wit no TV, current or running water, had to bathe at the police station."

"But me pay ya back ya money," Camille swears.

"Pay me wha? Me ain't never get a brown penny from ya!"

"Lord, all dis time I tink me pay ya back. Gil, me memory done leave me."

"You does know what dey say; 'A friend in need is a friend indeed!'"

"Me ain't never know what dat mean. Sound too stupidy!"

"It mean take you ass down in dat bush and get me clothes!"

Camille gets out of the car and throws her shoes in the backseat before crossing the road barefooted into the bush.

Denisha softly yells out of the car window, "Camille, look in the refrigerator, and you'll find something special for ya head. Dere should be at least a pound."

Denisha feels an ant in the crack of her behind. She starts hitting that area as it bites her.

"Oh me God, Oh me God! One of dem ants in de crack of me butt!"

Camille does a little dance as she quickly crosses the road, so happy to hear about the pot in the vegetable bin.

* * *

While en route back to the police station, Officer Sydney Huggins spreads the word by radio about the murder of Shakoi and that Denisha is responsible.

The police in St. Thomas and St. John have been alerted that Denisha and another woman have been spotted boarding the boat from Red Hook to St. John, heading to the carnival village.

* * *

Looking forward to getting some much-needed rest, Fitzroy enters the house from his yard, carrying bananas and coconuts he just cut from the tree. He finds Faith snoring very loudly in their overstuffed chair. Her teacup is empty.

"Let's put you to bed, snoring beauty."

Faith, in a deep sleep, manages to get up and stagger down the hallway to their bedroom.

"That soursop leaf is a serious knockout drug! I'm so sleepy! I hope you gave some to my mother. I've never seen her so upset. Will you please check on her before you go to bed, honey? It's been two days since she got the news, and it doesn't seem like she's getting any better." Faith yawns. As soon as her head hits the pillow, she is snoring again.

Fitzroy smiles at his beautiful wife and exits the bedroom; his cellphone rings.

"What can I do for you, Sergeant Pena? Denisha Liburd? No way! If you have a lead that she's in the Carnival Village, I'll go and check it out. I'm going to need you to make sure no one fires on that girl. I know her, and murder is not her style. The only thing she's good at killing is a hair weave."

Fitzroy removes his revolver from the locked box in his kitchen cupboard and straps it on. Just as he turns to leave, his father Roy enters the house.

"Looks like you're in a hurry, son," Roy says with a tired look on his face.

"Yeah, I need to get down to the Carnival Village and pick up someone. How's Mother Gloria?" Fitzroy asks in concern.

"The bush tea finally knocked her out. She put up a good fight. I had to give her the whole kettle of tea," Roy says, smiling.

"I thought you would stay the night," Fitzroy says.

"Yeah, I thought of staying, but didn't think it would be appropriate. Don't worry; I'll be there as soon as the sun rises. Besides, Lisa and the little ladies are there and Dot and Marlin are just next door. Let's talk in the morning. It's been a long day. Be safe, son." Roy hugs Fitzroy and tiredly heads down the hall to his bedroom.

\* \* \*

Fitzroy drives to Cruz Bay and enters the Carnival Village. It is packed with people young and old dancing and drinking like there is no tomorrow. The group Spectrum is on stage singing their Road March song, "We Brokes." The lyrics tell of the financial situation of the local people and the island's government, how there is no money and everyone is broke.

Fitzroy is talking and laughing with a group of police officers standing next to a concession booth that has a big sign above it reading, *Bump Dat Ting! Booth 7* There are about fifteen booths and each has a catchy name and a booth number.

Fitzroy's phone rings, and he recognizes Officer Huggins' cell number. The music is so loud he can't hear. He sends a text that reads, *Music too loud, text me!*

Fitzroy continues talking and laughing with the officers until he receives Officer Huggins' text message, a bulletin about Denisha that is now being distributed to all officers with her picture. Fitzroy shares the text and picture with the other officers.

"We'll circle the crowd around the perimeter, then work our way into the center. I know some of you guys over here don't work much with the office staff in St. Thomas, so take a good look at the picture. We don't want to take the wrong person into custody," Fitzroy tells his St. John officers.

One of the other officers speaks up right away with a smirk on his face. "Well, we have two things working in our favor, sir; one, is we know most of the people here, other than the tourists, and the second is that…"

He pauses to chuckle before he continues.

"You can see that big-ass hair piece sitting on top of her head from Google Earth!"

Fitzroy nods his agreement and continues to admonish his team. "Just so you know, this young lady is my receptionist at headquarters, and I know she wouldn't hurt a mosquito!"

"Yeah, I know her," another officer chimes in. "She's always on the phone! They should have sent a picture with a phone attached to her ear; then everyone would know her!"

"Okay, boys, let's move in and do this as discreetly as possible. Whoever apprehends her will bring her back to the station, and I'll take it from there."

All the men agree as they take their positions and move into the crowd. The music is loud, and the partiers are having a great time, including Denisha and Camille. The ladies are dancing wildly together and singing the words to the song.

Fitzroy spots Denisha and moves in to apprehend her. He taps her on the shoulder. She looks up, so surprised she falls to the ground. Camille quickly picks up Denisha's purse before the crowd steps on it, pretending it's hers.

"Get up, Denisha. I need to have a few words with you," Fitzroy says.

Camille continues dancing like she doesn't know Denisha and works her way deep into the crowd, hiding behind an extremely large man who welcomes her as his new dance partner. Fitzroy signals to the other police officers in eyesight that he has Denisha.

Denisha, with tear-filled eyes, gets up off the ground and allows Fitzroy to handcuff her without a struggle.

Fitzroy leads Denisha as they walk around the block a short distance to the front door of the police station. The door is locked, and there is a foul odor coming from the building. Fitzroy and Denisha jump over raw sewage that is running out of the building. Across the street from the police station is the fire station. Two men sit on the wall that surrounds the building. One of the men is a police officer and the other is a fireman.

"Fitzroy, over here!" Officer Williams yells.

Fitzroy and handcuffed Denisha cross the road to where the men are sitting.

"What's going on, Officer Williams? I need to book this lady and hold her in custody until we can transport her to St. Thomas in the morning."

"Me boy, de woman will die 'for morning if ya try ta put she in der! De main sewer line bust all de way from Abrams' farm to town!" he says, shaking his head in disgust. "We just now calling for all the firemen in Coral Bay ta come and help evacuate the eight patients at de clinic. The sea too rough ta take dem over on de hospital boat! The governor gon let the nurses and patients stay at he house. Dem dat ain't too sick, dey sending home."

"Officer Williams, what did you do with the criminals you were holding?" Fitzroy inquires.

"I let them go home. Wasn't but two. Mr. Lark, the town drunk, and Bishop Wells."

Fitzroy shakes his head. "Bishop Wells? What the hell, no pun intended, was he doing in jail?"

"Sad story! Da Bishop say dat woman, Lucinda Bramble, tell he she might be HIV positive and him need to get tested. All the man religion gone out the window and he lose it and start to choke de girl. She nearly die. Dem gon move she from de hospital to de governor's house, too," the officer sadly reports.

"Jesus! Fitz, wasn't dat your woman?" the fireman asks.

Fitzroy is shocked but manages to answer, "A very, very long time ago!"

"Dat sickness does have a long incubation period," Officer Williams comments.

"Hello, anybody know I 'ere? Can I please sit down while all you discuss other folks' personal business?" Denisha cuts in the conversation.

A fire truck comes around the bend and stops in front of them.

"My ride is here. Good luck, Fitz. If she were me type, I'd try and help you out! A little too "Ghetto Fabulous" for my taste!" the fireman says and jumps onto the fire truck, laughing.

The siren is blaring as Denisha screams over the noise. "You nasty face goat! You're not me type either!"

"Officer Williams, what time is your shift over?" Fitzroy asks.

"Not until seven a.m. Why?" he asks, puzzled.

"Great, then you're coming with us." They all jump over the raw sewage running down the street and climb into Officer Williams' police cruiser since they are on official business, headed to Fitzroy's house.

Once at the house, Fitzroy removes Denisha's handcuffs and places her in his cottage guesthouse with Officer Williams on guard at the door. Denisha and Fitzroy enter the cottage.

Denisha is impressed with the large beautiful room, complete with king-sized bed, sitting room and kitchenette. The bathroom is outfitted with double sinks, a jetted tub and a glass tile shower. Denisha takes a seat in the sitting room of the cottage.

"Dis 'ere is a nice place, Agent Fitzroy… Me could never kill anyone. Shakoi was mix-up wit some bad police. Me got video of dem coming ta Shakoi shanty, looking for dem money! Me hide in de bush and take it wit me cellphone."

"Do you have the video?" Fitzroy inquires.

A sad look comes over Denisha as she remembers her friend Camille picking up her purse, which has her cellphone in it.

"Me friend pick up me bag when me fall ta de ground in de village. I gon get de phone from she and prove what me say is true," Denisha says with excitement in her voice.

"Well, not tonight. In the morning, I'm going to have to take you over to St. Thomas and book you. If what you say is true, then justice will prevail," Fitzroy assures her.

"You does mean if me live to see it. Dem bad officers say dey gon kill me! Dem also say de chief gon be pissed 'cause half de money he money!" Denisha cautiously reveals.

"Get some sleep, Denisha. Now if you try and leave this cottage, I'm giving Officer Williams permission to shoot you in the foot." Fitzroy smiles as he exits, leaving Denisha with a look of fear on her face.

She walks toward the bathroom, closes the door and cries a river of tears.

\* \* \*

In the Carnival Village, people are still dancing to the sound of Jam Band as raw sewage slowly streams in. People are starting to notice the wet ground and smell the stench. One of the ladies selling food from her little shanty named *Feel The Groove Up In Here*, looks down and notices the sewer water on her open-toed shoes and can hardly breathe because of the horrible smell.

"Wha de hell going on 'ere! Lenny, come! Wha dis? Smell like coo-coo!" the lady vendor screams.

"Oh me God, dat is shit!" her husband responds.

"Shit? How shit come up in we booth?"

"Gil, me ain't know but move ya ass from 'ere now! Close up de place!"

Many of the carnival participants are running to the nearby sea to wash off their feet. Camille, Denisha's friend, holds tightly onto Denisha's handbag as she washes her feet in the seawater. Some people are so drunk they just fall in the water, bottle of beer in hand. The band continues to play until the power is short-circuited by the sewer water.

* * *

Back at Fitzroy's house, half-asleep Faith finds herself walking toward the kitchen and looks out the window toward the guest house to see who is crying. As she adjusts her eyes, it appears as if a man wearing a police uniform is asleep in a chair outside the cottage door. The crying continues. Faith uses the bathroom and returns to her bed but is unable to sleep because of the crying.

She gets up and finds Fitzroy sitting at the kitchen table, processing his thoughts. The sound of ambulances and fire trucks can be heard in the distance behind Denisha's crying.

"Fitzroy?" Faith cries out.

"Yes, darling; are you okay?" he asks.

"I'm fine, but I keep hearing someone crying," Faith says with a puzzled look on her face.

"Go back to sleep, honey. There's a lady detained in the guest cottage."

"What? Why is there a lady crying in our guesthouse?"

"It's Denisha Liburd. I need to hold her until I can take her to St. Thomas tomorrow and book her. Get some rest; we'll talk about it in the morning."

Fitzroy can see that Faith is completely bewildered, and realizes he needs to provide more of an explanation.

"Denisha Liburd? Isn't she your receptionist? I see a sleeping police officer sitting in a chair outside, and I hear a woman crying nonstop in between reciting the Lord's Prayer, and you want me to go back to sleep?" Faith has her hands on her hips.

"I'll put on some tea," Fitzroy says as he gets up from the table and turns on the kettle.

"Tea? I'll have coffee. I think I need to be wide awake to understand what's going on."

Fitzroy prepares coffee for himself and Faith. While the coffee is brewing, Fitzroy opens the kitchen back door and hollers out to Officer Williams, who jumps in his chair.

"Hey! No sleeping on the job!" Fitzroy yells and closes the door back.

"Now, I try not to get involved in your police business, and I hate that you feel obligated to explain what's going on to me but... this is my house and so I guess whatever it is just became my business too," Faith worries aloud.

Fitzroy takes three coffee cups from the cupboard, rests them on the counter by the coffeepot then takes a seat at the table with Faith.

"Faith, the lady in the cottage, as you know, is the receptionist at my job. Shortly after you fell asleep, I got a call saying she had murdered her boyfriend and was said to be in the Carnival Village. I went to the village and found her there."

"My Lord! You have a murderer in our guesthouse! Why didn't you take her to the police station?" Faith asks with a frightened look on her face.

"I did, but the police station is closed because raw sewage has seeped inside the building. The sewage is running down Main Street all the way to the sea, hitting the Carnival Village as well. My next move was to take her to the clinic and have an armed guard posted until morning but the clinic has been evacuated. The sewage line broke just above the hospital at the Abrams' Farm. They believe a group of cows trampled the pipe and busted it. Faith, it's a stinky mess out there."

"I hope those people at the clinic are okay!" she sadly says.

"The governor is allowing everyone from the hospital to setup a triage center at his house. My other plan was to take her over on the medical boat to St. Thomas, then I found its not running because the sea is too rough. I went to the firehouse and those boys are out helping to move people and clean up the mess. Just about everyone who uses water and plumbing from the government is having sewer problems. Thank God we have our own septic tank and cistern," Fitzroy says.

"This lady might kill us!" Faith cries.

"Denisha wouldn't hurt a fly! I'm sure this murder thing is a big misunderstanding. I've known this girl since she was in elementary school," Fitzroy reassures his wife.

"Did you talk to her?" Faith calmly asks.

"Sweetheart, I can't talk to her without a lawyer. All I can do is read her rights to her and hold her until she's officially booked," Fitzroy explains.

Getting up from the table, he pours the three cups of coffee, one of which he takes outside to Officer Williams, who is still having a hard time staying awake. Denisha is still crying and praying.

"Can I go and talk with her? Maybe I can help calm her down," Faith says after Fitzroy comes back inside.

"I don't know about that, Faith. I don't want to get you involved in police business."

"You said she's not dangerous; sounds like she could use a friend and this could be a great ministering moment where she can get to experience love and compassion."

Faith walks out the back door toward the cottage. Fitzroy signals the police officer to allow her to enter.

# Chapter 6
## Lisa and Lucille Confront Cathy

Unable to reach Billy on the telephone, Lisa decides to go to Tortola to confront Cathy, Billy's flight attendant. She asks Gloria to take care of the children while she's gone.

"The kids can stay here with me, I certainly don't want them in any foolishness," Gloria replies.

"I'll go with you, Lisa, in case a beat-down is necessary!" Lucille chimes as Wally gives her a look of disapproval.

"Lucille, like I said before, I really think you need to let Lisa and Billy handle this," Wally stresses.

"I heard you before, Wally! Now tell me why is it that I must do what you say when you have been turning a deaf ear on all the suggestions I've been offering to you about Wally, Jr. running the club? Sounds like some male chauvinist crap!" Lucille shouts.

"Lucille, you're crossing the line here!" Wally cries.

"Crossing the line! What line? Hell, I didn't know there was a line. It must be invisible when it comes to matters concerning you and your son! Wally St. Clair, I am and will always be my own woman and nobody tells me what lines I can cross!"

"Lucille, I only asked you to give my son a chance. His mother would have wanted that," Wally states.

"His mother? His mother is not here, Wally. It's me and you now! You know, that's the problem: you have not let go of your ex-wife. I have held my tongue on this matter long enough, and I just want to tell you I am sick and tired of competing with your dead wife and your… your drug-dealing son, who has managed to pull the wool over your eyes."

"Lisa, you ready? 'Cause this conversation is over. We got some lines to cross!" Lucille leaves Wally standing as she walks out the door swearing and Lisa runs to catch up with her.

* * *

Both the ladies follow the crowd into the immigration and customs area as they disembark the Road Town Fast Ferry. One line is for visitors and another line is for British Virgin Islanders and residents. Even though she is a resident, Lisa decides to stand in the longer visitors' line with Lucille. Visitors are asked to stand behind a yellow line until they are called. When Lucille is called to the immigration officer's desk, Lisa steps up with her, only to be insulted by the officer.

"Dis here is a big woman! I don't think she need you to come up here and hold her hand! Miss, you can just go back behind the line until I call you!"

"Damn, do you talk to everyone that rough? It certainly doesn't sound tourism friendly!" Lucille says, just as a spot becomes available in the residents' line and Lisa changes lines.

"Excuse me, lady; what did you say to me?" the customs officer says in her authoritative voice.

Before Lucille can answer her, the officer notices Lisa has changed lines and yells out to her, "Hey! What are you doing in that line?"

"I'm clearing customs," Lisa says.

"You need to get out of that line now! That line is for residents and British Virgin Islanders! You are out of place; so move it now!" the officer yells.

Lisa ignores her and hands her passport to the customs agent, who turns her passport to the page that shows she is a resident. Once the agent sees her status, she hollers over to her colleague, "Rest you mouth, Estelle! The woman is a resident!"

"Is your supervisor here? I really need to speak to someone about your horrible disposition, because I can't understand why you are talking to us like we stole your man or might be members of a terrorist group," Lucille screams.

Lisa and the customs officer who is attending to her shake their heads, laughing at Lucille.

"Don't worry about it, Auntie, let's just go. Some people you just are not going to change."

Lucille takes her stamped passport from the customs officer. "Have a better day!"

The customs officer sucks her teeth as Lisa and Lucille continue through the screening process and out into the streets.

Lisa's BMW SUV is parked in an adjacent parking lot. The women climb into the hot car and turn on the air conditioning full blast as they exit the lot heading east toward Little Mountain, Beef Island.

Lucille falls asleep during the ride, and Lisa is grateful for the quiet time. It gives her an opportunity to think about what she's going to say or do if Cathy is still at her house. Tears swell in her eyes as she thinks about Billy having an affair after all she has sacrificed in their marriage. Her pain is all the more raw because of what has recently come to light about Faith's father, Reverend Davis. As self-professed men of God, he and Billy are the last people she would expect to be unfaithful. *All men are liars and can't be trusted.*

As Lisa turns off the main road and drives through the Little Mountain Estates gates, she is greeted by the beautiful flowers that line both sides of the road and the spectacular view of the sea, a reminder of why she agreed to purchase this beautiful home. Lisa drives slowly down the steep driveway that hides their home from the road, revealing a beautiful view of other Caribbean islands; a view that inspires awe every time she sees it.

Lisa spots Billy's car pulling into a parking space. He must have just arrived. Billy gets out of the car with a smile on his face, happy but surprised to see his wife and Lucille in the car. He walks to her car and opens the door for her.

"Hey, sweetie! What a surprise." Billy reaches in to kiss her, and Lisa turns her head.

Lucille wakes up. "Hey, Billy boy! This place looks more beautiful every time I come here." Lucille stretches as she gets out of the car and hugs Billy.

"Is everything all right?" Billy asks with concern in his voice, looking at Lisa then at Lucille.

"Hell no!" Lisa says as she proceeds toward the front door of the house, stopping in her tracks as she sees Cathy coming up the stairs by the side of the house where the guest cottage is located, wearing her flight attendant uniform.

Cathy freezes, not sure if she should move forward or retreat down the stairs.

Billy sees her and calls out, "Hey, Cathy! Lisa and Aunt Lucille are here. Come and join us," he says in a warm and friendly voice.

"Don't you dare invite that bitch into my house!" Lisa screams.

Billy is shocked. Cathy runs back to the cottage.

"Lisa, I have just about had enough of your foul mouth and unbecoming disposition. What is wrong with you?" Billy sternly asks.

"Why don't we go inside and talk, guys," Lucille calmly says.

Lisa storms into the house like a spoiled child, flopping down on the living room couch, looking out onto a spectacular sea and chain of islands.

Billy walks briskly into the living room, standing over her. Lucille takes a seat on a nearby couch.

"What is that woman doing in my house?" Lisa screams.

"Cathy found herself in a terrible situation with Justin, her boyfriend, and nowhere to stay. I offered her our guesthouse until she could find a place to stay."

"And you didn't ask me if it was okay!" Lisa says in a nasty tone.

"Lisa, it was late last night. I told Cathy I would call you in the morning and let you know the situation," Billy explains.

"I don't remember getting a call from you, Billy," Lisa says.

"I overslept and barely made my scheduled run, so I planned to call you as soon as I reached the house, before I had to make my turn-around flight in thirty minutes."

"Are you fucking this woman, Billy?" Lisa screams at him.

"What? How dare you ask me something like that! We're married! I took solemn vows!"

"That doesn't seem to mean a damn thing these days! Look at Faith's father, a pastor who we just found out has a daughter who wants to come and meet the family! He took vows, too, Billy!"

"Oh no! I'm so sorry. Mother Gloria must be a wreck!" Billy says, looking at Lucille.

"That's putting it mildly!" Lucille replies.

"You didn't answer my question, Billy!" Lisa stares at him, waiting for an answer.

"That's a crazy question! I would never cheat on you!" Billy is upset at Lisa for asking him something like that.

"Then tell me, Mr. Holy Man, what in the hell was Cathy doing wearing my nightgown and lying on our bed when I called the house using my video connection?"

"What?" Billy asks, very puzzled.

"You heard me! That heifer was lying on our bed wearing my nightgown," Lisa says with tears streaming down her face.

Realizing that departure time for the next flight is soon approaching, Cathy cautiously knocks on the already opened door, sticking her head inside.

"Come in, Cathy, we need to speak with you," Billy says with authority in his voice.

"You sure that's a good idea, given Lisa's condition?" Lucille interjects.

"There has been a big misunderstanding and this matter has to be addressed so we can move on. Cathy, I need you to tell Lisa and me what you were doing lying on our bed wearing Lisa's bedclothes?" Billy takes a seat on the sofa next to Lisa, who slides over as if she doesn't want him to touch her. Billy shakes his head at her childlike behavior.

Nervous, Cathy stands in front of Lisa and Billy to explain herself. "Lisa, please allow me to apologize for any misunderstanding."

"Misunderstanding?" Lisa yells. "There's no misunderstanding here! I saw what I saw and there is no way you can clean that shit up!"

Billy cringes when Lisa cusses. "Honey, please let her explain herself. Let's be fair."

"Oh, so we're taking sides now! Well, you can kiss my—"

Lucille cuts her off as she is about to stand and leave. "Sit down, Lisa. We came all this way to get to the bottom of this situation, and you need to zip it up and listen. If you don't agree afterward then… we'll take it from there."

Lisa sits down and Billy looks at his watch, knowing they only have a little while to resolve this before he and Cathy have to leave and board his plane for Dominica.

"Lisa, I came upstairs looking for a charger for my phone and found myself in you and Billy's bedroom. Your closet door was open, and I was amazed at how neat and orderly you had everything hung. I spotted this white nightgown that was identical to the one I wore to a pajama party at the Bat Cave years ago, the night when my Justin and I became one; the night I lost my virginity. I put the gown on, trying to relive a very happy moment in my life. Before I went in your closet, I had called my girlfriend Yvonne on your bedside phone because while we were talking earlier downstairs, my cellphone died. Yvonne was telling me that my boyfriend Justin, who put me out and threw all my things on the street last night, is now in the hospital with ten fingers missing. You see, when Justin didn't pick me up from the airport last night when our flight came in, Billy gave me a ride home and witnessed all the confusion and he saw I had nowhere to go, so he offered your guest house. On the way here last night, I called my cousin and told him his young daughter was at my house with Justin. Well, Claude went over there with his machete and chopped Justin's fingers off and now he's in jail," Cathy cries.

"And just what the fuck does that have to do with me? You think I want to hear your pitiful story? Get your shit and leave my house now!" Lisa screams.

Billy is shocked, as well as Cathy and even Lucille.

"Whoa! What are you saying, Lisa? Cathy has just explained to you what happened and you respond like that! Unacceptable!" Billy is up and pacing.

"Unacceptable, my ass! I want her to get her stuff and leave my house now!" Lisa cries.

"I think you need a little time to think about this, Lisa. Let's go, Cathy, our flight leaves in ten minutes."

Cathy looks confused as she and Billy walk toward the door to leave. Lisa throws a beautiful vase in their direction, just missing her husband's head.

Lucille is shocked; she and Lisa sit quietly until Lisa's uncontrollable sobbing breaks the silence. Lucille rocks her in her arms until she is able to compose herself.

Lucille, for the first time in many years, finds herself lost for words. She is wondering how you tell someone they are wrong, especially when you know a few years ago or maybe even now, given the same situation, you would have reacted the same way. It's so much easier to see the light when you're on the outside looking in.

Lucille believes every word Cathy said, and she feels sorry for her, just as she does Lisa, who because of all the hurt and lies in her life, has become hard and finds it difficult to believe any man. Her last mistake, Trevor, really took her for a loop. She was so gullible and believed every lie that came out of his mouth until she was face to face with a woman who was pregnant just like herself, saying she was having Trevor's baby, too. Trevor died before Lisa's baby was born, leaving her to raise his daughter Kamari, who she adopted alone. Thank God Billy turned out to be the father of the baby she thought she was carrying for Trevor, as well as the fact that Billy loved her adopted child Kamari just as if she was his birth child.

Regardless of Billy being a man of God and just about a saint, Lisa has put him in the category of all the men she's let her guard down for and got hurt; including her first husband Jason, who she found out preferred men instead of women and took her to the cleaners for everything she owned.

The ride back on the ferry to St. John was very quiet. Lucille becomes very concerned about Lisa. She has never seen her this depressed before and has no idea how to help her. Her sister Gloria is still in shock upon finding out her deceased man-of-God husband of over thirty years has an out-of-wedlock child who wants to come and meet her is out of her mind and not speaking to anyone, and now Lisa.

Lucille thinks of her own marriage of three years, which seems to be a little rocky now. She tries to remember the last time she and Wally hugged, said I love you, had sex, or went out on a date. Then it hit her, she is so busy trying to help everyone else that her own marriage is in serious need of repair.

Lucille immediately calls Faith. She's Lisa's best friend, and it's time she steps up to the plate and helps her as well as her mother Gloria. Lucille needed to go home and repair the damage she made at her own house. As soon as the boat pulls into dock, Lucille calls Wally and asks if he will meet her for dinner at their favorite restaurant. Wally is surprised, and Lucille hears it in his voice.

"Mister, if you don't mind, I'd like to date my husband tonight!" she says with laughter in her voice, something he hasn't heard in a long time.

"Well, I have to think about it and it all will depend on who's paying the bill, 'cause I'm very hungry and it could be very expensive!" Wally says in a playful voice.

"Baby, you can order anything on that menu your precious heart desires and don't worry about the bill because the sister got this! Ain't nothing too good for my baby!" Lucille laughs.

"Didn't Diana Ross say that?" Wally chuckles.

"Whoever said it, stole it from me… so, what you gonna do… Baby?"

"I'm getting dressed right now as we're talking! You can call me a lot of things but never late for a meal," Wally teases.

"Mmm! Listen, baby, do me a favor… while you're getting dressed… leave off the underwear!"

# PART TWO

# Chapter 7
## Denisha Flees

Denisha, wearing sunglasses and an old-lady style wig, finds a pay phone at the St. Thomas Airport and calls Fitzroy.

Fitzroy is in his backyard, whacking weeds with his machete. The sun is beginning to set, and the beautiful colors in the sky are so vibrant. Fitzroy stops to take a sip from a glass of lime-aid, resting on a stump of wood when his phone rings.

"Special Agent Brown…this is Denisha Liburd."

"Miss Liburd. How did you get this number?"

"Sir, you forget me de receptionist at the police department? Me have access to everybody's phone numbers."

"Okay. And I guess you also have you own personal cellphone in jail?"

"Me ain't in jail, sir. Me get out."

"Wow, Ms. Liburd. You were able to raise one million dollars for bail?"

"No, sir. Me just call a friend and explain de situation me in and day call a friend and den me get out. But me ain't call you ta discuss all dat."

"Why did you call me, Ms. Liburd?" Fitzroy asks.

"Me know you an honest man. Me try ta tell ya when me was at you house dat I ain't kill Shakoi. Me went to he house to give he back some money he throw in me car dat him owe me. Me know dat money gon put me in trouble. Before me could reach he house, two police officers get dere first and I 'ear dem talking about money an tings and how dey gon kill me 'cause dem tink me got de money. Dem say half de money belong to de chief. When dem leave, me see Shakoi sittin' in he chair, buck-eyed dead wit a joint in he mouth," Denisha manages to say without tearing up.

"Do you have any witness to corroborate your story?" Fitzroy inquires.

"Sir, me ain't know what "corroborate" mean, but me done email ya de video dat me take on me phone, of de police officers at Shakoi's house. Me video it while me hide in de bushes. Sir, me tell you dis before. Check ya email and you gon have all de evidence," Denisha calmly says.

"Please deposit fifty-cents or your conversation will end in twenty seconds," a recorded voice interrupts.

Denisha dumps her purse out and finds two quarters.

"Sounds like you're at the airport, Denisha. If you're planning on leaving the island, I can have an officer there to pick you up in one minute or less."

"Listen ta me, sir. Me ain't kill nobody and me never will. Der are bad people… bad cops trying to kill me and if me stay 'ere… me dead. Now unless we does have a witness protection program, me gon have ta leave. Check ya email, den you can see de video and find de real killers. Me know Wally Jr. from he fadder Supper Club is part of dis mess 'cause him drop de box at de police station, wit Officer Olga Hernandez' name on it. Shakoi call me and ask me ta meet he on de parking lot and she gon come fa de box. Me meet he and somebody in a smoke-window car come fa he an' de box. Whoever dat was in de car me believe kill Shakoi, take de money an' frame me." Denisha pleads with Fitzroy to believe her.

Fitzroy recalls what he saw outside the window of his office while Denisha is telling her story. "I believe you, Denisha. What we have here is one officer trying to double cross the other officer and frame you. The car Shakoi jumped into belonged to Officer Sydney Huggins," Fitzroy divulges. "I'll take care of the problem. Now, Denisha, I can't tell you this, so it's off the record… Be safe!

"Please tell Faith t'anks for comin' ta visit me in jail. Me will never forget she kindness."

Fitzroy is surprised that Faith went to visit Denisha.

Denisha hangs up the phone and walks through the immigration clearance area to her gate, to board her plane to Hawaii.

"Hawaii. Sounds like a wonderful place to be going," the customs officer says.

"Yes, sir, it does!"

Pushing her way through the customs line, wearing a grass skirt, straw hat, platform sandals and Hawaiian shirt is Camille, Denisha's friend.

"Excuse me, excuse me! Me trying to catch up wit me friend! Excuse me. What a lovely pair of shoes you're wearing," Camille says to a lady standing in line. "Denisha! I'm coming!"

Denisha shakes her head, smiling at her friend as she works her way through the crowd. Finally, Camille reaches her, out of breath.

"Now you don't know a damn soul in Hawaii, so how you tink I gon let you go over der by yourself!"

The two ladies hug, then continue rolling their carry-ons to their departure gate.

* * *

Back at Wally's Supper Club, Junior finds himself in a bad situation.

Wally Jr., Officer Olga Hernandez, and Officer Sydney Huggins are in the office of the Supper Club, along with the chief of police, who is out of uniform, neatly dressed in a pair of slacks and a button-down designer shirt.

"Tell me again wa happen? It's 'bout ta get real ignorant up in here!" the chief says with a mean look on his face.

"De dead boy, Shakoi, get de box wit de money from he gilfriend, and she go to he shanty an kill he an take de money," Olga explains.

"Dat don't make no sense. De gil already had de box wit de money in she office so she ain't got ta kill nobody. If she want de money, she just had ta open de box and take the shit out!" the chief screams.

"Me ain't never look at it like dat. Sydney, why you tink de girl kill de boy? Dat's what you say," Olga asks.

"Me agree. Dat don't sound right. Besides, me does know de girl. She ain't so book smart but she ain't no thief. Denisha always help people. When me mudder was dying from cancer, she would come to we house and read de Bible to me mudder. De girl had a fish fry in de police station parking lot to raise money fa dat officer dat got killed last year family. No, dat don't sound right," Wally Jr. chimes in, shaking his head in disbelief.

"Don't try to bullshit de bull-shitter. Me done run dis 'ere scam before meself! Now one of you done get de money and tying ta blame it on de gil. Me know it can't be Wally Jr., 'cause he's a punk-ass and know me would kill he; besides, everybody does agree he give de box ta de girl. Now, ya got tree days ta come up wit me $200,000 or de drugs you was supposed to buy, or me gon kill everybody." The chief points his finger at each of them and turns to leave.

"Excuse me, Mr. Chief of Police, but you not gonna kill me, are you? Remember we all agree me ain't have nothing ta do wit de money being missin'," Wally Jr. pleads with a big humble grin.

"No, me ain't gon kill you, but me gon whoop ya ass so bad dat you gon wish ya was dead, 'cause dat was some dumb shit fa you ta listen to dees assholes and put $200,000 in a box and deliver it to de police station! And ya know I does tell all de officers I best not catch dem at Wally's, and look me 'ere." The chief rants.

The chief walks out of the office. Officer Sydney quickly follows him, leaving Wally Jr. and Officer Olga in the office.

As the chief and Officer Sydney step out on the porch of the supper club, Fitzroy cruises by in a van. He waves to his colleagues, and they nervously wave back.

"Shit." The chief mutters under his breath.

"Listen, Chief. I need you to know it wasn't me. Dat Spanish bitch probably got the money. I'm going to search her shit, and I'm sure I'll find evidence proving she took it."

"Man, me ain't give a flying fuck about the shit ya talking! Just get me ma money! Me ain't need no evidence! Me need me money! Ya got tree days!" He walks down the stairs to his car parked in front of the supper club.

Officer Olga steps on the porch. "You're trying ta put da shit on me, Sydney!"

"Hell no! We're partners! I know dat girl take de money!"

"You full of shit, Sydney, and me ain't going down like a punk!"

As Sydney tries to say something, Olga puts her hand up to his face to stop him. She continues down the stairs to her police cruiser. She flips him off.

He continues talking. "Dey catch she in de Carnival Village and put she in jail. Let we go to de jail and rough she up! De girl will tell we where de money is."

"Your dumb ass don't know; de girl gone!" Olga retorts with anger.

Sydney stomps his feet and throws his hands up in the air in disbelief and frustration. "Hell no! It can't be true!" he screams.

# Chapter 8
## Roy Counsels

Kamari opens the door to Gloria's home for Roy, who picks her up and showers her with tickles and hugs. Little Sarafina toddles over to them, and Roy knows the little lady does not want to be denied his affection. Roy picks her up and balances two happy children in his arms as Gloria enters the living room from the terrace, delighted to see Roy and the happy grandchildren laughing.

"Hey, Roy! Now don't let those babies cause your back to go out!" She smiles as Roy lowers the girls to the floor.

"Would you look at that smile? I don't think I've seen it in weeks! Praise the Lord!" Roy teases as he notices Gloria.

"Poppa, my daddy bought me a new tea set. Sarafina broke my old one. Would you like to have a tea party with me?" Kamari inquires.

Sarafina, not wanting to be left out, says, "Tea...tea!" She grins, showing all four of her teeth.

"Sarafina, you're not invited. You make too much of a mess. It's just going to be me and Poppa!" Kamari says.

Sarafina has a confused, sad look on her face.

"Well, Kamari, don't you think we need a guest at our tea party? I think if we put your little sister in her highchair that would minimize the amount of damage she will be able to do to your new tea set," Roy ventures to suggest.

Kamari thinks about it and nods her head.

"But first I need to talk to your grandmother. Maybe we can persuade her to join us?" Roy says with a big grin on his face.

"Please, Grammy, please?" Kamari is jumping up and down.

"Lord, Roy, what are you trying to get me into? These old knees have trouble bending down to that little table," Gloria says, hoping she will be excused.

"Then we'll change the venue! We'll have the tea party on the terrace," Roy says.

"Great idea, Poppa! Right, Sarafina?" Kamari is delighted.

Sarafina, not sure of what is being said, lets out a big cackle while flapping her arms, trusting that they must have said something good and she is included. Everyone laughs.

"But listen, sweetie, I'm going to need you to give me a little time to talk to your grandmother before we have our tea party." Roy bends down to the children's level as he talks.

"Okay, Poppa," Kamari agrees.

"Kamari, you and Sarafina go in the room and wake your mother up and tell her to put on your *Veggie Tales* video. We should be ready for the tea party after it's finished."

Kamari skips off toward the bedroom with Sarafina toddling behind her, falling down and getting back up several times until she decides to crawl.

Gloria and Roy make their way out onto the terrace where Gloria has a pitcher of ice water and sliced limes on the center of the patio table with glasses and a tray of tarts.

"Are those guava tarts?" Roy asks as he joyously reaches across the table for one and a napkin.

"Yep! Sister Claudette at the church said they were your favorite and insisted I buy them at the bake sale she organized for the K-5 students yesterday," Gloria says, teasing him.

"Yes, Sister Claudette… what's one to do? She dropped off a dozen of the same guava tarts at the house last night, inviting herself in for tea," Roy says, laughing and shaking his head.

"I certainly hope you didn't give her any of that bush tea that knocks you out like a bolt of lightning! If you did, then I know all memory of what happened last night is gone," Gloria says, teasing Roy.

"That's why I woke up and found her asleep on the sofa wearing my house robe!" Roy says.

Gloria has a look of shock on her face. "Roy!" she hollers.

"Just kidding! You set yourself up for that one, Gloria." Roy is bent over laughing.

Gloria jokingly hits him. "You are a terrible pastor! I can't believe I fell for that! Let's see who will have the last laugh. I know Claudette has her eye on you and if she has things her way, we'll be having a wedding real soon!"

"Well, I have not heard anything from the Lord leading me in that direction! And I truly believe Him when He says 'Wait on the Lord…' I say wait!"

Both Roy and Gloria are laughing.

"Enough about Claudette. What I need to know is how you are doing. This young lady who says she is Faith's sister is arriving tomorrow to meet everyone and as your pastor and most importantly friend, I have to be sure you are okay. It's been a rough few weeks for you since you found out about this child. Are you ready to meet her, Gloria?"

"How do you ever get ready to meet a child who was conceived with a woman your husband was having an affair with? Am I ready? No. Am I angry? Yes! Do I blame the child? No. I've thought about nothing but this for the past three weeks, and I think I've finally found peace. Besides, what can I do about it? The damage has already been done," Gloria says with sadness and resignation in her voice.

"Well, that's true, but we are human and as humans we do sometimes hold bitterness and anger," Roy presses.

"I'm not going to lie to you, Roy. I am so angry with the Rev that if he were here, I'd divorce him in a heartbeat right after I smacked his face! How dare he make a fool out of me? For over thirty years, I sat on the front row of Solid Rock Baptist church as the First Lady and supported him," Gloria fumes. "I wonder how many people in the church knew about this affair and were talking behind my back. What a fool I was. And to add insult to injury, I found out the mother of that child was the President of our Altar Guild, Barbara Bedford, who sat right behind me every Sunday during service! The woman was pregnant the same time I was pregnant with Faith! When the Women's Auxiliary Committee gave me my baby shower, I insisted they make it a duel shower for the both of us." Gloria is upset and hyperventilating.

Roy pats her back to calm her down.

"That dirty dog! And what kind of woman was Barbara to accept the invitation of having her baby shower with me? I always thought she was a strong Christian woman grounded in the Word and stood on the principals of God. Roy, you can't trust a soul! Another thing that has been made clear to me is I saw that woman arrive at the hospital to deliver her child the same day Rev was taking me home from the hospital with Faith. Rev and I stopped and prayed with her! No wonder he dropped me home so fast and told me he would be right back! The man went back to the hospital to help deliver Barbara's child!"

Gloria starts crying and Roy comforts her.

"Now, now, Gloria, calm yourself down. You don't know all that. Let's not add anymore to a terrible situation."

Roy pours a glass of lime water for Gloria, who gulps it down in between sobs.

"I had my niece Debbie go to the Office of Vital Statistics and pull the child's birth certificate. Rev is listed as the father and the baby was born that same day we checked out of the hospital."

Roy hands Gloria several napkins and pulls his chair close to Gloria and takes her hand in his. "Gloria, believe it or not, but by the grace of God we are going to get through this! Now, it's killing me to see you hurt like this! I feel so helpless but I need you to know that I am here with you; you are not alone." Roy holds Gloria in his arms as she stops crying and gives him a big smile.

"Now that's my Gloria, strong and a survivor! God won't give us more than we can bear."

"I'm going to have to have a talk with God about that one when I get to heaven, because I swear He gave me my burden and a whole lot of other folks', too." Gloria says, shaking her head.

"That's because you're a strong woman like I said; and you will have a testimony for other women who think they can't make it, starting with the mother of our grandchildren." Roy points toward the bedroom where Lisa is.

"Oh, buddy! Now that's one hard knot to untangle in there. She almost made me lose my religion last night. And I'm sure that's why she's been locked up in that room all morning."

"Did the two of you have a fight?" Roy wants to know.

"That's putting it mildly. If she was twenty years younger, I would have put her across my knee and gave her one good whacking! Billy has been calling Lisa day and night and all she does is hang up the phone on him. Roy, God is my witness, the man is going to get enough of her stubborn ways, and she is going to run him into the arms of that woman. Now, I said it and that's that."

"I rebuke that in the name of Jesus, Gloria. Those children need their father," Roy says.

"You know it, and I know it. Now all we need is for Lisa to know it!" Gloria gets up and paces the floor. "I think it's time I had a talk with her. I was hoping you, Faith, Dot and Lucille might have been able to get her back on track, but doesn't look like that's happening," Roy ponders aloud.

"I don't know what you're going to say that will be any different than what we've said already. Lisa is stuck on what Trevor did to her and that little sissy husband she married in

Los Angeles. Another example of her hard-headedness. We all asked her in our own way, before she married him, if the man was a homosexual and she denied it! Now she has become bitter and hard toward a man who doesn't deserve it all because of the bad choices she made in her life way before Billy even knew her," Gloria says with frustration.

Their conversation is interrupted by a knock at the door.

"Are you expecting anyone, Gloria?" Roy asks.

Gloria leaves the veranda and heads toward the front door with Roy following her.

"No, everyone who comes here is family and they just walk in," she replies.

"Maybe it's the Jehovah's Witnesses?" Roy says, laughing.

"Good luck to them climbing this mountain, and they better have on some serious hiking boots because there isn't a paved road to be found!" Gloria laughs as she opens the door and finds Cathy, Billy's flight attendant, standing there with a worried look on her face.

Roy stands next to Gloria at the opened door.

"Hi. We met at Kamari's birthday party; I'm Captain Billy's flight attendant," Cathy says.

"Well, I know who you are, but what I don't know is why you're here," Gloria says with a terse tone, not inviting her inside.

"Why don't we talk inside?" Roy says as Gloria cuts her eye at him in disapproval.

Roy ignores her and leads Cathy to the veranda with Gloria following behind them.

"Can I offer you something to drink?" Roy desires to be a gracious host.

"A glass of water would be great. I took a taxi up here from Cruz Bay when I got off the ferryboat. The cab driver was not very courteous; he complained about the roads not being paved. I told him the road is not paved but it's graded very well. Halfway up, he refused to go any further, saying his van was too big to climb the hills and that I need a four-wheel drive vehicle to come up here. He opened the door and put me out, so I had to walk the rest of the way," Cathy says, as she quickly drinks down her water.

"Well, I certainly hope you didn't pay him a single penny!" Roy says, smiling as he refills Cathy's glass.

"I did offer to give him something for his troubles but he wouldn't take anything. He said he didn't want to face Pastor Roy in church on Sunday morning and hear that he had taken money from me and didn't drop me to my destination," Cathy says as she puts her water glass down on the table.

After a brief pause to take in her surroundings, Cathy continues, "You have a beautiful home, and one of the best views!"

"Thank you, Cathy. So what brings you all the way up this mountain?" Gloria asks frankly.

"Well, I was hoping to speak to Lisa," Cathy says.

"Lisa? Are you sure? You're probably the last person next to Satan that she wants to see or talk to," Gloria says, raising her voice.

"Gloria, there is no need to raise you voice. We are all right here," Roy says, trying to calm the situation.

"I apologize if I'm raising my voice but I'm a little upset at you, Cathy, for having the gall to bring yourself up here to talk to Lisa after all that has happened. Don't you women have any shame?"

"All that has happened? Nothing has happened! I don't know what you've heard or who's been filling your head with lies but I'm a Christian woman!" Cathy says with hurt in her voice.

"So was the woman in my church who sat behind me every Sunday, who I just learned had a baby with my husband, the pastor!" Gloria screams at Cathy like it was her fault.

"Whoa! Everybody take a Selah. We need to pray. This conversation is starting off wrong." Roy puts his arms out in a referee position.

"That's because the whole situation of her living in Lisa's house with Lisa's husband is wrong! You can't make a right out of a wrong!" Gloria insists.

"Well, you just made a wrong assumption about me, Ms. Gloria! I am not involved with Billy – at all! He was kind enough to offer me their guesthouse when I was homeless. If you know anything about your son-in-law, you would know he is a true man of God who loves his family and would never cheat on his wife and those beautiful children!" Cathy screams with tears in her eyes.

Once again, Roy takes a napkin from under the guava tart tray and hands it to Cathy to wipe her tears.

Gloria is quiet until she looks up and sees Lisa with Sarafina on her hip and Kamari standing in the doorway to the veranda. Kamari pushes her way past Lisa and runs to hug Cathy.

"Miss Cathy, did you bring me another doll from Dominica like the one you gave me for my birthday?"

Cathy smiles and sits Kamari on her lap. "No, I didn't, Kamari, but I did see one like it in Trinidad but it was dressed in their country's costume. Do you think you might like that one?"

"Yes, Miss Cathy! And do you think you can get a baby one for Sarafina?"

Upon hearing her name, Sarafina pushes herself out of Lisa's arms and toddles over to Cathy with her arms raised for Cathy to pick her up, too. Cathy is overwhelmed with joy.

"Baby doll, baby doll!" Sarafina repeats over and over.

Everyone laughs except Lisa, who is not happy that Cathy is there. Seeing Cathy holding her children only irritates her more.

Roy sees the expression on Lisa's face. "Hey, little ladies, what happened to our tea party?"

Kamari jumps off of Cathy's lap. "It's time, Poppa and Grammy! Miss Cathy, would you like to come to our tea party?"

"Princess, Miss Cathy is here to speak to your mother. Why don't we let them talk while we go inside and have our tea party?" Gloria says.

"Okay, Grammy." Kamari gives Cathy a hug as Sarafina climbs down from her lap.

"Go and get everything set up for us, honey, while I pray," Roy says as Kamari happily obeys and Sarafina follows her big sister into the kitchen.

"Come on, Sarafina, I'm going to show you how to set the table for a tea party... but you have to listen and promise to be careful with my dishes," Kamari says to her sister, who is all smiles because she is being treated like a big girl.

Roy prays with the ladies then he and reluctant Gloria join the children in the kitchen, leaving two uncomfortable women on the veranda to work out their problem.

"I heard what you said to my parents, Cathy, and I don't believe a damn word of it! Did Billy send you here?" Lisa asks, standing by the veranda railing with her hands on her hips.

"No! And I hope he doesn't find out I've been here," Cathy says.

"So why exactly are you here?" Lisa asks in a vicious tone.

"To tell you how much your husband loves you and those little girls and to try and make it clear to you that there is absolutely nothing going on between Captain and me," Cathy pleads.

"Look, Cathy, I've been stupid too many times in past relationships not to recognize when it's happening again. So you can just trot your ass back down this mountain; and whatever you have to say to me, save it for Dr. Phil!"

"Wow! Who would have ever thought?" Cathy says, shaking her head.

"Who would have ever thought what? Don't talk to me in that condescending tone!" Lisa says, feeling offended.

"You have really surprised me. When I first met you, I said to myself, 'that's one classy lady!' I was so proud of my boss for marrying such a beautiful, smart woman. You were a role model to me. You have a husband who loves the Lord unequivocally, loves you and his children, and his job. All Billy talks about is you and his little princesses to everybody! Whoever hasn't met you yet would think you were the First Lady of the entire world, the way he puts you up on a pedestal. What happened to you? All I see is a foul-mouthed, insecure woman who's using her past hurts as an excuse to blame an awesome man for helping me when the piece of shit man I was living with kicked me out on the street. Well, you stay right there with your foolishness, because you are going to lose that awesome man if you don't check yourself, and it won't be to me. I don't do seconds and especially married men!" Angry, Cathy gets up to leave.

"Wait. I… I don't know what to say," Lisa says in a low voice.

"Look, Lisa, I don't have all the answers either. I'm trying to figure this thing out myself. My boyfriend threw me and all my stuff out on the street so he could be with my underage cousin, and it hurts! My family isn't speaking to me because my little cousin's dad is in jail for going over to my ex's house to get his daughter but not before chopping off all ten of Jason's fingers with his machete and telling him to keep his hands off his daughter. The surgeons were able to attach nine of the fingers back but the paramedics were not able to find the right thumb. My Jehovah's Witness parents had already shunned me because I left the faith, and after hearing about what happened with Jason, they don't even look me in the face if I see them on the road. I literally have one friend to my name, and she's so involved with her new man who's hitting her spot twenty-four/seven, she barely has time to take my calls. But you know what, I'm going to keep on stepping and I'm not going to blame the next man in my life for what happened, because if I had paid attention to all the warning lights that were flashing telling me to stay clear of Justin in the first place, I would not have found myself in this situation. I really thank you and Billy for allowing me to stay in your guest house and in about two more weeks, I will have enough saved to move into my own place. However, if my staying there until then is going to keep you from coming home, I can move out today and sleep on the plane for two weeks," Cathy sincerely says.

"Cathy, you are the last person I wanted to see – ever, and who would have thought you would be the one to show me what a fool I've been? My entire family has been preaching to me and doing everything short of knocking me in the head for the way I've been acting. They even started a 'cuss jar' because of my choice of words lately!" Lisa says, smiling.

"A cuss jar?" Cathy is confused.

"Yeah, every time I cuss, I have to pay a hundred-dollar fine." Lisa is embarrassed.

"Woo-hoo! Now that's a lot of money, especially if you cuss a lot." Cathy shakes her head.

"Let's just say I have at least twelve hundred dollars in the jar, not counting what Faith has on her tablet the last time we went out to lunch. She's coming over tomorrow to record it and hold me accountable." Lisa sighs.

"That bad, huh?" Cathy looks at Lisa with a sad look.

Lisa shamefully nods her head. "I don't know when all this cussing started. I was never like this. I mean I would say a few little 'shits' here and there, but now it's grown into something vulgar and downright nasty! Sometimes I feel like a street woman. Lord, I'm so ashamed of myself! And the look on Billy's face when I cuss just condemns me straight to hell! Thank God there is no condemnation in Christ Jesus! But look at the mess I've made of my marriage."

"It's not too late, Lisa, to do something about it. That man sings your praises from the back of the plane to the front! He's so lost without you. Do you know he once told me that he knew you were going to be his wife the first time he laid eyes on you?" Cathy says, smiling.

"Yeah, he told me that, and I thought he was crazy. At the time, I was involved in a going-nowhere relationship built on lies with Kamari's dad Trevor, and I was too blind to see the truth," Lisa says, reminiscing.

"Tell me about it! Been there, done that, and got the scars to prove it!" Cathy chimes in.

"I almost lost Billy because of Trevor, but the Lord gave me a second chance. And look at stupid me, about to blow it again." Lisa shakes her head.

"Isn't it amazing how we tend to gravitate toward those suave-talking bad boys? Well, once was enough for me. I lost my virginity to Justin with the promise of a marriage that never happened. I'm putting this girl on lockdown until the Lord sends a Billy my way! Lisa, you are so blessed." Cathy gets up and walks toward Lisa, who is still standing by the veranda railing.

"I've been blessed all my life but never walked in it. I had a dad who loved me, and a caring mother who I don't think knew what love was. Nice lady, but was not into hugging and saying things like 'I love you.' No, not Mom. But, they did send me to a great college, where I went crazy over every disgusting, lying, popular guy on campus. Why stop when you're on a roll? I married Jason, who was more interested in men than me. He was so fine, dressed to the hilt and was so sensitive, just like a woman. I suspected he might have a little 'sugar in his tank,' but I wasn't sure, or maybe I just didn't want to know. I would come home and find a bunch of little West Hollywood sissies lounging around my house like they lived there, using my perfume and wanting to borrow my clothes. Jason still denied being gay until my girl Faith caught him kissing a football player one night on a dark parking lot behind a gay nightclub next door to a comedy club she attended," Lisa sadly says, as if in a daze, telling a story of long ago.

"Good Lord, no wonder you're all twisted! But, my dear, you have been delivered from all those past relationships into the arms of an angel, sent from God and his name is Billy," Cathy says, holding Lisa.

"I'm asking myself, do I deserve him? I have been such a... witch! Please notice I dropped the 'b'," Lisa says, chuckling.

"Praise the Lord! Now I do have a pen and pad in my purse if you think I need to keep tally for the cuss jar." Cathy pretends to reach for her purse.

"No, that won't be necessary! I'm sick of hearing myself cuss!" Lisa surprises herself by saying so.

"Good! So, what's the plan for you and the girls going back home?" Cathy moves on to the business of reuniting Lisa, Billy and the girls.

"Well..." Lisa hesitates.

"Well, what?" Cathy raises her voice, causing Gloria to run out on the veranda, carrying a little teacup in her hand.

"Is there a problem out here?" Gloria sternly says as if ready to protect Lisa.

"Not at all, Mother Gloria," Lisa calms her.

"All right, then let's keep our voices down; we're having a tea party." Gloria turns and goes back into the house.

Lisa and Cathy laugh.

"What I wouldn't give to have a mother like that!" Cathy points toward Gloria.

"Now that's another example of how blessed I am. Mother Gloria is my best friend Faith's mother. They took me in just like I was their own child when I lost my parents." Lisa smiles.

"So, what's the plan?" Cathy gets to the point again just as dishes fall to the floor.

"Sarafina, look at what you've done!" Kamari screams. "You were supposed to sit in your high chair like a big girl and enjoy your tea! Now you've broken another one of my teacups and the teapot!"

Sarafina cries for her mommy.

"Calm down, sweetie. She didn't mean it," Roy says to Kamari.

Sarafina, crying, toddles out to the veranda, holding her arms up for Lisa to pick her up. Lisa takes a seat at the table on the porch as Sarafina pulls up Lisa's blouse, takes a breast out and begins to suck.

Cathy is amazed by what she is seeing. "I tell everyone these aren't even my breasts; they belong to Sarafina, she just allows me to carry them around until she needs them." As Sarafina sucks, she grabs a lock of Lisa's hair and twists it to comfort herself. Lisa bounces Sarafina on her lap to calm her down.

"Oh, Lisa, what a beautiful sight; you are a lifeline to this little innocent darling. What an honor it is to be a mother who nurtures her children. There is no job in the world that is more important." Cathy looks on with loving envy.

"Girl, you are just full of golden nuggets today. I have been complaining non-stop about being left home with the children for days at a time while Billy enjoys flying all around the Caribbean! I never looked at my role with the children as a nurturer. All I could think about was 'I'm not using my nursing degree!' Billy even suggested I hire a nanny to sit with the kids while I work but I never could find anyone good enough to leave my babies with. Now I see it's because I'm the one who's supposed to take care of them. Wow! What a complaining fool I've been."

"If you only knew how many women would give their right arm to walk in your shoes!" Cathy says.

"If you only knew how many women would give both their arms to be as beautiful as you, Cathy!" Lisa counters.

"Girl, please!" Cathy modestly says.

"Come on, Cathy, I know men are always after you. I bet you can't walk a block without at least ten men trying to hit on you! Tell the truth!"

"Yeah, and eight of them are probably my cousins and the other two are usually married and have a few extra women on the side! Do you know how happy I was to learn Justin and I were not related! His father came to Tortola from St. Lucia and his mother from Barbados. Trust me, there are not a lot of men to choose from for me. And then I have another problem that might scare off any possible suitors. So, I'm just going to work on me, and not focus on any man right now."

Lisa is curious about Cathy's statement and wonders if she should pry, and decides to go for it. "You're not sick, are you?" she asks with concern in her voice.

"You mean like AIDS or cancer? No." Cathy pulls a chair closer to Lisa and sleeping Sarafina, who has milk from Lisa's breast dripping down her chin.

"When I was born… I was born with both genitalia. I think that's how I managed to stay a virgin so long. I mean, how do you explain that to a guy?" Cathy shrugs her shoulders with a sad look on her face.

"Oh! Damn! Sorry, Cathy! Now I'm not sure if I should have to contribute to the cuss jar for my response to that!" Lisa smiles.

Cathy laughs. "You're not getting away with that, Missy! You owe the cuss jar a hundred dollars!" Cathy teases.

"You're a hermaphrodite? Wow! We had a newborn baby at Children's Hospital in Los Angeles where I worked who was born with both male and female sexual organs. Do you know that some say as many one in every 2000 babies is born that way?" Lisa shares.

"Stop lying! Then there certainly must be more people in the Virgin Islands like me than I would have ever thought. Of course it's not like someone will start a 'Hermaphrodite Support Group' or host a coming out party, and expect everyone to be accepting! No, what you'll get is the whole island calling you a freak!" Cathy sadly projects.

"I'm surprised you haven't had the surgery done to correct this," Lisa matter-of-factly says as she tucks her breast into her bra and shifts sleeping Sarafina to her lap.

"Well, now that I have health insurance, I think I'm going to do it. Quite frankly, Lisa, I've had this all my life and it just seems like an extra digit on the body, you know what I mean?"

"No! Girl, you need to get that little penis whacked off; especially now that you know what sex you are. You do know, right?"

"Just when I thought I might like you again, you ask me something crazy like that!" Cathy laughs.

"Hey, these days you have got to ask. Like I told you, I married someone I thought was a man and he acted more like a woman than me; I'm sure he's probably traded his thing in for a vagina by now." Lisa shakes her head.

"Well, I'm one hundred percent sure I'm a woman, but don't ask my parents because what answer you'll get depends on which one you ask. My dad swears I was supposed to be a boy, but my mother pushed and pushed for me to be a girl. My mother said boys just don't have vaginas and the penis part is just a big clitoris." Cathy laughs.

"Okay! And what did Mr. Justin think it was?" Lisa inquires.

"For the first few months, he didn't even notice it and when he did, he freaked out and didn't want to have sex with a half-man half-woman. Man, did that hurt! So I just ignored him. Then one night I woke up to him playing with 'little boy.' That's what I call him. I just laid there pretending I was asleep; I wanted to see what he was going to do," Cathy says.

"Well, tell me! What did he do? And then tell me how he missed seeing that thing for months?" Lisa asks.

"It ain't like it hangs down like a "ding-ding." For the most part, my hair covers it. Besides, all that man cares about is jamming it in and making sure he's satisfied! Now, I have never told anyone this before, not even my girl Yvonne. Justin put little boy in his mouth!" Cathy screams.

She and Lisa are laughing so loud Sarafina wakes up, reaching for Lisa's breast. Gloria runs out on the veranda once again to see if everything is okay. She finds Cathy and Lisa bent over laughing with tears running down their faces.

"Who would have ever thought? Roy, you have got to come out here and see Muhammad Ali and George Forman; they have stepped out of the boxing ring and laughing like bosom buddies!"

Roy and Kamari run out to the veranda to watch the two ladies try and compose themselves, but they look at each other and burst out laughing all over again.

"Hey, I could use a good laugh... you want to share?" Roy asks.

Both Cathy and Lisa at the same time yell, "No!"

In between laughs, Lisa says, "Mother Gloria, can you start packing up the girls? We are going home!"

"Sure... I mean okay! Right away!" Gloria is so happy, she bumps into Roy as she turns to leave. Kamari gets a good laugh out of this.

"Shall we dance?" Roy says.

"We're going home! We're going home! Yeah!" Kamari yells.

"Well, try not to act too excited that you're leaving your poor old Grammy all alone!" Gloria teases.

"I'll be back, Grammy! Poppa doesn't have anything to do. He'll keep you company!" Kamari tries to smooth things over.

Roy chuckles.

"Don't worry, sweetie, Grammy was just teasing. I'm a big girl. I'll be all right until you come back." Gloria kisses Kamari.

"Can I help you pack, Grammy?" Kamari begs.

"Of course! Let's do it." The two of them head into the house.

"Well, God certainly answers prayers!" Roy says, smiling at Cathy and Lisa as he goes back into the house.

"I know someone who is going to be one happy man tonight!" Cathy teases.

"Yeah, right! I am going to have to accept the fact that my husband's first love is his plane and I will see him when I see him," Lisa says.

"Now see, there you go thinking you know everything!" Cathy slyly says.

"What? You know something, don't you?" Lisa pries.

"Yeah, but I'm not telling you! So, take that little tittie out of that baby's mouth and let's head out. If we hurry, we can make the next boat," Cathy says, smiling.

"Girl, tell me, and I'll let you have my white nightgown!"

Both ladies are quiet and sad. Lisa regrets saying it.

"Wow! That's how this whole stupid thing got started. I'm so sorry, Lisa."

"No, girl, you had nothing to do with me and Billy's disconnect. We were having problems long before you went in my closet and put on that nightgown, so don't go beating yourself up about it." Lisa reaches her hand out to Cathy in friendship.

Cathy smiles. "Thanks for the offer, but that nightgown will only haunt in more ways than I like to think of; I have closed that chapter of my life! What I'm more concerned about right now is whether I'll be sleeping on the plane or do I still have a spot in your guesthouse for the next two weeks?"

The ladies laugh.

Gloria hollers out to them from inside. "Will you hens stop cackling and come in here and help pack!"

"Forget the packing! We can leave everything right here. All I need is a diaper and some wipes for Sarafina! We have a boat to catch!" Lisa screams as she, the baby and Cathy head for the door with Kamari running behind them, struggling to put her overstuffed backpack on her back.

"Lisa, would you like me to pick up your car from Cruz Bay and bring it back to the house?" Roy asks.

"Thanks, Dad; unless Mother Gloria would like us to come back over tomorrow to be here for support when... Hope arrives?"

Gloria becomes solemn for a second. "Child, I almost forgot about that. No, no, you go and do you! Dot, Faith, Lucille and their husbands will all be here, and Roy."

Roy pats Gloria's hand and smiles. "Go now, if you want to make the boat! And don't be speeding off this mountain with my babies!" Roy kisses the little ones and Lisa as they head out the door.

Cathy looks on, smiling; Roy takes her in his arms, squeezing her, and whispers in her ear, "Thank you."

Once everyone is out the door, Gloria and Roy stand smiling, unable to believe what just happened.

"I wonder if those guys left the old man some guava tarts?" he says, walking toward the veranda very happy.

"If not, you know I can make a call and have some more up here in seconds!" Gloria teases as she follows Roy, laughing.

"All right, Gloria! Don't start any foolishness," Roy says as he pops a mini-tart in his mouth, making a moaning sound, letting Gloria know how good they are.

"Hey, why don't I fix us some real food? Enough of these tarts before they give you diabetes!" Gloria says as she removes the tarts from the table.

"Just one more, Gloria… Just one more!" Roy says, chasing Gloria into the house with the tray of tarts.

Gloria quickly steps on the trashcan pedestal and dumps them inside, laughing.

Roy stands there surprised, looking at the empty tray where the tarts were.

"Well, sir! What does one say to that?" he asks with a confused look on his face.

"We say no more of Sister Claudette's tarts are coming up in here! Now what do you want for dinner?"

"Some fried chicken, mashed potatoes, pumpkin, boiled bananas, yams and kalaloo," Roy says, grinning and licking his lips.

"You must think you're back in Nevis somewhere! We'll do the fried chicken and mashed potatoes, and I have some greens from Dot and Marlin's farm, but you can forget about all that other stuff." Gloria has her hands on her hips, ready for an argument.

"Okay! What do you need me to do?" Roy asks.

"You can get the potatoes out of the refrigerator and peel them while I cut up the greens." Gloria gives him his orders with a smile on her face as she takes the greens and chicken out to season.

Roy is whistling. "This is a good day! My soul is happy."

"Roy, would you mind staying over tonight? I don't think I can bear to be alone, knowing the hurdle I'll have to face in the morning."

Roy pauses as he takes the potato peeler out of the drawer. "I'm always here for you, Gloria, and I've been dying to try out that Sleep Number bed in your guest room."

"I think you'll like number fifty the best; that's the number I keep mine on."

Roy continues whistling an old hymn and Gloria joins in as they busy themselves with preparing dinner.

## Chapter 9
## Hope Arrives

Fitzroy and Faith are standing at the passenger arrival gate at the St. Thomas airport, waiting for Hope to enter the terminal. Faith squeezes her husband's hand nervously as she stares out onto the tarmac, watching the arriving passengers deplane.

"Oh my God! Oh my God!" Faith screams, causing Fitzroy to worry.

"What's the matter, sweetie?" He turns to her, waiting for a reply.

Unable to speak, Faith points to Hope, who is walking among the other passengers, pulling her carry-on bag.

"It's her! Fitzroy, she looks like my daddy!" Faith has a frightened look on her face.

"And you!" Fitzroy says, as he waves to Hope so she will see them and know it's them.

"I feel like I'm going to faint. This is unbelievable." Faith holds on to the Tourist Board's bar for support. They are passing out rum punch samples to the arriving passengers.

"This is exactly how I felt the first time I met your mother and aunties right her at this very airport. When Mother Gloria walked through that gate, and I saw how much she favored my mother, it was like I'd walked into the *Twilight Zone*. Come on, honey, be strong; let's go greet your sister." Fitzroy squeezes Faith's hand for reassurance just as his cellphone rings.

"Please don't take that call. I need you," Faith begs.

"It's your Aunt Lucille. I'll get her off the phone quickly." Fitzroy answers.

Faith shakes as if she has to go to the bathroom, watching Hope as she comes closer and closer to where they are standing.

"You did what?" Fitzroy screams.

"What? Please, no drama right now! My plate is full!" Faith says as Fitzroy continues listening to Lucille on the phone and walking nervously back and forth. Faith's attention jumps back and forth between Fitzroy and her sister, who is less than twenty feet away from them.

"Lucille, whatever you do, do not go inside the club! I'm on my way there!" Fitzroy has a worried look on his face.

Faith is even more worried as she stares at her husband, waiting to hear what's more important than what's going on right now that he has to leave her.

"Lucille put web cameras in the club without telling Wally so she could prove to him that Junior. was still up to no good. Well, she is witnessing a drug deal going down inside the club and the Chief of Police is the ring leader."

"Oh my God, honey!" Faith screams just as Hope walks up to them.

"Is it my outfit or my hair?" Hope asks, feeling out of place.

"Oh no, nothing like that. Fitzroy just got a really unusual emergency call, and I was surprised by it," Faith apologizes.

"Hello, Hope, welcome to the Virgin Islands." Fitzroy hugs her. Faith attempts to do the same, but the two women are awkward and their arms flap in conflicting directions.

Hope decides to extend a handshake. "With a little practice, I'm sure we will get it straight." She chuckles.

"Hope, I'm going to need you to excuse me while I run off to take care of some urgent police business. Faith, you and your sister can get a cab to the Green House, and I'll meet you there. Have John the porter secure Hope's luggage, and we'll come back to pick everything up." Fitzroy kisses Faith and darts off, leaving her looking worried and out of her element.

"Be safe, honey!" Faith yells as Fitzroy races toward the parking lot while calling for reinforcements to meet him at the club. The two sisters continue to the baggage area, walking like strangers.

"I hope I didn't come at a bad time?" Hope politely says as Faith looks at her with a puzzled look on her face.

"I'm not sure if there would ever be a good time for you to come. I mean the whole family is still in shock and trying to wrap their heads around your existence. Do you have a lot of luggage?" Faith asks shortly.

Hope ignores her crassness, still reflecting on the awesome beauty she just experienced when her plane was gliding onto the runway, mere inches from the beautiful Caribbean Sea. *You're in the islands! You're in the islands,* keeps echoing in her head; this is a long way from her project townhouse in Atlanta.

"You know how we roll; afraid to leave anything behind in case we might need it. Yep! I have five suitcases and this carry-on," Hope says.

"Exactly how long are you planning on staying?" Faith asks with obvious surprise.

"Hey, looks like one of my bags is coming around the belt now." Hope picks up speed, ignoring Faith as she works her way deep into the crowd to grab her bag before it goes back around the belt.

Faith follows, feeling annoyed. Hope's suitcase is heavy and a nice gentleman helps her pull it off the belt. Faith waves to John the porter to come and help load Hope's baggage. John is more than happy to oblige, knowing his boy Fitzroy will take care of him generously. Once all of Hopes bags are loaded on the trolley, Faith and Hope follow John to the airline terminal office, where the baggage is secured and they are given a receipt for the luggage.

"Say, are you ladies twins?" John asks. Both Faith and Hope are embarrassed.

"No!" Faith says as she snatches the receipt out of John's hand and heads toward the taxi area.

Hope thanks John and follows fast-walking Faith to the awaiting taxis. Once inside the crowded taxi, Faith instructs Hope to take the passenger seat up front. The taxi van is packed with tourists all going to different locations. Faith tells the driver they are getting off at the Green House. Another passenger is confused about what boat to take to Tortola. A couple with two hyperactive children tells the driver they are going to St. John.

The driver looks at his watch and tells them they have twenty minutes to make the boat leaving from town. Their stop will be right after he drops the people to the Road Town Fast Ferry leaving for Tortola and the pretty little twin ladies to the Green House. Hope laughs, and Faith makes it a point to let the driver know they are not twins!

One of the hyperactive children is trying to climb over the seat to sit next to his mother, who is seated next very close to Faith. The dad tries to restrain him and he starts screaming, "Let me go! I want to sit with my mommy!"

"Honey, we're almost there please sit with your daddy... Sweetie, there is no room for you to sit with Mommy. Just be a good boy and sit still. The driver said it's only a few minutes from here."

"No!" He bites his dad and throws his leg over the seat, hitting Faith on the side of her face.

"Hey!" Faith yells, holding her face in pain.

"I am so sorry. Hunter, tell this lady you are sorry right now!" the mother pleads as the little boy tries to squeeze between them on the seat, not listening to a word she's saying. Everyone in the van starts to mumble in disapproval of the child's behavior and the parenting methods being used.

"Hunter? Say you're sorry."

Hunter busies himself with trying to find some candy in his mother's purse. "Mommy, where is my candy!" he yells.

"No more candy until you apologize to the lady."

The little boy yells, "No!" and smacks his mother.

Hope turns around and faces Faith in the seat behind her. "Faith, would you like to borrow my gun?" she asks casually.

A dead silence is felt in the van. The little boy stops tugging at his mother's purse and with a frightful look on his face he stutters, "I'm sorry!"

Faith nods her head in acceptance.

"Now climb your bad ass back in your seat and don't let your feet touch my sister!" Hope quietly says then turns around in her seat and continues enjoying the tropical view.

The van driver smiles as he picks up speed to ensure everyone makes it to their destination in a timely manner.

When Faith and Hope pull up to the Green House, it's crowded, as Faith expected, since there are four cruise ships in town.

Hope is like a child in a candy story, trying to take in everything at one time; the cruise ships, the seaplane taking off just across the street, the barkers trying to steer shoppers into their stores.

A homeless man, who makes birds on a stick out of palm leaves, approaches the ladies to purchase one of his unique one-dollar items. Hope smiles and gives the man a dollar. Faith continues up the stairs to the restaurant.

"Why would you buy that? He's probably going to take the money and buy drugs or alcohol!" Faith scolds Hope.

"Would you rather he steal from the shops or maybe snatch your purse? The man is not begging and whatever money he earns will be the same as anyone else who works and decides how they are going to spend their money."

"We're talking about a bum! Not an executive on Wall Street!" Faith counters.

"Now that's a great comparison. This man makes birds from palm leaves and sells them for one dollar, and a Wall Street executive gets hundreds of thousands of dollars and rips the American people off for all their savings. Hmm, now who's the real bum?" Hope laughs.

Faith rolls her eyes at her, just as she hears someone in the Green House call her name.

"Faith! Faith! Over here!" A middle-aged woman looking out onto the parking lot and stairs where Hope and Faith are walking calls out. She's sitting at a table close to the porch with an overweight young adult.

"OMG! That's Miss Claudette from my church. She is the nosiest person I have ever met. Please, whatever you do, don't tell her any of our business," Faith begs as she waves.

"Come and sit with us!" Miss Claudette hollers over the crowd.

Reluctant, Faith obeys and excuses herself as she and Hope push past the crowd. There is an extra chair at the table, and Miss Claudette orders her daughter, who is busy eating a large slice of cake and ice cream, to go and find another chair. The young woman obeys but not before she manages to stuff another mouthful of dessert into her mouth. The ladies take a seat. Faith doesn't introduce Hope.

"Hello, my name is Hope, and I just arrived to your beautiful island from Atlanta." Hope shakes Miss Claudette's hand and attempts to shake her daughter's hand, but there is ice cream running down her fingers. They just nod and smile at each other.

"Faith, did you get to try any of my tarts I left at your house for your father-in-law?" Claudette asks, beaming with pride.

"No, not yet, but if there are any left, I'll try them when I get home. I hear they are the best," Faith kindly says as she reaches for the menu on the table.

"Did Pastor Roy tell you that?" Claudette waits anxiously for Faith's response.

"Yes, I do believe I did hear him and my mother talking about how good they are." Faith smiles and continues looking at the menu.

Hope slides the other menu out from under Claudette's daughter's arm.

"So, Hope, how long will you be here with us?" Claudette inquires.

"I'm not sure yet. But I sure hope I get to try some of those tarts before I leave," Hope says, causing Claudette to smile.

Talking with food in her mouth, Claudette's daughter chimes in, "My mudder makes dee best tarts ever! Nobody can do it better dan she!"

"Thank you, sweetie. Now don't talk with food in your mouth. Shavon is my only child. She was my change of life baby. Everybody thought I was crazy having a baby at such a late stage in my life, but God knew she would be my blessing. You have any kids, Hope?" Claudette pries.

Faith looks nervous. She worries about what Hope might disclose in response to Claudette's relentless inquiries.

"No, none yet. I think I'll wait until I find my Mr. Right, if he's out there." Hope smiles and continues studying the menu.

"Well, your friend Faith here certainly snatched up a good one! Yes sir-ree!" Miss Claudette says like she's ready to drool over a piece of steak.

"Thank you, Miss Claudette," Faith says, hoping she will be quiet. No such luck.

"Hope, have you met her father-in-law yet? He's the new pastor of our church. They threw the mold away when they created that man, too!"

"No, I haven't had the pleasure of meeting him yet. So, what's good on the menu?" Hope asks, trying to change the subject.

"Everything!" the young lady says as she slurps the remainder of her ice cream, turning up the cup.

"Shavon! Mind your manners. Lord, I tell you, one would think I didn't teach her a thing. Young lady, that's the last sweets you'll be having for the rest of the day," Claudette admonishes.

"I think I'm going to have the Chicken Cesar Salad," Faith says and closes her menu.

"This Mahi Mahi sounds good. I'll have that," Hope says and closes her menu.

Faith waves the waiter over to their table. Shavon is licking her ice cream cup.

"Put the cup down, Shavon, and push away from the table now!" Claudette tries to say it politely but you can tell she is embarrassed and wants to yell at her daughter.

"But, Mommy! There's still a little bit left in the bottom," Shavon whines.

"We just left the doctor's office, and they said if she doesn't lose weight, they are going to start her on the diabetic shots. You want to take injections for the rest of your life? Is that what you want, Shavon?"

"No, Mommy. Me ain't like needles," Shavon says like a little child.

The waiter comes to the table to take their orders and give Claudette her check.

"Don't leave. Let me pay you now. I need to get home and finish my baking before it gets too late." Claudette looks at the bill and takes money from her purse and puts it with the bill and hands it to the waiter. "Let's go, child! Hope, it was so nice meeting you. Will we see you at church on Sunday?"

Hope smiles and doesn't answer. Shavon waves. As she gets up to leave, Claudette notices Shavon has a large grease spot on the back her dress, apparently from food that amazingly didn't make it to her mouth.

"Oh Lord! Let me have you ladies' napkins."

Claudette takes the cloth napkins and a few safety pins from her purse to fasten them over the soiled spot on her daughter's skirt. Shavon goes along with what her mother is doing like it's routine. Once pinned, they say goodbye and leave.

"Well, that's a first!" Hope says as she gives the waiter her order.

"That woman is a pain in the butt! Thank God they left, and she really needs to get some therapy for Shavon. The girl is twenty-two years old and can't spell cat!" Faith verbalize her annoyance.

Faith's phone rings, and she fumbles around in her purse to find it. It's Fitzroy.

"Listen, you guys go up to the house, and I'll meet you there in an hour. Things are kind of crazy," Fitzroy says in a calm voice, trying not to get Faith nervous.

"You're okay, right?" she belts out.

"Yeah! Junior's been shot, and the chief is in bad shape. I'm going over to the hospital now," Fitzroy says with sadness in his voice.

"Oh no! How bad is Junior?" she whispers.

"He'll live. Wally is a wreck, and he's angry with Lucille for planting the web cameras. Anyway, sweetie, Lucille took the earlier boat from Red Hook, headed up to the house. Wally doesn't want her to go to the hospital, so if you could catch the next boat home so you will be there to calm her down, I would appreciate it," Fitzroy says in a tired voice.

"What about our meeting with the family?" Faith desperately asks.

"I just spoke to Dad and your mother and told them we would call them, Dot and Marlin and let them know what time to come over. Look, honey, I have to run. Love you." Fitzroy hangs up, leaving Faith with a puzzled look on her face.

The waiter places the ladies' food on the table. Hope stares at Faith with compassion. "Is everything okay?"

"Things are just a bit crazy right now. But, this is what life is like when you're the wife of a detective," Faith says with sorrow in her voice.

"I'm sure everything will be all right. Things have a way of working themselves out without us worrying too much." Hope pulls her food toward her and starts to eat.

Faith looks at her like she just committed a crime. "You're not going to bless your food?" Faith asks in a scolding tone.

"Uh…no! But you can go ahead and bless yours. I'm not into religion." Hope puts a fork full of food into her mouth.

"And how did that sit well with my dad?" Faith sarcastically says.

"It came up the last time we were in Israel, when I didn't want to visit all the holy sites with him, and we decided to agree to disagree," Hope casually says.

"You were in Israel with my daddy!?" Faith is flabbergasted.

"Yeah," Hope casually answers and continues eating.

"And when exactly did you and *my* daddy go to Israel?" Faith is upset.

"Don't get yourself all bent out of shape, Faith. *Our* father was living a double life. Whatever he did with you, he did with me. The only difference was he was a 24/7 father to you and a Monday, Wednesday, Friday and special occasion dad to me."

"No, sister, don't you get it twisted. My daddy was a husband to my mother, and I was his legitimate child, recognized by God and everybody. Your mother was his whore, and you were their bastard child!" Faith screams.

Hope puts her fork down and leans closer to Faith. "I need you to listen to what I have to say, Faith, because it's very important and can determine how the rest of this visit and our getting to know each other goes. Now, if you ever call my mother a whore again, I will smack the taste out of your mouth. My mother was a real lady and everyone who knew her would say the same, including your mother, I'm sure. If there is anyone we need to question about their moral conduct, it is our father, the man of God." Hope continues eating.

"Please, forgive me. I don't know where that came from. I've never called anyone's mother a whore before, even if they were one. Not to say your mother was. You're right, we need to start with my dad. I just don't understand how a man I've looked up to as my role model of a man could be living a double life!' Faith is very emotional.

"Maybe the letter will answer a lot of our questions," Hope says.

"Letter? What letter?" Faith inquires.

"After Dad passed, I went to the bank and closed our account, as well as cleared out his safe deposit box. In the safe deposit box was a letter addressed to Gloria, Faith and Hope. It said *do not open* until the three of you are together." Hope stares into Faith's puzzled eyes.

"You had a bank account with Daddy!" Faith cries.

"Yes, didn't you? I told you, whatever you had, I had! Get over yourself and let's move on. Now, are you going to eat, 'cause I'm starving and I can eat that!" Faith slides her plate over to Hope as she stares out of the Green House porch toward the sea with tear-filled eyes and notices people boarding the boat to St. John.

"Oh my God! Oh my God!" Faith screams.

"What, more drama?" Hope says as she swallows her food.

"Our boat is boarding!" Faith flags the waiter as she collects her purse and cellphone off the table.

"You mean we have to run?" Hope asks.

"If you want to go to St. John, where we live. We have food at the house so you can leave that there," Faith says as the waiter approaches the table.

"What can I do for you?" he asks.

"We need to pay you quickly. Our boat for St. John is boarding." Faith has her wallet out to pay; Hope is standing up to leave, while taking a last sip of her drink.

"Mrs. Brown, Detective Brown left his credit card number for us to charge your meal. Everything is taken care of." The waiter smiles as he clears plates and glasses from their table.

Faith walks fast with Hope in awkward close pursuit, trying to keep up as they race across the street filled with tourists and busy traffic. They arrive safely at the boat just as two crewmembers are loosening the ropes that hold the boat to the dock. Upon seeing Faith, they whistle up to the captain to hold the boat.

The captain sticks his head out of the window, where he sees Faith and Hope and hollers down to her. "Mrs. Brown, how are you? Come up here and ride with me."

Faith and Hope jump aboard the boat as it pulls out of the harbor. The ladies climb the stairs, passing sunburned tourists sitting on the top level of the beautiful commuter boat before they arrive at the captain's house, unlocking the port door they walk inside to a very comfortable seating area that surrounds Captain Lamar's chair.

"Ladies, have a seat and if you're thirsty, there are drinks in the cooler under the seat. Mistress Brown, your husband didn't tell me you had a twin sister! I'm going to have to have a serious talk with me boy for withholding vital information! So, pretty lady, how long will we have the pleasure of seeing your beautiful face on our island?" Lamar asks in his sexiest voice.

Faith, frustrated and angry at being mistaken as a twin again, forces an insincere smile, knowing Lamar is a ladies' man and tries to hit on every new female who comes to the island.

"I don't think you told me your name," Hope answers.

"Please forgive me. I'm Captain Lamar. And what is your name, beautiful?"

"Hope," she says, as she stares out of the boat's window in awe of the beautiful different hues of blue in the sea and the coral deep down below the clear water. Hope is enjoying this bird's eye view from the captain's house. It feels as if she's driving the boat and she hopes Lamar will be quiet so she can enjoy every second of this awesome experience. She only dreamed of this, and now it's happening.

"Hope… that sounds promising! As in there is Hope that I will get to take you out tonight when I get off work." Lamar has a giant grin on his face.

"No, Hope as in I hope you will drive this boat and allow me to enjoy the view without having to answer any more of your questions!" Hope lets out a loud laugh and hugs Lamar. He's confused, but she thinks nothing of it since this kind of greeting is common among folks from Atlanta.

Faith tries to contain her laughter but can't. Soon, all three of them are laughing, then Lamar is quiet and allows Hope to enjoy her ride. She looks out the window until they pull up to the dock in St. John, where she thanks him so much for allowing her to ride in the captain's booth and see everything up close.

Lamar doesn't know how to handle Hope, so he just smiles and says, "Anytime."

# *Chapter 10*
## Everyone Meets at Faith & Fitzroy's

When Faith pulls into the driveway of her house, she sees their extra jeep parked in front. She and Hope walk in the house, and find Aunt Lucille pacing the floor with a large glass of rum and coconut water in her hands.

"Can you believe that shit? Here it is I helped his black ass and he has the nerve to be mad at me!" Lucille is mad and appears as if she's been waiting for someone to vent to.

"Aunt Lucille, this is Hope. I'm going to show her to the cottage in case she wants to freshen up." Faith heads out the back door of the house toward the cottage. She notices Hope is not following her and turns to see what the holdup is.

"I'm cool, Faith. I'm going to have to wait until my luggage gets here before I can do anything. I'll just chill right here, if you don't mind." Hope smiles and takes a seat in the living room.

"You want a drink, honey?" Lucille asks. Not waiting for a response, she pours a drink for Hope and hands it to her.

Hope smells the drink and it's strong. She puts it down on the table, so as not to offend Lucille.

"How long have you been here, Auntie?" Faith asks as she picks up Hope's drink off the table and pours it down the sink without Lucille seeing her and replaces it with coconut juice. Faith and Hope smile at each other.

"About an hour or so. I hope your guest room is available, because I ain't never going back to that man! The ungrateful…"

Faith cuts her off. "Can I get you something to eat, Auntie? Looks like Fitzroy or Dad made some oxtails, boiled bananas, rice and stewed tomatoes, here on the stove."

"Food is the last thing on my mind! I'm taking my ass back to Atlanta. I saved that man's life and this is the thanks I get! Faith, I told him Junior was running drugs out of his club, and he didn't want to believe me; so I had web cameras installed so I could prove it to him. I watched that shit happen on my phone! I thought he would be happy and we could kick Junior's ass out of the business and follow our dreams of having a classy supper club. But the shit backfired! This wasn't some little poot-butt operation! The chief of police and several of the officers in the department was in on this! Now everybody is busted, Junior got shot… I wish they would have killed his lying, cheating ass!" Lucille is drunk and decides to take a seat on the lounge chair.

Faith tries to take her glass out of her hand.

"What are you doing?" Lucille slurs.

"I'm going to freshen up your drink," Faith says.

"You think I'm drunk or something? I just poured this damn drink." Lucille raises her voice.

"Aunt Lucille, you are drunk and you don't need any more to drink." Faith pulls the drink out of her hand and some spills on the floor.

"Girl, if you don't give me my drink back, I will kick you little skinny ass!" Lucille tries to stand up but falls back down in the chair.

"Give her a few minutes, and she'll be out like a light," Hope whispers as she joins Faith at the kitchen sink.

"I know ya'll little bitches is over there talking…" Lucille is out. Her head is cocked back on the chair and her dress is hiked up in the air with her legs gapped. Faith and Hope look at her and shake their head.

"Mmm! She looks a tad bit trampish sitting over there like that," Hope says and Faith quietly laughs.

"I think we should try and get her to the guest room before everyone gets here." Faith tries to wake Lucille up. The ladies decide to carry her. They put Lucille's arms around each of their necks and their hands around her waist for support and slide her down the hall.

"Oh no! She's peeing!" Faith screams.

"Nothing a few wet wipes and some *Febreze* can't take care of. Let's keep moving and hope she doesn't do a number two," Hope says, laughing.

"What the hell are you laughing at? This is not funny!" Faith screams.

"It is to me. When I got up this morning, I never in my wildest imagination would have imagined this." Hope snickers as they lay Lucille on the guest bed.

"I can't leave her here all peed up!" Faith cries.

"You have any clothes she can fit in?" Hope asks.

"Fitzroy's jeans," Faith says.

"You might just want to change her drawers and put a housecoat on her. Putting a pair of jeans on a drunken woman is not easy," Hope says as they stand there looking at Lucille knocked out on the bed.

"You have a point," Faith agrees.

"Where are the wipes? I'll take care of the wet spots on the floor while you change her soiled clothes," Hope says as she turns to leave the room.

"Look under the kitchen sink." Faith proceeds to take off Lucille's wet underwear as Hope leaves the room to find the wipes.

Under the sink, Hope finds a plastic tumbler that reads, *disinfectant wipes, kills 99% of germs.*

*This should do it!* She pulls out several sheets and proceeds to wipe the trail of urine as Marlin and Dot enter the house.

"Faith, what in the world did you do to your hair, child! I don't know about this afro thing!" Dot screams.

"I like it, Dot! I think woman should be natural like God made dem." Marlin gives his opinion.

Hope gets up off the floor and turns to say hello. Dot feels embarrassed when she realizes it's not Faith.

"Hi, I'm Hope, Faith's sister. I would shake your hand, but I'm cleaning a little pee-pee of the floor," Hope says, chuckling.

"Oh my God! Marlin, the child looks like Faith." Dot's mouth is open as she stares at Hope like she's a specimen.

"Just like she! Dot, stop examining the young lady like she a prize mango or some ting." Marlin hugs Hope. "Hello, Miss Hope! Dis 'ere is Dot, she is Faith's momma's sister, and me is she husband."

Dot waves with a smile, being careful not to get any pee on her.

"Now me know you didn't come all de way from de states ta be cleaning up pee-pee. Wha' gon on 'ere?" Marlin asks.

"Faith is in the room changing Mrs. Lucille. She had a little too much to drink and when we were trying to move her to the bedroom she…!"

"Oh my Lord. My sister drunk! She hasn't been drunk since her fiancé Bedford was killed!" Dot walks quickly down the hall to investigate the matter as Hope finishes wiping the floor and Marlin takes a seat in the living room.

Hope washes her hands and joins Marlin in the living room.

"You ever had a mango before?" he asks.

"No, I can't say I have. I've had some watered down mango juice in a jar that said it was all-natural but once you read the label, mango is the last ingredient," Hope says, shaking her head.

"Well, me dear, you have come to de right place," Marlin says with a big grin on his face. Their conversation is interrupted by Dot running down the hall.

"Marlin, I'm going to need you to go to the farm and bring some of my clothes for Lucille to wear," Dot says with urgency in her voice.

"Baby, me ain't no nothin' 'bout picking out ladies' clothes! It's just down the road. Sweetie, you go and me will be right 'ere when ya get back."

Dot gives Marlin a stern look. "Marlin, please go. I can't leave Lucille here like this. She just vomited all over the bed. Faith needs me." Dot kisses Marlin, and he melts like butter.

Hope is smiling as she observes their conversation.

"Miss Hope, you comin' wit me. You know more 'bout woman clothes dan me care ta know. Let we go!"

Hope is surprised, but she jumps up and leaves with Marlin.

Dot yells out the door as they climb in the truck. "Marlin, you can show Hope your pigs and mangos another time… I need you to hurry back, you hear?"

Marlin toots his horn and pulls away from the house, heading to the farm. Hope is so happy; she hasn't seen this kind of love before except on television. Mabel would love these people. Suddenly Hope remembers promising to call Mabel as soon as she arrived in St. Thomas. Oh boy, she's in trouble.

As Marlin drives up the dirt road leading to the farm, Hope notices a stunning hotel with rows of fine-looking, well-manicured mango trees lining its entrance and golf carts darting around the grounds adjacent to the road they are traveling on.

"Wow! That's one beautiful hotel!" Hope says.

"Now dat dere hotel is built on me land. Me fadder tell me never sell me land, so me lease it to dem people fa ninety-nine years, den it go back to me family! Dem tink day so smart. You see dat der little house wit de galvanize roof next to it? Dat was me house till me brother die and me take over de family farm and me move over 'ere. Me and me sweetie Dot, we does live 'ere and up on de mountain, too, where she does have she house before we marry. Now dem hotel people had me plant all dem trees to hide me little house from de rich folks but what dem don't know is me plant all mangos and me mangos win blue ribbons all over de world. Me can't ship dem fast enough ta all de gourmet stores in de states and Europe," Marlin brags.

"You are a smart man, Mr. Marlin! Oh my God, I just love that little house. I bet when the rain hits the galvanized roof, it sounds so relaxing. I once saw a picture in a magazine of a house that looked like that. The husband and wife were in the yard chopping sugar cane and the children were helping load the cane onto an old truck while their dog sat on the porch sleeping without a care in the world. One day I'd like to go inside and see what it looks like." Hope smiles.

"Now, me is ya uncle, so me would appreciate it very much if you would address me as Uncle or Uncle Marlin. Dat would make de old man happy." Marlin grins, showing his big false teeth. "And when every ting calms down, me gone show you me old house."

Hope is quiet.

"Some ting wrong?" Marlin asks.

"Well, I've never had any family before, other than my mother, Dad and Miss Mabel, my neighbor, so to call you Uncle makes my heart smile. Thank you, Uncle Marlin." Hope chuckles.

"Well, me dear, you gon find out you have a lot of family 'ere. Some by blood and most by the need to belong." Marlin smiles.

Marlin parks the truck by the farmhouse porch, and several baby sheep and goats run to greet him.

Hope is in awe.

"Now Lucy, Bambi and Billy, you guys gon have to go and find ya momma, 'cause Big Momma Dot have sent me on a mission and she timing me." The sheep and goat make baaaa sounds.

"Oh my goodness! They are so cute." Hope gets down to the ground to pet them.

"Come on, Hope, let's be about the business we does come 'ere ta do." Just as they are about to enter the house, Marlin hears his name being called by the farmhand Dominique from across the field.

"Monsieur Peters! Monsieur Peters!" Dominique calls as he runs toward them.

"What is it, son? Me on a mission, talk fast," Marlin says.

Dominique nods a hello to Hope, who nods back.

"Sir, the mother pig Greta is in labor. Five of the piglets have arrived, but there are a few stubborn ones that refuse to drop. I think we might have to call the veterinarian. She's in distress."

"I guess dere is no good time fa dees tings ta happen… do ya tink you could give me a nudder hour or so? Me really got ta get dees tings ta me wife fo' she get vex wit me," Marlin pleads.

"Sir, I think I can get the babies out but I just need someone to rub Greta and let her know everything is okay," Dominique pleads.

"I'll do it!" Hope says, surprising herself.

Both Dominique and Marlin are surprised as well.

"I'll run inside and find some clothes for Mrs. Lucille, and you can take them back to the house and come for me later." Hope continues.

She runs inside the house and up the stairs to the bedrooms, making herself familiar with the surroundings immediately so she can go and help the distressed pig. She opens the small closet door and retrieves a frock-like dress and in the only dresser in the room she sees underwear. She grabs two pairs of panties and a bra then runs back down the stairs and gives the clothes to Marlin.

"Uncle Marlin, this should do. I'm ready," she says to Dominique.

Marlin smiles and scratches his head as he jumps into the truck and speeds off, leaving Hope and Dominique racing across the field toward the pig pen.

Once inside the pen, Hope is wondering what the hell she has gotten herself into. Seeing a host of grunting giant pigs and little piglets in various stalls is a sight to behold.

"Come, over here!" Dominique calls as Hope pauses at one of the stalls to watch a pig drink from a nozzle attached to the wall. Dominique climbs over the interior fence, where Greta is struggling. Hope follows.

"Please, forgive me, Madam, I am Dominique and I did not get your name. On first glance, I assumed you were Madam Faith, but I can see now that is not true."

"My name is Hope. I'm Faith's sister." Hope follows Dominique's lead and drops down to the ground, where the pig is lying on a mound of hay and blankets. The little piglets that have managed to make it into the world are stumbling and stepping on top of each other to find their mother's nipples to nurse.

"Please, Madam, I need you to pat Greta and rub her stomach. Most importantly, talk to her in a low kind voice and let her know everything is going to be all right."

Hope attempts to rub Greta but find her skin very rough. Dominique notices this and gives her a work glove to put on. Once Hope is comfortable, Dominique puts on a pair of arm-length plastic gloves and enters the mother pig's birth canal, pulling out a stuck pig.

"There you are, little one! Now go over and nurse so your other siblings can make their way out!" Dominique places the piglet at his mother's nipples, only for him to be pushed out of the way and stepped on by the other piglets waiting for a chance.

"Welcome to the world, little buddy! Get in there a fight for your spot!" Dominique chuckles as he pulls another one out.

Hope has tears running down her face as she talks to Greta. "You're doing a great job, big momma! Your babies are all doing well! Hang in there, Greta," Hope gently says.

Dominique notices the tears and smiles because he knows the feeling she is having. He felt the same way the first time he came into the pen and watched the birthing take place. To watch a life come into the world is such a wonderful feeling, and it can bring you to tears. Hope sees Dominique looking at her, and they both smile and continue with the task before them.

After about fifteen minutes, Dominique pulls his bloody gloved hands out of the birth canal and announces to Hope, "I think we got them all out." He disposes of his gloves and shakes Hope's hands.

"Great job, Madam! I could not have done it without you!"

Hope smiles, experiencing a sense of purpose she's never felt before. "Thank you for the opportunity." She pats Greta one last time before climbing over the stall fence.

"I'll walk you back to the house," Dominique says.

Just as they reach the house, Marlin's truck comes up the dirt road in a cloud of dust.

"Madam Hope, it was a pleasure meeting you. I see Monsieur Marlin has arrived. I will return to my duties," Dominique humbly says.

"The pleasure was mine. Maybe while I'm visiting here, I can come and get to know the animals. Believe it or not, I've never been on a farm or any closer to an animal than the zoo's fence." Hope lets out a chuckle.

"Well, you carried yourself today like an animal whisperer!" They both laugh as Marlin gets out of the truck and Hope walks to meet him.

"Everything is in order, sir! Madam Hope was just what we needed!" Dominique waves and continues across the field toward the pig pen.

"So it does seem like you's a regular farmhand, me dear!" Marlin pats Hope on the back as they walk toward the truck.

"I don't know about all that. But what I do know is I can certainly use a long hot shower," Hope screams.

"Hot is good but long, no sa! Water is like gold in dees islands. We get our water from the rain. If you does run out, den you have to buy a truckload of water. So we does get wet, turn de water off, soap up, turn de water back on, rinse we skin, den we get out! Now some folks are hooked up to de government water and have der cistern where de water does store. Me dear, you might be in luck 'cause me believe Faith and Fitzroy does have both."

"No disrespect, Uncle Marlin, but I don't care what water system they have, I'm going to take a long hot shower today! And if I have to pay for a truckload of water, then so be it! This girl is funky! I've literally been lying down in a pigsty with pigs!" Marlin and Hope both laugh hard.

"I say you take dat long hot shower and if anybody don't like it, den dem can come see Uncle Marlin 'bout it!" Laughter continues as they pull up to Faith and Fitzroy's house, where Fitzroy has just arrived and is unloading Hope's luggage.

"Not a second too soon! Now I have clothes to change into after my extremely long shower I'm about to partake! Now, Uncle Marlin, if the shower police try to arrest me, I need to know you got my back!" Hope says, laughing as she gets out of the truck to help Fitzroy with her luggage.

"Me child, Uncle got you covered, even if me got to thief Fitzroy's gun!" Marlin chuckles.

"Hey, little sis, Marlin; what's so funny? I have your luggage, Hope," Fitzroy says as Marlin helps him lift them out of the van. Hope attempts to help, but Fitzroy directs her into open the door. "The men have this."

"Now dat's one sweet young lady!" Marlin says to Fitzroy as they carry the heavy luggage into the house.

"Must be in the bloodline," Fitzroy says, continuing inside, where he finds Faith and Dot sitting at the kitchen table, eating. Fitzroy says hello to Dot, kisses Faith and continues out the back door to the guest cottage.

Faith gets up to show Hope where she'll be staying.

"Come on, Hope, let me show you your room. Something smells like… the pig pen. Uncle Marlin!" Faith cries.

"Not me, darling!" Marlin counters with a smile on his face.

"Sorry, it's me! I was helping Dominique deliver Greta the pig's little piglets. What an experience! I will treasure it for the rest of my life. Now if you can point me in the direction of the shower, I'm sure we'll all be happy campers." Hope laughs while Dot and Faith are shocked and trying to process what Hope just shared with them.

"Marlin, you had that young lady delivering pigs?" Dot screams.

"Sweetie, she volunteered!" he says, smiling.

Hope can hear them talking; she turns back and peeps her head in the door. "And I enjoyed every minute of it!" Then she turns to leave, smiling.

Once inside the guest cottage, Fitzroy places Hope's suitcases against the wall and starts out the door. "Baby, I'm starving! I'll see you guys back in the house."

"Hope, there are towels in the linen closet in the bathroom. Please make yourself comfortable." You can hear it in Faith's voice that she is tired from dealing with Aunt Lucille.

"Faith, everything has been happening so fast since I first stepped foot on the island that I didn't get to tell you what a lovely warm home you have," Hope sincerely says.

"Thank you. My mother and father-in-law will be here soon," Faith says with trepidation in her voice.

Hope ignores her uneasiness. "It's going to be a pleasure to meet your mother, Faith. I'm sure she is as kind and sweet as everyone I've met so far." Hope smiles.

"Well, I guess that's a good way to look at it," Faith says as Hope stands, taking off her shoes being careful not to sit down and soil the beautiful furniture.

"Hope, I'm excited to find out what my father had to say in the letter addressed to the three of us," Faith says as she stands by the door to leave.

"Me, too, big sister; I've been waiting for this day for three years now." Hope lets out a big sigh as she walks into the bathroom, closing the door.

Just as she turns the water on and is about to step in the shower, Hope's cellphone she placed on the nightstand rings. With a towel wrapped around her, she races into the bedroom to answer the phone, knowing it's the only person in the world who would be calling: Mabel.

"Girl! If you didn't answer this phone, my big ass was about to book a flight and come down there and see if you lost your mind or something! What the hell is going on? I hope those people haven't tried no crazy shit with you. 'Cause I'll be there on the next flight and open up a can of whoop-ass; you know I will!" Mabel screams.

"Calm down, killer! Everything is fine. I have been running since my foot hit the Caribbean soil. Mabel, you will love this place! Oh my God, it's everything I thought it would be and more." Hope is so excited.

"So I guess that means you haven't met Mrs. Mother yet?" Mabel sarcastically says.

"No, not yet, she should be here any minute now. You will never believe this: I just left my Uncle Marlin's pig farm, and I helped this French-speaking farm hand deliver baby pigs! It was the most exciting thing I have ever done in my life!" Hope hollers.

"Okay! You're right; I never would believe anything like that. Five minutes on the island and you're a regular Dr. Doolittle and have inherited an Uncle Marlin!" Mabel is laughing very loudly.

"Oh, you got jokes! Look, I'm standing here in my sister's beautiful guesthouse with a towel wrapped around me. I need to jump in the shower before everyone gets here. I smell just like a pig. I love you, don't worry about me and I'll call you tonight after I've had a chance to meet everyone and read them the letter my dad left for us." Hope kisses the phone.

"Please call me right after that. If I could just be a mosquito on the wall, I'd promise not to bite anybody just to be in the room to hear what's in that letter! Go on, girl, and get you naked ass in the shower. I love you!" Mabel hangs up, and Hope laughs as she makes her way into the running shower filled with steamy water pulsating from the shower head.

While Hope is in the shower, Gloria and Roy enter the house, carrying food containers. Faith can tell her mother is nervous. Faith gets up from the table, kisses her mother and takes the food container out of her hand. Fitzroy waves to his dad and mother-in-law from the table where he is devouring a large plate of food.

"Is there anything in those food containers that I need to be concerned with?" Fitzroy asks as he swallows a mouth full of food.

"Well, son, I don't think you can fit another morsel of food on that already overflowing plate." Roy smiles and places the container on the counter.

"Give me a few minutes and there will be a space opening up!" Fitzroy continues eating.

"You know, Lucille is here in the room sleeping," Dot says as she gets up to help take the foil off the food.

"What is she doing sleeping so early?" Gloria inquires.

"She's drunk!" Dot says with disgust.

"Don't you ladies work yourself up into a hissy. Give Brother Wally a minute, and I know he'll come to his senses," Fitzroy matter-of-factly says.

"Lucille drinks wine occasionally these days and no hard liquor at all; whatever happened between the two of them is no small thing if my sister is drinking to the point of getting drunk." Gloria asserts.

"My exact thought!" Dot says.

"What happened, son?" Roy asks.

"Can I please tell you guys the details after I finish eating?" Fitzroy continues eating.

Faith laughs. "You know how serious my husband is about his food. Go ahead, baby, enjoy your food. I'll give them the short version of what happened."

"The short of it is, Aunt Lucille planted a camera in the club so Wally could see what Junior was up to, not knowing the operation he was running included the chief of police and several officers. When she showed the video to Fitzroy, a team of highly trained narcotics officers went in and arrested everyone, but not without incident. Junior was shot, nothing serious but Wally is freaked out and blames Lucille for his son getting shot and wants nothing to do with her."

"How dare he? Ungrateful cuss! After all Lucille did to help him get back on his feet! My sister saved his life!" Gloria screams.

"Calm down, Gloria. It's all going to work out. God didn't put the two of them together to have this situation break them apart," Roy counters.

"You can say whatever you want to say, but Mr. Wally has some explaining to do," Dot chimes in just as Hope enters the room from the back door.

Gloria looks at her and becomes weak. Roy helps her to a seat.

"Oh my Lord! Look at Rev." Gloria whispers.

"Hi, I'm Hope." She walks over and shakes Roy's hand and hugs Gloria.

"Hello, my dear. Welcome to St. John," Roy says, smiling.

Gloria is shaking her head in disbelief.

"Gloria, she looks just like Faith and Rev," Dot says in amazement.

Faith cuts in. "Mother, Daddy gave Hope a letter to share with us upon his death. It was important to him that the three of us meet and read the letter together."

"I'm going to have to sit down for this one. I never thought I'd be hearing from a dead person in the form of a letter," Dot says, shaking her head as she takes a seat next to Marlin.

"I don't want to be the one to read it! Seeing this child looking just like him is more than enough to bear!" Gloria says, sighing.

"I'm way too nervous to read it!" Faith admits.

"Maybe someone else other than the three of us should read it?" Hope suggests.

"Dad, will you do it?" Faith asks in a loving voice.

Roy hesitates. "Yes, but only after we pray."

"Good idea, me boy! Good idea!" Marlin says.

"Guess I'll finish eating afterward." Fitzroy puts his fork down and joins Faith on the sofa in the living room, holding her hand.

Surprisingly, Hope sits next to Gloria and takes her hand. Gloria gives her an awkward smile then covers her hand over Hope's as Roy prays.

"Holy Father, it is by Your divine appointment that we find ourselves assembled here at this time. We come from different places, have different experiences, and yet we have at least one important thing in common, that our lives have been impacted mightily by the life of Reverend Davis; some of us without ever having met him.

"Mighty God, as we prepare our hearts and minds for the reading of Reverend Davis' Epistle to the three persons dearest to his heart, I pray that by the power of Your Holy Spirit, You will impart a peace that will transform our souls so that we can hear, understand and honor all that was in Rev's heart to share with us now that both You and he foresaw before his home-going.

"Lord, I pray that the words of this letter will lift our burdens, quiet our fears and minister grace, unity, faith, hope and love. In the matchless name that is above every other name – even Jesus Christ our Lord.

"Amen."

The room is pin-drop quiet as Roy opens the letter and begins to read aloud:

> "To my beautiful wife Gloria, I know it will be difficult for you with me gone, but it is my sincere prayer that you will find happiness in the next passage of your life. When the Father calls us home, I know it is not His will for our loved ones to live a life of perpetual grief or stay stuck in what once was. Hold on to your memories, but don't be afraid to create new ones. You still have a lot of years left, and I expect you to live them to the fullest.
>
> "I will assume that you, Faith and Hope are together reading this letter, as requested.
>
> "Please listen carefully to my words and understand how important it is to my memory that you know it was never my intentions to hurt or deceive any of you. I'll start first by explaining my relation with Hope's mother Barbara. I'm sure this is a question everyone has wondered about.
>
> "Barbara was a dear friend I met in college; she, a student at Spellman and me at Morehouse. Barbara

and I were on the same debate team and attended the same bible study group. My roommate Ademola was smitten with Barbara and hounded me every day to introduce him to her. I was a little apprehensive, because he was involved in a Pan African Movement radical group but I knew he was from a good family with means, so I introduced them to each other and they became joined at the hip. Where you saw Barbara, you saw Ademola. I was happy for them and gave them my blessings when Ademola announced he wanted to marry her."

Hope gasps as Roy continues reading.

"After graduation, the two left for Africa, where they were wedded. It was a year before I heard from Barbara and the news was not pleasant. Ademola was from a tribe of people that believed once a woman is married, her clitoris was severed to keep her from experiencing sexual pleasure, which in his tribal culture is only for the men."

Tears are running down Hope's face. Gloria embraces her. Roy continues to read.

"Barbara was drugged on her wedding night with powerful painkillers and woke up realizing this barbaric ceremony had taken place. Afraid and alone in a foreign country, she almost lost her mind but pretended to go along with their customs until she could figure out how to get back to America, which took a year to come to fruition.

"Finally, there was a breakthrough; Ademola was going on a business trip to London to sell textiles from their family business and his mother insisted Barbara go along with him, saying she would be a blessing when it came to negotiating, with her accounting and business expertise. Prayers had finally been answered. She would make her escape once in London.

"Barbara called me and asked that I arrange a ticket for her to come back to America immediately, saying that she would explain everything to me when she arrived and that I was not to let anyone know she was coming back. From the tone in her voice, I was scared but did exactly as she instructed me.

"Barbara was not a violent woman but the morning she left London, with Ademola still asleep, she stuffed his mouth with a sock, tied him to the bed post and cut his penis, leaving him to bleed and boarded her flight to America.

"As much as I wished he had died, he didn't. For years, he called me, asking if I had seen Barbara. He was afraid to come to America because of the atrocity he had committed, so Barbara was safe for the most part but always lived in fear that someone from his tribe would seek her out and therefore decided to live in the projects, knowing that would be the last place they would look for a highly educated woman.

"Gloria and Faith, please comfort my sweet Hope. I know that thus far this is a lot for her to handle.

"I know you are wondering what happened next. Well, I was overwhelmed with grief and guilt. It was me who introduced Barbara to Ademola. I felt as if I had sent her to her demise. In that horrific act of barbarism he and his tribe's folk had killed that bright smile she always wore, and robbed her of her lifelong dream of raising a child in a loving family.

"I tried to assure her that God would send the right man to her in His time, but my words just fell on deaf ears. A man was the last thing Barbara wanted. She wanted a child. After finishing school her aspiration was centered on being a wife and mother. Ademola deprived her of the first, and she desperately wanted the latter.

"One day, Barbara asked me the unthinkable. She asked me if I would be a sperm donor and help her realize her dream of motherhood. She said there would be no strings attached, and she would be forever in my debt.

"My first thought was "oh heck no!" I know she felt my reservations and asked if I would donate my sperm and if she did not find a suitable donor before she got too old that would be the only way she would use it.

"I was so overcome with guilt for introducing her to that African butcher that I agreed, believing that she would find a suitable person, maybe even a husband. Barbara was still young and had a long life ahead of her. We were just twenty-three years old.

"For years, I didn't hear from Barbara until she called and told me of the murder of her cousin, her only living relative, Bedford Jennings. The same Bedford Lucille was engaged to marry. Barbara was devastated because now she had no one. That's when she joined our church, Gloria, and became head of the Altar Guild.

"So much time had passed that I never thought about the donated sperm until I noticed she was good and pregnant one Sunday and the Spirit led me to ask her. Barbara smiled and said, 'Yes, but this is my blessing and thank you for your contribution.' Then she left the church. The next time I heard from her was when I saw her going into the hospital in labor the day I was taking you and Faith home from the hospital.

"I dropped you home and went back to the hospital as a friend to make sure she was okay and the baby entered the world safely. Once I saw that precious little five-pound nine-ounce baby girl, I knew I had to be a part of her life. Hope was me; bone of my bone and flesh of my flesh.

"Barbara was upset with me for a long time because I didn't keep my part of the deal. I was only supposed to help her reach her dream and then disappear.

"Gloria, Faith and Hope, please forgive me for the pain all this has caused you. I'm going to have a long talk with the Father once I'm on the other side and maybe by and by He will help me to understand.

"I only have one request and that is that you love each other as I have loved you."

Without another word, Roy returns the letter to its envelope and lays it on the table; silence fills the air. Gloria finds herself wiping tears of joy, then notices everyone else in the room is doing the same. Attempting to compose herself, she finally says, "Well, sir, would you just look at God?" Searching for words, she mutters mostly to herself, "I'm ... I'm just in awe." She rises to her feet, lifts both her hands, and begins to worship God with one of her favorite choruses – half singing, half sobbing, "I stand, I stand in awe of You; I stand, I stand in awe of You; Holy God to whom all praise is due, I stand in awe of You."

The overflow of emotion in her voice is electric, and one by one, Roy, Faith, Dot, Fitzroy and Marlin spontaneously join in the second and third time around.

Overwhelmed, Hope races out of the room and Faith moves to follow her, intending to offer comfort until Roy intervenes, admonishing that Hope should be allowed to have some time to herself to process this new revelation. Fitzroy reaches out for Faith, giving her a familiar reassuring look, as they embrace.

Voicing the amazement he is experiencing, Fitzroy turns to his father. "Dad, you and Mum raised us to always tell the truth, the whole truth, and nothing but the truth. But for the first time in my life, it seems that there are some truths that cannot be told entirely except in retrospect. I just cannot imagine that Mother Gloria, Faith, Barbara or Hope could possibly have been able to hear of all this until Reverend Davis had gone to be with the Lord. Can you?"

Roy looks reflectively at Gloria, then at Faith, then at Fitzroy. "Son, before this very minute, I would have gone to the Father myself believing that truth delayed is no truth at all. I guess even an old man like me still has lessons to learn. I'll tell you this, though. The life of a pastor is very often a lonely one, even when he's surrounded with loving, supportive family, there is no earthly person he can safely tell his troubles to. While at the same time, you have no idea how many stories from the members in our parish we as pastors listen to and counsel them on, very private things I could not share even with your mother, Fitzroy.

"Trust is the stock-in-trade of a pastor, my son, and that sometimes means making the complex distinction between the truth that heals and the truth that destroys."

Just as Roy finishes talking, Lucille staggers down the hall, wearing a flowered frock housedress of Dot's. Everyone turns as she enters the room.

"What, ya'll having a wake? Did somebody die? And please tell me who the hell put this ugly-ass bag lady muumuu on me!"

"No, darling, no one die… it's a celebration!" Marlin shouts.

# Chapter 11
## Walking While Black

Mabel woke up to the sound of someone banging on her door. She glanced at the ticking clock on her nightstand and it said 3:06 a.m. Who the hell could be at her door this time of morning? Without giving it a second thought, she reaches into the nightstand drawer and takes out her small revolver and makes her way to the front door, stopping to look out the window first to see who she might have to shoot.

Kesha, her young neighbor, is calling her name with fright in her voice. "Miss Mabel, please open up the door. Your son has been shot!"

Unable to process what Kesha is saying, Mabel flings open the door with a look of terror in her eyes. "What did you just say?"

"Miss Mabel, your son and Day Day both got shot; day lying in a pool of blood in the street on the boulevard! You need to come now, Miss Mabel."

"Oh Dear God!" Mabel cries as she races out the door in her nightgown, house robe and sleep bonnet, with her gun still in her hand.

"Miss Mabel, you might want to leave your gun in the house. There are a lot of policemen down there," Kesha cautions her.

Mabel puts the gun in her house robe pocket and keeps stepping. Kesha runs to keep up.

A crowd of angry people has assembled, and they are cursing at the police. "You didn't need to shoot them! When ya'll gon stop shooting black people!"

Mabel pushes her way through the crowd, where she sees her son lying on the ground next to Day Day and starts to scream out of control.

The police are afraid of the big woman, who is running toward them screaming, "You killed my child! Look at what you did to my son! You cold-blooded bastards!"

Two police officers try to hold her as she approaches her son's body. Mabel pushes them off of her, and they fall to the ground, Mabel continues toward her son, crying out, "Baby, please don't die... baby, please!" She is cut off mid-sentence as one of the officers tases her.

Mabel reaches in her robe pocket in the midst of being tased and fires her gun, hitting the officer in the neck. Two officers run toward Mabel with their guns drawn and fire multiple bullets, killing her. An angry mob closes in on the police officers just as a backup group of officers armed in riot gear climb out of the back of a van, pushing the angry crowd back to the sidewalk to watch four bodies lying in the street. The ambulance arrives and immediately starts to try and resuscitate the police officer, ignoring Mabel and the others. Kesha screams out of control!

The sun is just starting to rise as a news team arrives and finds white sheets covering three bodies in the street. Police barricades hold back the angry crowd. A news reporter approaches Kesha to get information on what she saw happen.

"They killed Miss Mabel! Miss Mabel was the rock that held these projects together. They did not have to kill her, she was only trying to get to her son, who the police shot down dead because he was fighting Day Day! It wasn't like dem was fighting the police. Day was fighting each other and the police shot them because day would not stop fighting! When a black man is fighting, day can't hear nothing, not even the police! Dem don't know us! Day Day and Miss Mabel's son Butch have been fighting since day was kids! The two of them fight one day then the next day them drinking buddies. Dee's police don't know us and now day done killed Miss Mabel, her son and Day Day!" Kesha cries.

The news reporter continues to ask Kesha more questions. "Why do you think Mrs. Brown was carrying a gun? They are saying she shot the now-deceased police officer with the intent to kill." The reporter positions the microphone in front of Kesha's face.

"Hell, just about everybody in these projects have a gun! When I knocked on Miss Mabel's door to tell her what happened to her son, she already had her gun in her hand when she answered the door. She probably thought I was someone knocking on her door to do her harm. Once she saw it was me, I told her she might want to put the gun in the house because there were police down on the boulevard, but she was in such a hurry to see about her son she just kept running and put the gun in her housecoat. When someone tell you your son have been kilt, you don't be thinking. But none of this would have happened if they didn't tase Miss Mabel when all she was trying to do was get to her son. She wanted to hold him, tell him everything was going to be all right! None of this had to happen! None of this! The police is too quick to shoot us! If this had been two white men fighting; you think they would be lying dead in the street! Hell no! This shit has got to stop! Black lives count, too!"

"'Black lives count, too,' is what the crowd is chanting. 'Black lives count, too!' I'm Michelle St. Jacques, reporting from the last standing projects in Atlanta where three African-Americans have been gunned down by white police officers."

Back at Mabel's house, her ten-year-old grandson wearing his pajama bottoms is walking from room to room, calling his grandmother. Mookie notices the front door is opened, and he ventures out into the yard, where he can hear people chanting just a short distance from his house. He walks toward the noise and sees a crowd of angry people.

His grandmother always taught him to go in the other direction of trouble but somehow this chanting is drawing him in. Just as he reaches the boulevard, the first person he sees is Kesha and wonders what she and all these people are doing up so early; school doesn't start for another three hours.

Kesha sees Mookie approaching the crowd. She steps quickly to stop him. The panic in her face tells the young man something terrible has happened and in some way it has to do with him and his family.

"Mookie! You don't want to come over here! Stay right there!" Kesha yells.

"Why?" Mookie continues walking toward the street.

"Honey, something terrible has happened to your daddy and your grandma! Please, sweetie, don't go any further."

Hearing this only propels Mookie to run toward the crowd, where he pushes his way up to the front of the police barricade. Kesha is right behind him as he looks on in horror, seeing one of his grandmother's house shoes on her foot sticking out from under a blood-stained white sheet and the other on the ground a few feet away. The young man's eyes comb the scene, examining the other bodies in the street and an arm that is not covered up that has a silver ring with a lion's head on its middle finger. The ring Mookie gave to his dad a year ago on Father's Day.

Kesha turns Mookie's body away from the carnage in the street and hugs him. No words are coming out of his mouth. Suddenly, Kesha feels hot urine splattering on the ground. Mookie is in shock and peeing on himself.

"Come, Mookie, let me take you home and get you cleaned up. Come on, sweetie," she cries. Realizing the child is in shock, summons one of the tenants standing nearby to help her carry the child home.

Roscoe, a neighbor, who lives on the other side of Kesha, puts Mookie on his back and the three of them head for Mabel's house.

"You know Social Services gon take him. The boy can't stay here by his self," Roscoe says.

"He ain't gone be by his self. I'm going to get him cleaned up, take him over to my house until I can find his momma," Keisha says as they enter Mabel's house.

"His momma! Ain't she in jail?" Roscoe screams.

"No, I heard she in a halfway house and done got saved. She wit' T.D. Jakes an dem. Put him on the bed," Kesha instructs Roscoe, who puts the still in shock wet boy on the bed. Kesha notices Roscoe looking around the house at Mabel's things.

"Thank you, Roscoe, you can go now and shut the door."

Roscoe pauses, still looking around.

"Don't even think about touching any of Miss Mabel's shit or she will come from her grave and kick your ass! Everything in here belongs to Mookie or Miss Mabel's brother Bobo."

"Kesha, how you gone say some shit like that? Miss Mabel was my girl; I would never take anything from her when she was alive and I damn sure ain't gon take nothing from her since she dead," Roscoe says with hurt feelings.

"Den I glad me and you are thinking alike. Do me a favor and see if you can get in touch with her brother Bobo. Danny Green who lives at the end of the bricks should have his number. They used to be boys. I'm gon try and find a number for Hope. She down in the islands, but I know Miss Mabel must have a number round here somewhere."

"I gon check Danny out, and I'll hit you up on your cellphone wit Bobo's number. You need me to give you a ride to go check for the boy's mother?"

"Please, if you could." Kesha smiles.

"Okay," he says; and just as Roscoe turns to leave, he turns back around.

"I'll borrow a few dollars to get you some gas," Kesha says as if reading his mind.

"Thank you, Kesha." Roscoe leaves and Kesha runs a bath for Mookie. She puts the quiet pensive child in the tub, being extra careful to keep a close eye on him in between searching through Miss Mabel's papers for Hope's phone number. Consumed with grief and unable to fight back the tears, Kesha sits on the couch and wails out, sobbing uncontrollably; not only for Miss Mabel but for all the people she's lost in the past years to senseless murders. Kesha wipes her eyes with the tail of her tee shirt as her ten-year-old son Sean walks in the door.

"Momma, why you crying and what you doing in Miss Mabel's house? Momma, you know the police and a bunch of people are down there on the boulevard? Momma, I'm scared." Sean doesn't stop talking long enough for Kesha to answer his questions.

"Momma, did somebody else get killed? Momma, why you in Miss Mabel's house?" he repeats.

"Sean, please stop asking me so many questions at once. Something happened to Miss Mabel and Mookie's father. I'm trying to find Hope's phone number so I can call and tell her. Now do me a favor and go check on Mookie; he's in the bathtub."

Inquisitive Sean can tell by the tone of his mother's voice he better do as she says and not ask any more questions. Sean finds his way to the bathroom to check on Mookie, where he calls out to his mother from the bathroom.

"Mommy, you need to come! Mookie done slip down in the tub, he under the water!"

# Chapter 12
## Hawaii Ain't The Virgin Islands

The breakfast diner where Denisha works as a waitress and Camille as a grill cook is located on the road close to the Hawaiian airport. They could hardly believe their good fortune for both of them to find work right away, and at the same place. The diner is always busy and filled with people from five in the morning until three in the afternoon. Mr. Zoni is their boss and his first priority is to make the money. Nobody eats for free, not even his mother, unless it's Mother's Day or Christmas.

Denisha has been watching the clock for the last two hours, and it seems like it's not moving at all. A party of six has just been seated at her station. A couple with four children ranging ages eight to sixteen. From looking at them, Denisha can tell they are on their way to the airport headed back to one of them cold states because of the way they are peeling from the sun and sporting a bunt red color similar to that of a cooked lobster. These snow bunnies were trying to drain every bit of the Hawaiian sun before they headed back home.

"Welcome to Zoni's, what can I get for you?" Denisha stands close to the table with her pen and pad ready to write down their order.

"We hear the pineapple pancakes are to die for!" the mother screams as if their pancakes have magical powers.

"Yep, dem real good. Would you like dat wit sausage or bacon?" Denisha writes her order on the pad.

"I'll have the sausage. I hear they are made at a local Hawaiian plant right here on this island." Again, the woman is excited over the sausages she's about to order. Denisha gives her a fake smile.

"Yep. And what can me get fa you, sir?" Looking up from her pad, Denisha stares at the man, hoping for less excitement.

"I'll have the waffles with the homemade Hawaiian syrup, plenty of butter, sausage, an egg over easy and one percent milk with my meal." He closes his menu and hands it to Denisha, along with his wife's menu.

"Now, children, decide what you want or I'll decide for you," the mother admonishes her kids.

"I'll have the same thing Dad ordered except I want scrambled eggs," the sixteen-year-old boy says, closing his menu and immediately taking his iPhone from his pocket, tuning everyone out.

"Mom, I told you I'm not eating until he calls me. I'm on a love hunger strike," the fifteen-year-old girl says as she takes her brush out of her bag and proceeds to brush her red hair.

"Young lady, you are going to eat something even if I have to force-feed you! Now don't make me embarrass you in front of all these people. I'd bet you a new iPhone that that stupid boy is feeding his face right now as we speak, and he isn't giving a damn about you not eating! Now pick something!" the dad says between his teeth as if he is tired of this child and she has been a problem the whole time during their vacation.

"Fine, Dad! Miss, I'll have a cup of coffee and some toast with butter! How's that, Dad!" She continues brushing her hair.

"Put the brush away, Missy. If you want to brush your hair, go into the bathroom!" the mother says.

Denisha cuts in. "And what can me get fa de two little ones?" Who look like they don't have a clue, Denisha is thinking.

"Give them your mini pancakes. Sweetie, you want strawberries or blueberries on your pancakes?" Mom asks.

"Strawberries for me, if they're fresh!" the eight-year-old says.

Denisha has a blank stare on her face.

"Me, too, if they are fresh!" the child who looks like she goes along with anything her sister says shouts.

"Are they fresh?" the eight-year-old asks.

Denisha's feet are killing her, and she's doing everything not to be rude to these people.

"Honey, I'm gon go to the strawberry patch out back right now and see if I can pick dem fa ya. Any ting fa ya ta drink?"

Shocked, the little girls quietly say milk at the same time. Dad has a smile on his face, as if he wants to chuckle but he can see is wife is not amused, so he quickly removes the smile from his face.

"Was she serious or just rude? I know they grow pineapples here in Hawaii, but I'm almost sure they don't grow strawberries and especially at this roadside dinner!"

"I think she was just kidding, honey. Relax yourself," the dad says, trying not to get his wife upset.

Denisha returns, carrying a tray filled with drinks and sets the drinks down in front of them.

"Excuse me, young lady, but do you have a strawberry patch out back?" the mother asks.

"No, the chef apologizes, he forgot to till the soil last season so dem not gon come up again. But him say he does have de next best ting… frozen strawberries. Would dat work for de little ladies?" Denisha musters up a fake grin.

"Frozen is fine." The little girls shake their heads. Denisha turns to leave.

"Excuse me. Your accent… where are you from? Jamaica?" the mother inquires.

"Actually, I'm from Russia," Denisha whispers. "I'm here in a witness protection program so I use this accent. I'll be right back with your meal." Denisha turns to leave but the husband talks.

"Russia? What part? I lived in Russia for a year as a foreign exchange student."

Denisha looks annoyed but smiles. "Oh, you wouldn't know our little goat-herding village. Only 3,000 people live there and just about everyone is family. I'll be right back." Denisha turns to leave again.

"What's the name of your village?" the dad pries.

Denisha is surprised and quickly rattles off the first thing that comes to her head. "It's called Anna's Retreat, named after me great, great, great grandmother." She walks off toward the kitchen, leaving dad and mom suspicious.

"Son, Google Anna's Retreat on your iPhone and tell me what you come up with," Dad says.

"There's something about that girl that just isn't right! I think she's a liar," Mom says.

"You guys are all up in her business like you're with the FBI. For god's sake, she's a waitress. Can we just order our food, catch our plane and go home!" the son screams.

"Just do what I ask you. Google Anna's Retreat and see if there is a town in Russia called that!" Dad says.

"I didn't know black people even lived in Russia," Mom chimes in.

"That is so racist! Black people live all over the world, Mom! That's the reason why I don't want you guys to meet my boyfriend!"

"Are you saying he's black!" the dad screams.

"As black as they come, straight from Africa! One hundred percent uncut black!" the teenager says then puts her ear bud in her ear.

Her mother reaches across the table and snatches them out of her ear. "You never told us this boy you are so stupid over is black!" Mom is pointing her finger in her face.

"Anna's Retreat is located in the U.S. Virgin Islands, okay!" The young man puts his ear buds back in his ear and relaxes, patting his feet to the beat playing on his iPhone, totally tuning out his parents and the fight that's going on between his sister and them.

"Mommy, my history teacher is black and I think he's the nicest teacher I've ever had," the little sister chimes in.

"That's nice, sweetie. It's okay to have a black teacher, just make sure when you pick your husband he looks like daddy," the mother says.

"For god sakes, we have a black president! It's a new day, Mom and Dad! Wake up!"

"If we had it our way, his black ass would never have gotten elected!" Dad spews with venom in his heart.

"Well, guess what? He got elected twice in spite of you and your Tea Party Bigots!" the daughter yells.

"This is not the place to discuss this. We will talk to you when we get home, young lady!" Mother shouts at a whisper.

The teenager's phone rings. She smiles.
"Excuse me, I'll take this call in the ladies' room."

Her younger sisters move out of the way so she can slide out of the booth.

Dad, talking through his teeth, says, "You'd better end that relationship now!"

The young lady just smiles and continues to the restroom.

Denisha arrives with their food. "Two orders of mini pancakes with frozen fresh strawberries, two orders of waffles with the homemade Hawaiian syrup, plenty of butter, sausage, one egg over easy, one scrambled and one percent milk, order of toast with coffee, pineapple pancakes with manufactured sausage made right here on our beautiful island! Is there anything else I can get you?"

"Excuse me, Miss, but my son Googled Anna's Retreat and it's located in St. Thomas, U.S. Virgin Islands. You're really not from Russia, are you?" the dad attacks.

Denisha looks at him with a smile. "Sir, as I earlier said. I'm in a witness protection program and if you dig any further into me background, me gon have ta call de special protection agency ta investigate you. Now tell me, what is your name and where are you from?" Denisha takes out her ordering pad and pen, ready to write his information down.

The couple is speechless and has a shocked look on their face. Dad finally speaks. "Thank you very much. The waffles and pancakes look good, and we'll have our check when you get a chance."

Denisha turns and walks away. Their son, with a smirk on his face, shakes his head and turns up the volume to his music.

Later that evening, we find Denisha and Camille sitting on the upper porch of their duplex apartment. Palm trees are swaying in the background as they talk and eat hamburgers just off the grill where Camille is cooking.

"Akoni does wants me to move downstairs wit he," Camille tells Denisha, grinning like she just won the lottery.

Denisha's feet are soaking in a footbath while she eats. Surprised at what she just heard Camille say, she puts her burger down and looks at her like she's lost her mind.

"Camille, you ain't known he but five seconds! Dat man might be some serial killer. Slow your friggin' roll, me son! We ain't come to Hawaii to get into stupidness. Pour a little more Epson salt in me footbath and hand me some ketchup. I tell you dis, if dat man don't let me take a break tomorrow, me gon quit! How him tink me gon waitress on me feet for ten hours straight wit out no break?"

"If you quit, I gon quit, too. Him got me at dat hot ass grill wit no break. I tell he me got ta pee and he gon tell me to wait until de lunch crowd finished! I tell he me pee pee don't know nothing 'bout no lunch crowd and if him don't want me ta wet the floor right 'ere in front of dis 'ere grill, him better move out me way 'cause me got ta go now! Ya ever ''ear of such a ting? Den the fool gon tell me when we was leaving ta go home dat me need ta cut me weave hair; it too long and gettin' in de customers' food. I ask he who tell he dis 'ere is a weave."

Denisha is laughing at Camille and almost choking on her burger. "Gil, what him say?" Denisha continues laughing.

"First, him no answer me. I put me hands on me hips and study he up and down, like dis." Camille reenacts her moves.

Denisha is rolling with laughter. "You push your butt out an' ting too wit your hands on your hips!"

"Gil, I give he de black woman pose you give when people in you business where day ain't got no business being wit out cussing dem out," Camille yells.

"What da man say?" Denisha hollers.

"What could him say wit' out being out of place? He shut he damn mouth and say see you tomorrow, Camille, and he walk he ass to de back of de store!"

"Gil, you know one of me customers did find a blond hair in she French fries. I tell she it's a potato string," Denisha says, laughing.

"What de hell is a potato string?" Camille looks puzzled

"Me ain't know! But you got ta give me points for coming up with something ta say to cover your butt," Denisha jokes and Camille laughs.

"So what da woman do wit de potato string?" Camille says like it's a gourmet food.

"She put some ketchup on it and ate it wit' the rest of she fries." Denisha and Camille are rolling with laughter.

"Gil, you know you crazy! And dat's why me love you 'cause you's me girl and you always got me back!" Camille hugs Denisha.

"Yep! And dat's why you need to listen and not move your big behind downstairs wit dat Hawaiian man!"

"Now, see, you two faced. I ain't say nothing when you park your ass up in Shakoi's raggedy little shanty all dem years, shacking up in de ting. Me just shake me head and pray dat you would come ta ya self one day an realize da man wasn't shit."

"True dat! True dat! An dat's why me don't want ta see you go through de same ting me went through," Denisha pleads.

"Akoni ain't like Shakoi. Akoni work a good job. Him an engineer at de Navy base on dis 'ere island. Da man finish college and got he degree and ting."

"Okay. Now don't take dis de wrong way or nothing and me is probably de only person and I mean de only person who could ask you a question like dis, being dat I'm your best friend and we been friends since second grade and we never lie or hold tings back from each other... So, Camille what dat man want wit you?" Denisha bluntly asks.

Camille puts her hands on her hips and pushes her butt out, pointing her finger at Denisha before she speaks. "So you saying I'm dumb?"

"No, but you're not the brightest bulb in de lamp. Camille, the man is an engineer! You can't even spell it. Men like that marry girls name Muffy, Trish, Megan, Taylor and shit like that. Not no ghetto big mouth woman from the projects. Name three reasons why that man should want you?"

"One: he said he like my island accent and the challenge it is trying to figure out what I'm saying." Camille smiles like what she just said makes her special.

"Now that some dumb shit. How long you think it gon be before him get tired of trying to figure out what you saying?" Denisha pounces back.

"Whatever! Number two: him say he loves my hair. The color is like a ray of beautiful sunshine on a cloudy day. Isn't dat sweet? No man never tell me dat before." Camille smiles, looking dreamy.

"Now I know you crazy. Camille, dat ain't your hair! Now if Mr. Zoni down at the restaurant can see your weave tracks, den how long before you think Akoni gon be all up in dat hair and feel the thread? What you gon do, tell he it's potato string? Gil, just 'cause you bought the hair don't mean it's *your* hair!"

Denisha takes her feet out of the soaking tub and dries them as she continues her conversation with her best friend.

"Well, you asked for tree reasons. Number tree is enough to cover any of the other shortcomings." Camille smiles.

"I hope it's you have boatloads of money that none of us know about that will shadow over all your flaws," Denisha jokes.

"No! Better dan dat! De man say my cookie is de best him ever had! Denisha, you should hear how dat man be carrying on when we make love. I be like damn, is it all dat?' Me ain't know I was dat good. Da man is whooped!" Camille attempts to high-five Denisha, who leaves her hanging and slips on her back-out sandals.

"Now, dat's cold. Denisha, you gon leave me hanging? High-five me! Me answered your crazy questions with the bomb answer." Camille does a little winner dance.

Denisha shakes her head, unable to believe her friend can be so slow. "So you saying number tree is de reason you should go and shack up wit de man?" Denisha stares her friend in the eyes.

"Yeah! What man doesn't want some good coochie when him wake up in de morning fa lunch, dinner and at bedtime? Coochie is what makes the world go round!" Camille's hands are back on her hips.

"Camille, 99.9 percent of every woman's coochie is good if you know how to move it! If you tink that and that alone is what's going to hold that man's attention, then you better tink again. Just let some other woman who knows how to work it and have a few more tings going for dem; like a degree, good job, house or car get Akoni's attention, den you gon be yesterday's news. Men want a woman with substance, not just a good coochie. Dem can buy that at the strip club!" Denisha says.

"Well, you sure know how to make me feel worthless! T'anks!" Camille pouts as she takes a beer out of the cooler next to the grill.

"Well, Denisha, how do you tink dat went?" she asks herself.

"Maybe you should open up a relationship counseling office and ting! 'Cause you does seem to know all de right stuff dat make a relationship work. I guess dat's why you and Shakoi was doing so good up till him get killed," Camille sarcastically says as she takes a seat on the reclining lawn chair with her beer.

Denisha rolls her eyes. "No, me an' Shakoi wasn't doing good a-tall! De man was a cheating, lying, self-centered, stealing idiot and I was a bigger idiot for staying wit he so long! Camille, if me tell yah de world is round, you ain't got ta go walk ta de end ta see if yah gon fall off or keep going around! Me don already walked it for yah! I see me casting me pearls in de wrong direction. Me mudder say, 'a hard head makes a soft behind.' So go head and fall on yah ass if yah like. I gon be right there to help you up 'cause dat's what friends do, just like you do for me when me run from dem people trying ta kill me over Shakoi's stupidness."

Denisha is quiet after she speaks. Camille doesn't talk either for a while.

"I guess Shakoi liked your coochie, too, huh?" Camille finally says, smiling.

"Me son! You could hear he screaming from Agnus Fancy Hilltop down to Crown Bay and de man still cheated! De relationship wasn't blessed and started out wrong. Me was desperate to have a man and I settled for a selfish boy."

"And now you can't go home 'cause of he and he dead. Life crazy!" Camille says as she takes a swig of her beer.

"Who say me can't go home?" Denisha has a sly look on her face.

"You can go if you have a death wish! Der is a lot of people dat want you dead! Ain't dat's why we 'ere? I mean unless we come ta learn how ta hula dance and surf an ting." Camille laughs like that's out of the question.

"I know you miss St. Thomas, don't you?" Denisha asks.

"I ain't gon lie; me miss salt fish and dumplings at Victor's Hide Out, Texas Bar-be-Que truck on de waterfront on the weekends, Miss Viola's goat water, johnnycake and bush tea…" Camille keeps going!

"Gil, shut your mouth! You gon make me swim dis ocean home!" Denisha screams.

"Well, let de records show dat one of us can go home! Me could go an' bring some food back. Ain't nobody trying ta kill me." Camille laughs.

"Don't trouble yah self, Camille. I gon go home! I mean what de hell we doing 'ere. You about ta make a stupid mistake and move in with Akoni, me feet killing me working at de dinner, and any day now somebody gon choke on your potato strings at the restaurant and we get fired; besides, me got me desk job in St. Thomas. I does miss me family der, and I sick of looking at you all day every day! I want me life back!" Denisha cries.

"Life back! You crazy! You ain't gon have no life if you go back to St. Thomas, you gon be dead! No buddy, me can't let you go home 'cause dat gon be suicide!"

"We gon park we big asses right 'ere and try and make a life as Hawaiian women. I gon sign us up for one of dem belly dancing classes or scuba diving. Hell, we can even do dat zipline ting in the rain forest dey advertise on television! Please, Denisha, don't go home and die. I won't move downstairs; I gon tell Aknoi I'll come downstairs and rock his world, den bring me ass back upstairs when me done. We just can't go home," Camille pleads with her friend.

"Gil, you're the best friend I ever 'ad. T'anks so much for being a true friend." Denisha gets up and hugs Camille. Camille gently pushes Denisha away.

"What's wrong, gil?" Denisha asks Camille, who has a puzzled look on her face.

"Denisha, I know how pigheaded yah are and if yah decide ta go back ta St. Thomas and die I would kill mah self for keeping a secret from you. Being dat we are best friends and nothing will ever change dat, me need to tell yah some ting." Camille lowers her head.

"Gil, don't tell me yah got cancer or nothing like dat. Me ain't ready to hear dat!" Denisha screams nervously.

"No, no! Me ain't got cancer. It's just dat me ain't ever want ta keep nut ting from yah and me been concealing some ting," Camille sadly says.

"Whatever it is, we gon get through it," Denisha calms her friend.

"You see... de week before Shakoi die, I see he in town and he tell me he got some bomb weed just come in from South America. Gil, me eyes pop open and me tongue stick out, panting like a dog for a bone! I tell he, 'slip me a spliff no?' Him tell me he gon drop da ting pass me house later, 'cause him ain't got none rolled and somebody waiting for he. Him say him gone come around nine o'clock.

"Me forget Shoki was coming fast as him say so and me just go on about me business. Well me peas, round ten o'clock me 'ear somebody knocking at me door. Me look out de window and it's Shakoi. I cuss he for coming ta me house so late and me thinkin' you dere wit he. Shakoi tell me him got de shit and it's good. I tell he come on in. We sit dere and drink Guinness beer and smoke weed dat was stronger dan any shit me ever smoke! Gil, dat weed had me hallucinating! Me can't tell you when night ended and morning came. But me can tell you me wake up naked wit Shakoi in me bed all lockup together an' ting. Denisha, I beat he ass black and blue and swell up he eye when I knock he wit me shoe." Camille is crying. "Please forgive me before you die! I'm so sorry 'cause you's my best friend."

Denisha is shocked but she sits down on the lawn chaise chair and rocks her best friend in her arms. "So dat's how him get he black eye. Don't worry, Camille, Shakoi don't deserve your tears or mine. Let's agree to never talk about this nightmare again."

"So you not mad at me?" Camille asks tearfully.

"Absolutely not! And you don't have to worry about me dying. Dem bad people who want ta kill me is in jail or dead. We can go home if we want to," Denisha calmly says.

Camille jumps up, pacing de porch. "Who tell ya so? Dis could be a set up! Yah didn't tell anybody where we live, did yah? Lord dem gon come to Hawaii and kill we!"

"Rest yourself, gil! Detective Fitzroy call me an' tell me him want me ta come testify. Him say dere is $25,000 reward money, too," Denisha casually says.

"Oh, hell yeah! When we leaving? Does him want me ta say something, too? Reward money! Oh yeah! But, Denisha, does dat mean we have ta give back de money we come 'ere wit?"

"Him ain't say nothing bout dat. Me ain't tink nobody know bout dat but Shakoi," Denisha says.

"Denisha, der is one more ting me need to come clean wit!" Camille smiles.

"What else?" Denisha looks at her friend with a puzzled look.

"You remember de time you does tell me ta go in de bush and get ya some clothes and de weed out of Shakoi freezer?" Camille explains.

"Yes. How can I forget it was when my naked butt get ant bitten up and me was sitting in de car waiting for yah ta bring me some clothes," Denisha recounts.

"Well, dere was more dan weed in de freezer. Dere was a big wad of money inside de bricks of weed. When me count it later, it was $20,000. Me ain't want ta tell yah since you was so hell bent on we giving back de money you got from Shakoi so me put de money under de floorboard in me room." Camille points toward the bedroom. Nervous that Denisha is going to be mad, she waits to hear what her friend is going to say.

"Well, my friend, spend it wisely because we going home!" The ladies embrace just as Camille's friend Akoni calls out for Camille from the downstairs apartment.

"Camille, my island flower… Daddy's home!"

Denisha and Camille burst out laughing.

"His ass is just going to have to wait. Me got some packing ta do."

# PART THREE

## Chapter 13
## A Celebration For Hope

Hawksnest Beach, the place where almost all beach parties are held in St. John is packed! Wall to wall people occupy every inch of the beach. Steel pan players are pounding out melodious tunes; men, woman and little ones are jumping up to the music. Marlin pulls Hope out onto the covered patio dancing area.

Hope pulls away from Marlin. "I don't know how to dance," she squeals.

Marlin is not taking 'No' for an answer. "Me darling, dis 'ere is your celebration, and Uncle Marlin gon teach ya a few moves. You's a part of dis 'ere family and me job is ta teach ya what we island folks do when dem steel pans is playing sweet music. Tell she Dot!"

Smiling, Dot shakes her head as she flashes back on the day she met Marlin when she was visiting Faith from Atlanta during an ugly separation from her ex-husband; it's like déjà vu. Marlin insisted she dance with him and from that day forward they have never been separated. Dot eggs Hope on, and she finally relents to having Marlin give her West Indian dance lessons on the beach. Fitzroy and Faith are amused at Hope's shyness.

"You can do it, girl! You're a Davis. We can do anything we put our minds to! Rock it, Hope!" Faith screams.

Hope is so touched by Faith comments a sense of belonging overcomes her. She is smiling and following Marlin's instructions to the tee!

"Well, sir, you's me best dance student! Dot, watch she! De

girl got moves," Marlin cries.

Fitzroy, Faith and Dot join them on the dance floor. Gloria and Lucille are sitting at a picnic bench nearby. Lucille has a large plastic cup in her hand filled with rum and coke. Gloria is laughing and clapping as everyone dances.

Roy is sitting at the far end of the same picnic table. He is trying to get away from Miss Claudette and her special needs daughter so he can fix himself a plate of food and enjoy the party.

"Reverend Brown, I just don't know what to do. The doctors, dem tell me de girl is two weeks pregnant. Now who would take advantage of me child, knowing she special?"

"Sister Claudette, I am so sorry to hear this news. There are bad men out there who will take advantage of any woman, special or not. Now, if I can excuse myself, I'm going to go and fix me a plate. My belly is talking in other tongues." Roy gets up to leave.

Miss Claudette starts talking again, trying to hold him there. "Reverend, I was wondering if it would be possible fa you to come pass me house later on dis evening so we could continue dis 'ere conversation? Ya see, me is in distress and ain't got nobody I could talk to about de situation."

Miss Claudette gives the Pastor a pitiful damsel-in-distress look. She may have even fluttered her eyelashes.

Roy pauses and gives her a very serious look. "Miss Claudette, I don't think it would be appropriate for me to visit you at your home this evening. Now, what you can do is make an appointment with the church secretary and the three of us can meet in my office, Monday – Friday 9:00 A.M until 5:00 P.M.

My secretary will take notes as we talk, then that way I will have a detailed list of all the things we need to do going forward to resolve this situation or I can have one of the Deaconesses come over tonight and pray with you. With that said, I'll wait to hear from you." Roy gets up and heads toward the food table.

Miss Claudette hollers at him. "It's mighty funny you always at Mrs. Gloria's house in the late hours! I bet she ain't had to make no appointment wit your secretary. If I ain't mistaken, you been sleeping over some nights… Reverend. You think she better den me?"

Roy pauses for a second then decides to ignore her and continue to fix his plate. Gloria and half-drunk Lucille turn toward the end of the table where Miss Claudette and her daughter are sitting.

"How desperate!" Gloria whispers.

"Did that heifer just call you out like you some kind of adulterous slut?" Lucille slurs.

"Don't worry about it, Lucille. Desperate people say and do desperate things."

"I will beat the black off her desperate ass if she says one more damn word about my sister!" Lucille stands up, ready to head down to the end of the table.

"Lucille, please sit down. We don't need two ignorant people adding fuel to a dead fire." Gloria pulls Lucille down on the bench.

Miss Claudette is angry at Roy for walking away and is searching for words to throw his way.

Lucille covers her mouth with her hands like she's making a megaphone and screams in Miss Claudette's direction. "Say one more ignorant ass word to Roy, and I will drown your ugly ass and your retarded fat-behind child in the sea!"

Not sure if she will do it or not, Miss Claudette realizes that Lucille has been drinking. She grabs her daughter by the arm, stepping quickly, and they leave the beach area and head to her car.

"Give me whatever you have in that cup, Lucille! Have you lost your mind, threatening folks? You've had enough to drink!" Gloria takes her cup.

"You know you never could fight. And you better thank God I had your back!" Lucille says, laughing.

"God has my back, thank you!" Gloria retorts.

"Why you ain't tell me you and Roy been knocking boots!" Lucille teases.

"Because there is nothing to tell! You know I ain't 'knocking boots' with nobody unless they are my husband!" Gloria screams.

"That's true. I've been trying to get you to get yourself a little something-something since Rev died, and you just won't listen. So, when you and Roy gon tie the knot and you get to brush those cobwebs off the damn thing?" Lucille says, grinning up close in Gloria's face.

"Girl, you'd better get out my face with that stink liquor breath. Go find some Tic Tacs!" Gloria gets up to join Roy at the food table.

Lucille hollers out, "My damn breath don't stink!"

Just then, Billy, Lisa, Kamari and Sarafina arrive. Gloria turns around to greet them. Kamari runs and embraces Gloria, holding on tightly. Sarafina pushes her way out of Billy's arms to get to her grandmother. Roy, with food running over his plate, spots them and works his way toward the loving family.

"Would you look at my babies!" Gloria says, kissing them.

Roy sets his plate down on the picnic table and embraces Lisa and Billy.

"Poppa! Poppa, I have something very important to tell you!" Kamari lets go of Gloria and runs over to Roy.

"What is it, princess?" Roy asks, excited to hear whatever the news might be.

"I can swim! Auntie Cathy has been giving me swimming lessons every day in our pool and now I can swim and I can do cannon balls! Do you know what cannon balls are, Poppa?" Kamari doesn't wait for an answer. "Cannon balls are when you take off running really, really fast and you jump in the pool holding your knees up close to your chest!"

Sarafina makes her way over to Roy, tapping his leg for him to pick her up.

Roy smiles at the little toddler. "Well, hello, Miss Sarafina! Do you want to tell Poppa that you're doing Cannon Balls, too?" Roy teases as he tickles the little girl, who melts in his arms with laughter.

"She's just a baby, Poppa! She can't do Cannon Balls yet!"

Kamari tells Roy.

"He's just teasing her, Kamari," Lisa interjects.

"That plate looks mighty good, Dad. I think I'm going to fix me a plate," Billy says.

"That looks more like two plates' worth of food jammed on one plate," Lisa teases.

"As hungry as I am, when you see me next, my plate might look like three people's plates. Anybody want me to bring them something?" Billy laughs as he heads to the food table.

"No, baby, go for it!" Lisa says.

"Well, I must be wearing my invisible clothes, 'cause ain't a friggin' soul said hello to me!" Lucille slurs.

"I thought you were asleep. You got your head all down on your arms on the table," Lisa says.

"Mmmm hum! Whatever! So looks like you and the Puerto Rican gonna make it after all?"

"Yes, thank you. We are doing wonderful!" Lisa says with a big smile.

"Good! I'm going to send you my invoice soon as I get your address," Lucille says, not making any sense.

"Invoice for what!" Lisa asks.

"For helping you realize that you were being stupid and crazy and hard headed for even thinking about walking away from that man!" Lucille holds her head up and says.

"Lord, let me go get something to eat," Lisa says, laughing as she turns to join Billy at the food table.

Roy sits down with the children and shares his food with them. Gloria helps feed Sarafina. Kamari is sitting between Lucille and Roy.

"Poppa, something smells like doo doo," Kamari says, holding her nose.

Gloria checks Sarafina. It's not Sarafina.

"It's coming from over in that direction." Kamari points toward Lucille.

Gloria gets up with Sarafina and walks down to the end of the bench where Lucille is sitting and pushes her over so she can sit on the edge of the bench.

"Lucille!" Gloria whispers. "You didn't go to the bathroom on yourself, did you?"

"What kind of shit is that to ask a grown ass woman?" Lucille slurs.

Gloria sniffs Lucille. "Roy, would you mind holding Sarafina for me?"

Roy takes the toddler.

"Lucille, get your behind up and follow me," Gloria says, talking between her teeth.

Lucille reluctantly obeys. Gloria grabs her beach bag as she and Lucille walk down the beach away from the crowd, out of sight from the party. Gloria instructs Lucille to go into the water and take off her clothes and wash her bottom. Lucille's shorts and underwear float away with the current. Gloria meets her at the edge of the sea with a towel and a bathing suit bottom. Once she's dressed, the ladies sit on the sand and talk.

"I need my sister back. I lost you once before when Bedford died and it was no fun for any of us. When you go into these bouts of depression, you take all of us who love you there, too. I don't know what to say to snap you out of it but I do know this… you are very important in my life and I can't imagine waking up each morning or going to sleep every night without fussing with you, and sharing my problems and my triumphs with you. Because whether you know it or not, other than God, you are my earthly source of strength. When I feel weak, I know I have you to lift me up, protect me from my enemies and that you love me no matter what I say or do. Lucille, I need my sister back in her right mind; please don't take me down another spiraling road of despair, grief and hurt. Just tell me what I can do to make it better and I'll do it!" Gloria pleads with tear-filled eyes.

Lucille takes her grieving sister in her arms and rocks her. "I hurt so bad, Gloria. I hurt deep down in a place that's crying for mercy but has no ears to hear. I never thought I'd get to this point ever again after Bradford, but I let my guard down and allowed Wally to push the dagger into my already fragile heart and now I'm hemorrhaging!" Lucille cries.

Gloria takes her face into her hands. "You are more than a conqueror! Do not let anyone tell you otherwise. Wally is a weak man who never recovered from the death of his wife and from what I've heard, she was the one with the backbone in the family. You gave that man strength just like you give it to Dot, Faith, Lisa and me; when we are weak, so seeing you like this scares us, because we depend on you so much. Lucille, just tell me what to do and I'll do it!"

"First, I want you to give Roy a chance. If I can risk stepping out into another relationship after someone as wonderful as Bedford, then surely you can give another pastor a chance after the loss of Rev.

"Second, I want your blessings as I find my way back to Atlanta and continue with all my projects I stopped doing when I met Wally. I need to find myself again and I can't think of a better place that home.

"Third, I'm going to need you to find me a Tic Tac so I can kiss those beautiful grandbabies."

Lucille and Gloria walk back to the picnic area, hugging like childhood best friends.

"Girl, can you believe I shitted on myself? Please don't ever tell anybody about this. I thought I was farting. Damn!" Lucille begs.

"Your secret is safe with me. Especially after you make your contributions to the cuss bucket, 'cause you've racked up a hefty sum today alone."

"You can throw that damn cuss bucket in the trash, 'cause I'm going to write a check to Marlin and Dot to fund their project for two years. As long as I can cuss whenever I feel like it!" Lucille throws her head back and lets out a bellowing laugh as they approach Roy and the kids.

"Oh Lord, what am I going to tell that nosy, don't-miss-a-thing granddaughter of yours when she asks what was that smell?" Lucille stops in her tracks, looking at Gloria.

"She'll probably get a good laugh if you whisper in her ear and tell her it was a wet fart!" The two woman continue laughing as they join Roy and the grandchildren.

"Lord, you gon wear dis 'ere old man out! Let me sit a spell an catch me breath!" Marlin cries as he and Hope come off the dance floor.

Faith calls out to Hope to introduce her to Lisa and Billy, who are sitting at another table eating guava tarts and drinking homemade soursop juice.

"Man, these mini tarts are good!" Billy says.

"Yeah! That's your fourth one!" Lisa teases.

"And your fifth, not that I'm counting!" Billy says and Lisa punches him in the arm.

"Liar! For your information, I had six! Hey, Faith!"

"Lisa and Billy, I'd like you to meet my little sister, Hope," Faith says proudly.

Lisa and Billy both get up and hug Hope.

"Would you look at what the Rev did! He made two of you. No need for a blood test here!" Lisa says.

Billy cuts in, "So, Hope, how are you enjoying the Virgin Islands?"

"I love it! I'd like to share this place with some of the young people at home. It could be a life-changing experience," Hope shares.

"Hope has been helping Marlin and Dot set up the Youth Agriculture Program. And by the way, Lisa, we fell short on contributions this month without your donations to the cuss jar," Faith teases.

"Well, you better start working on a fundraiser, 'cause my baby has put all that cussing behind her." Billy kisses Lisa on the cheek as she blushes.

"Do you guys need to get a hotel?" Faith laughs.

"So where are you staying, Hope?" Lisa asks.

"I'm staying at Uncle Marlin's old place." Hope smiles.

"You're living at the old shanty? Faith! How could you let your sister stay in that place! You could have offered her my Chocolate Hole house!"

"Hold up, guys! I asked Uncle Marlin if it would be okay if I stayed in his shanty, and he graciously said I could and refused to allow me to pay him rent while I'm there." Hope smiles.

"He'd better not think about charging you rent for living in that sub-standard shack!" Billy nudges Lisa.

"Well why don't you say what's really on your mind, Lisa! Faith sarcastically says.

"So how long do you plan to be here with us, Hope? I'd love to take you up in my plane," Billy offers.

"Yes, Billy has his own airline company and flies to many of the Caribbean Islands. You'd love that! Maybe we all can fly with you to St. Martin and go on a shopping trip," Faith says with excitement.

"Wow that sounds really exciting! I'll be here for another week, then I'll have to go back to Atlanta to help a dear friend move. I also want to set up a program in Atlanta where I can provide teenagers the opportunity to be a part of the Youth Agriculture Program here in St. John for two weeks out of the summer and two weeks during the winter." Hope smiles.

"Well, you certainly can't fit them in your little house. Where will you house them?" Lisa asks.

"Aunt Dot, Uncle Marlin, Dominique and I have already cleared land on the farm to put up four cabins; each will sleep eight. We're waiting for the drawing to be approved by Public Works."

"Well, I'll say you've been busy. I really admire your energy and sense of purpose to get something like this going so quickly. Listen, I'm all for helping young people find their way. Why don't you allow me to take a few of them at a time up in the plane? Who knows, we might just have a couple of future pilots in the group," Billy says.

"How sweet, honey!" Lisa kisses her husband, who smiles and takes hold of her hand.

"That would be awesome! I can't wait to get back to the Bricks and sign the kids up for this life-changing experience."

"Did you say the Bricks?" Billy asks.

"Yes, those are the projects I was raised in," Hope matter-of-factly says.

"You were raised in the projects! How could your daddy allow that, Faith!" Lisa is repulsed.

"It's a long story, Miss Uppity!" Faith is upset at Lisa.

"It's cool. I may have lived in the projects, but I'm not the projects and living there has allowed me the opportunity to make a difference in a lot of people's lives. You see, something good can come out of the Bricks!" Hope laughs, raising her hands up in the air.

"Hope, when was the last time you turned on the television or listened to the news?" Lisa asks with sadness in her voice.

"It's been a few weeks. There is no television on the farm or in my shanty. I've literally tuned out the world since I've been on island and it feels so good," Hope says.

"Hope... they are rioting in Atlanta right now. Two men and one woman were shot down by police officers a couple of days ago and everyone is marching, burning and looting. On television, protestors are carrying signs with the slogan *Black Lives Matter!* I distinctly remember them saying it happened in the Bricks, because I hadn't heard that name before, and I'm from Atlanta. They said it was the last of the projects to come down where all this unrest took place." Lisa stops abruptly as she realizes the impact of this news.

Hope is visibly stunned.

"Hope, are you all right?" Billy reaches out to support her.

"Girl, I've got the video on my iPad, if you want to see it. You know they been playing it over and over again! I don't know why the news media think people want to look at three dead bodies lying in the street every five minutes." Lisa takes her iPad out of her purse sitting on the bench next to them and pulls up the video.

Hope immediately zeros in on the house slipper lying a few feet from the body of the woman covered up under a white bloody sheet.

"No! Something is wrong! Something is wrong! Mabel has not called me! Oh my God! That's Mabel's house slipper I bought her for Christmas! They've killed my Mabel!" Hope sits on the bench a weeps uncontrollably.

Roy, Gloria, Lucille, Marlin, Dot and Fitzroy, all surprised, run to find out what's going on. Many spectators on the beach circle around the grieving woman with puzzled looks on their faces. Faith holds on to her sister as if her life depends on it and rocks her in her arms.

"I guess this wouldn't be a good time to tell the family we're expecting another baby like we planned, huh?" Lisa whispers to Billy.

"No, darling, it wouldn't. Gather up the children," Billy says as he moves closer to help Faith and Fitzroy lead Hope to Fitzroy's van and take her to their house.

# Chapter 14
## Kamari Won't Go Into The House

Lisa and Billy, along with Sarafina, are sitting on the pool deck of Lisa's Chocolate Hole house that she used to share with her ex, Trevor, Kamari's biological father, who died three years ago. Kamari is sitting on the steps of the pool, pouting.

"Honey, I just don't think this is a good idea. We can't force Kamari to go into the house. Her fears are legitimate," Billy says as he gives Sarafina another piece of peanut butter cracker.

"Billy, we are the parents, not Kamari. Now I've talked with her until I'm blue in the face. I've explained to her that Trevor is not in the house hiding, waiting to scare her, and that he's in Heaven with God. Hopefully the last part is true." Lisa chuckles.

"So, what's the plan, Lisa?" Billy casually says as Sarafina runs toward the pool to be with her sister. Billy jumps up and swoops her in his arms. "And where do you think you're going, little lady!" Billy teases as he places the toddler on his lap at the patio table where he takes a seat.

"We tell her that we expect her to be an example for her little sister and to put on her big panties and stop acting like a baby!" Lisa looks at Billy, smiling.

"Yeah, right!" Billy chuckles.

"I don't know, sweetie; what do you suggest?" Lisa pleads.

"I say we sell the house and not subject the child to the trauma!" Billy matter-of-factly says.

"Billy, the house has been on the market for almost a year now!" Lisa says with frustration in her voice.

"Then maybe you need to think about lowering the price. I mean, the house is already paid for," Billy points out.

"I'm not going to just give my house away!" Lisa screams.

"Okay, that was my suggestion." Billy bounces Sarafina up and down on his knee.

"Do you have any more suggestions?" Lisa asks.

Billy stares at her and doesn't say a word.

"Billy, don't do that! I value your opinion. Just because I don't agree with you on lowering the price of the house doesn't mean I don't want to hear other suggestions," Lisa whines.

"Okay, then rent the house out. Maybe the tenant will love the house so much in time they will want to purchase it," Billy says.

"Then where will we live? I mean now that you've moved El Shaddai Airlines over to the U.S. Virgin Islands, we have to focus on selling the Beef Island house or getting a tenant for that house as well. And you know it's very hard to sell your house in the British Virgin Islands with all their stipulations," Lisa laments.

"Look, right now I don't want you stressing about anything, okay? I need you relaxed and healthy for you and my little boy you're carrying. Besides, I've been talking with a realtor, and I believe we might have someone to rent the Beef Island house. They are bringing in a new Chief of Police, and he and his family are going back for a second look tomorrow." Billy pats Lisa's hand, urging her to relax.

"Thank God! But, Billy, I still think we should not let Kamari get away with not facing her fears," Lisa states.

"The last time we were here, you dragged the child in the house after a three-hour standoff, and all we got was her screaming and crying! My princess had nightmares for a week. I'm not going to subject her to that again," Billy firmly says.

"Kamari, will you do Mommy a favor and go in the house and get your daddy a glass of water?" Lisa says with a big smile on her face.

Billy looks at her like she didn't hear a word he said. Kamari looks at her dad for guidance.

"What are you doing, Lisa?" Billy mumbles so Kamari can't hear him.

"I'm giving it one last shot, hoping we won't have to move," Lisa whispers with a smile on her face as the obedient child leaves the pool steps and approaches her parents.

"Excuse me, Mommy, what did you say?" Kamari asks with fear in her voice.

"Your daddy is really, really thirsty, sweetie. Would you mind going in the house and getting him a cold glass of water out of the refrigerator?" Lisa says as if nothing is out of the ordinary.

"Well, Mommy, I don't think that's a good idea. Maybe you or Daddy can go do it. You see, I asked God to make it so that I'd never ever have to go inside that house again, and I'm standing on his promise that He answers prayers. Poppa Roy told me to cast all my fears to the Lord and he would give me peace. And standing outside this house, I find peace, but going inside only stresses me out and gives me nightmares. I know my old daddy is still in that house and he is not happy that I am not his little girl anymore," Kamari says with tear-filled eyes.

Billy passes Sarafina over to Lisa and hugs and kisses Kamari. "Now that was spoken like a big girl who knows how to go to God in prayer. Wouldn't you agree, Mommy?" Billy smiles at Lisa.

"Absolutely! What do you say if we pack up, get in the car and go visit Grammy?" Lisa asks.

"Gram-mee, Gram-mee!" Sarafina repeats, bouncing up and down flapping her arms as Kamari races out the back gate to the car without another word. Lisa and Billy look at each other and laugh.

"Out of the mouth of babes… let's split this place!" Billy says.

Before Lisa, Billy and the girls reach Gloria's house to share their latest decisions about their living situation, Roy and Gloria relax on the veranda, looking out at the beautiful view of Coral Bay and several islands in the distance, sipping lime-aid and munching on mini guava and coconut tarts.

"So, what you think?" Gloria says.

"Think about what?" Roy asks.

"My tarts? You think they're better than Claudette's?" Gloria asks, holding her breath, waiting for a response.

"What kind of questions is that, Gloria?" Roy asks, laughing.

"Excuse me, but what's so funny, Pastor Roy!" Gloria turns from looking at the view and stares him in the eyes with a serious look on her face.

"Well, it sounds a little loaded, that's all," Roy teases.

"Just answer the question, man! Are my tarts as good as Sister Claudette's?" Gloria raises her voice.

"Well, let me try another one. Pass me the coconut one. I'm not sure if I've tasted that one yet." Roy smiles as he takes a tart on a napkin from Gloria, who stares at him, knowing he's had several coconuts tarts already.

"Roy, either you're losing it or you're just plain forgetful, because you already had several coconuts tarts already! Now, just answer the question!" Gloria says.

"I'm at a loss for words, Gloria. I mean, what's one to say about such a thing?" Roy stares into her eyes, smiling.

"Just tell the truth, man! I can take it!" Gloria replies.

"Well, the crust is nice and flaky; you couldn't ask for better. The guava is not too dry and has just the right amount of moisture; the natural syrup from the guava is present and the same with the coconut. There is nothing worse than a dried-up coconut; it gets stuck between your dentures and not to mention how hard it is to chew and swallow. Now as I survey the remainder of the tarts on the almost empty tray, I can see that you took extra care in making sure the top of the crust didn't get overcooked; they have just the right amount of heat applied to the butter that was brushed on top of them, giving them that wonderful golden color." Roy takes a bite of the tart and slowly chews it in his mouth, as if he's a connoisseur.

"Roy, if you don't answer my question, you just might find the rest of these tarts and the tray upside your smart head! Now, are my tarts better than Sister Claudette's or what?!"

Roy is rolling with laughter. Standing next to Gloria's chair, Roy gently pulls Gloria up out of her seat.

"Come here, lady," Roy softly says.

"Go on, Roy, I'm not fooling with you!" Gloria says in a playful way, with a nervous tone in her voice.

Roy pulls Gloria close to him. "I love you, Gloria, and it's time we do something about it," Roy says, while staring her directly in the eyes. Nervous, Gloria tries to pull away, but Roy holds on to her.

"Roy, you're talking crazy." Gloria chuckles.

"No... I'm not and you know it. It's time we stop lying to ourselves, Gloria. You know that you have feelings for me just as well. I loved you from the first time I saw you; I couldn't take my eyes off of you," Roy pours his heart out.

"Roy, you had a concussion and you thought I was Hannah, your deceased wife. Lord knows we look just alike." Gloria chuckles.

"Yes, I was a little off kilter for a minute, but it wasn't long before I realized you were not Hannah. You two might look like twins, but your personalities are as far apart as the east is from the west, morning is from night. No, my darling, you are a queen in your own right." Roy holds on to Gloria's hand.

"Roy, we've already talked about this before and didn't we agree we would just be friends?" Gloria sadly asks.

"And we are friends; best friends! It's a new day, Gloria. Before, you needed time to grieve the loss of your husband and we both needed time to get to know each other better. Well, now that I know you like you were my own sister and my best friend, it's time for us to take it to the next level. Enough of this pretending. Like I said, I know you want me just as much as I want you. Right?" Roy says, waiting for an answer.

"And what if I don't! You sound mighty sure of yourself, Mr. Brown." Gloria relaxes.

"Listen, darling, we are not getting any younger. Our kids are grown and have started their own families. Well, at least one of them has. It's time for us to work on spending the rest of our lives together. What do you say, sweetie? I've already talked to the Lord about this and received a bright green light. All systems are go."

"I will not make a decision as serious as this… until you tell me whose tarts are better, mine or Sister Claudette's!" Gloria says, laughing.

"You, my dear, are the Tart Queen." Roy pulls Gloria into his arms and hugs her just as Lisa, Billy, Kamari and Sarafina enter the house. Billy and Lisa are surprised and it shows on their faces.

"Busted!" Roy whispers in Gloria's ears, as Kamari runs to embrace them.

"Did we come at a bad time?" Lisa asks with a confused look on her face.

"No, no, no! Girl, give me my baby!" Gloria takes sleepy Sarafina out of Lisa's arms, kissing her and rocking her gently in her arms.

"Poppa! Prayer really works! I did just like you told me to do. Take my problems to the Lord. I said 'Dear God, you know I don't want to go in that house where my old daddy is living, so please give me the words to say to Mommy and Daddy that will make them see how scared I am!' Poppa, they heard me! I don't have to ever go in there ever again!"

"I am so proud of you, Kamari. Now, don't we serve an awesome God? You see, I have been praying to God, too, asking him for a big, big favor and he answered my plea! Young lady, we have some celebrating to do!"

Kamari is jumping up and down with Roy. Gloria, Lisa and Billy watch, smiling. Once they stop jumping up and down, Kamari looks at Roy with a puzzled look.

"Poppa, what did you ask the Lord for?" she asks with a big grin on her face, anxiously waiting his answer.

Roy stutters and looks at Gloria, who gives him a nervous smile.

Billy picks up on it and cuts in, "Sweetie, why don't you give Poppa a minute to give the Lord thanks before he tells what his blessings are?"

"Oh. I though Poppa would be just as excited as I am and want to shout it from the mountaintop! Like this!" Kamari runs to the end of the balcony and yells out toward the mountains and the awesome view of the valley before her. "I have been saved! I have been saved!"

Everyone laughs.

"My goodness! I didn't realize how traumatized the child was," Lisa sadly says.

"Bad Mommy!" Billy teases as he rubs Lisa's belly and gives her a kiss. Sarafina has fallen asleep in Gloria's arms.

"Mother Gloria, let me take her, she must weigh a ton!" Billy reaches for the baby.

Gloria holds on to her. "In case you've forgotten, young man, I know what to do with a sleeping child." Gloria smiles, kissing the sleeping child, as she walks Sarafina toward her bedroom to lay her down.

"It's your naptime, too, Little Missy!" Lisa tells Kamari, who pouts.

"But I haven't heard Poppa's praise report yet." Kamari looks at her grandfather.

"Well, the Lord hasn't given me the permission to share it just yet with any little people. I have to let the adults know first," Roy bends down and tells Kamari.

"But I'm six years old now, and I'm going to be in the second grade soon. Even Teacher Potter says I'm smarter than my age," Kamari states.

"Naptime, Kamari. I'm sure Poppa will tell you in due season. Now give Poppa a hug."

"Okay!" Kamari does as she is told, then leaves the veranda heading toward her bedroom.

"Make sure you use the potty before you get in the bed, sweetie!" Lisa hollers.

"Okay!"

Billy and Lisa join Roy on the veranda where they take a seat at the table.

"Man, these tarts seem to be following me." Billy pops one in his mouth. "Okay, these are clearly not the same tarts!" He takes the tart out of his mouth and wraps it up in a napkin. "Whoever made those tarts that were on the beach last month, you need to tell them to stick to the same recipe, 'cause this is not it!" Billy says.

"Gloria made those tarts and if you know what's good for you, you'd better act like you love them! Now, I need you to help a brother out... eat at least three more; I've been eating them all afternoon and I need some help. Lisa, you can knock off a few as well!" Roy whispers.

"Are you crazy, Dad! Can't you see she's with child!" Billy whispers back.

"You have a point there, son. Then you'll just have to eat her portion!"

Roy pushes the remainder of the tart tray toward Billy.

"Okay, but you owe me big time!" Billy says as he pops a tart in his mouth just as Gloria enters the veranda.

"Oh, I see you're enjoying my tarts! Make just sure you save some for Roy. They are his favorite," Gloria says as she joins them at the table.

Lisa and Billy both say okay at the same time.

"Now, Mother Gloria, you know I have never been one to pry into folks' business, but you and Daddy Roy are the only parents I have, so as your daughter, I need you to explain to me just what I saw when we walked into the house," Lisa says with her hands on her hips like she's questioning one of her children.

"First, you need to get that lie out of your mouth about you not prying into people's business, 'cause you know that is not true. You've been in these islands so long, you love melee just like the locals, so just take your hands off your hips like you're talking to Kamari or Sarafina. Roy and I are grown folks and we don't have to explain nothing to our children!" Gloria calmly says.

"Yes, we do, Gloria," Roy says.

"Roy!" Gloria screams.

"Honey, it's time we came out in the open with our feelings toward each other. Now!" Roy says, smiling and reaching for Gloria's hand.

"About time! I mean, everyone knew where this was going for years! We were just wondering why it was taking so long for you two to realize it," Lisa says.

"Everything happens in God's time, honey! Mom and Dad had to wait until they both heard from the Lord," Billy explains.

"Yeah right!" Lisa sarcastically says.

"Anyway, you two! Gloria and I are ready to take our relationship to the next level." Roy pats Gloria's hand and she smiles.

"Next level? You guys are a few days younger than water, so you'd better get to making this thing happen sooner than later!" Lisa says jokingly.

No one laughs.

"It's a joke!" she screams.

"So, do Fitzroy and Faith know about this?" Billy asks.

"Well, you know Faith just got back from Atlanta a few days ago, from helping Hope and Lucille set up the Black Lives Matter Foundation. We haven't seen her since she got back," Gloria says.

"And I've barely seen Fitzroy with this trial going on. He's been staying over in St. Thomas at Wally's house these past few days. I think Faith is staying over there as well," Roy shares.

"That's right! I've been watching parts of the trial on the news. Can you believe the police chief was the ringleader of that multi-million-dollar drug operation? And just to think they were running it out of Wally's Club and the police station! Mom, Dad, my heart almost skipped a beat when I found out Wally Jr. was part of the operation, and I thank God that He protected me and my business from being implicated in this foolishness, because a few months ago Wally Jr. asked me if I would be willing to pick up a package for him in Dominica waiting at the airport addressed to Wally's Supper Club in St. Thomas; thank God we were not flying to Dominica that day because of a terrible storm," Billy says with disgust and relief.

"Oh no! Baby!" Lisa hugs Billy, comforting him at the very thought of going to jail.

"Wally should have listened to Lucille! She told him the boy was up to no good! But no… he wanted to give the rotten apple another chance!" Gloria hollers.

"Now, that is his son and every father wants to believe his child is capable of changing," Roy says.

"Not when all you have to do is open your eyes and see nothing has changed since the last time the boy was operating an illegal business out of the club. Wally had his blinders on and believed the lies his son was feeding him over the truth Lucille was showing him," Gloria says with anger.

"Dad, Mother Gloria has a point. Wally didn't want to hear a bad word about his son. He told Auntie Lucille his deceased wife would have wanted him to give Wally Jr. another chance. Excuse me, but the ex-wife is dead and he should have been listening to the wife breathing up in his face who is alive, trying to get him to see the real deal-lee-o!" Lisa flippantly says.

"Hindsight is always 20/20. Do you think Junior is going to do time?" Billy asks.

"I'm sure he will have to serve some prison time. And it could be a good thing. The boy is young and it will give him time to reflect on his ways," Roy sadly says.

"Dad, have you been inside of that prison? Trust me, there is no kind of rehabilitation going on in there whatsoever! Those men come out ten times worse than when they went in. I'll never forget the time I was asked to go over to one of the jails and help out for six weeks. Their regular nurse was on maternity leave; I lasted one hour and twenty-five minutes and refused to *ever* go back up in there. If you didn't walk with all your supplies, including gloves, disinfectants, and masks, you would find yourself looking at a sick horny man and you couldn't do one thing to help. Well, there was one thing! I ran out of that place; they couldn't send the elevator up to get me fast enough so I took the stairs!" Lisa tells the story with disgust in her voice.

"I saw that frightened young girl on the stand yesterday, telling how she was in the bushes with her cellphone and videotaped the officers going to the shanty for the drugs. She also had them on video them saying the chief of police was going to be mad at them if they didn't come up with the money or the drugs. With these cellphones and tablets having cameras, you can record everything, even when you're hiding in the bush!" Gloria shakes her head in disbelief.

"Now the fashion police need to come up in there and arrest that girl. I mean she was ghetto fabulous. Calico colors and weave hair so long my girl was sitting on it! I'm sure that hair cost her a chunk-a-change! And the fake faux leopard painted with diamond-stud inlay on the mile-long fingernails. All I could think about every time I watched her take those nails and move her hair out of her face was how in the hell does she wipe her butt with those nails? Then she just started to look stink to me!" Lisa frowns.

"Lisa, if no one has ever told you before that you are a first-class snob, please allow me to be the first to say it. You are just too judgmental!" Gloria points her finger at Lisa.

"Actually, beyond all that long hair and nails, is a very beautiful woman who loves the Lord and has a kind heart," Roy says as everyone looks at him in wonder.

"And just how do you know all this, Roy?" Gloria asks, surprised, waiting for a response.

"Her name is Denisha, and we had the opportunity to host her at our house overnight. Faith stayed up all night in the cottage praying with her. The next morning, all of us had breakfast together, prayed and got to know each other quite well before Fitzroy took her over to St. Thomas to arrest her," Roy casually says.

"Say what?" Gloria screams.

"Gloria, you remember the night you ladies were having your meeting to try and help Lisa stop cussing? The night the Cuss Jar became a reality to help form the Youth Agriculture Farm and Fitzroy, Wally and I came in looking for food?"

"Yes, we remember that night very well, thank you! That was a very ugly time in my life, and I do not wish to revisit it," Lisa sarcastically says.

"Ugly is an understatement! None of us could stand you, Lisa! Thank God you had a patient husband like Billy willing to put up with that mess! All of us were ready to ban you from our homes with your negativity. The only reason you were not excommunicated from the family is because of the children," Gloria informs Lisa.

"Thank God that beautiful young lady Cathy found her way up this mountain to help save your marriage! God sent a ram in the bush, 'cause you were not listening to anyone!" Roy points out.

"How is Cathy doing? All of us were wrong in judging her. Once we got to know her, she proved to be the sweet Christian woman that she professed to be. I feel so terrible for being so accusatory!" Gloria admits.

"Cathy's doing great, Mother Gloria, and what a blessing she has been to Lisa and I, helping with the girls, demanding we go out on dates while she watches the children. As both of you know, I was having trouble with this local guy who I put on my trade license as my partner. He wanted more and more money each month as the company grew, simply because his name was on the license," Billy explains.

"Just greedy! I mean, the man did absolutely nothing for the business except collect his check each month!" Lisa points out.

"Are you still paying him his ransom each month, Billy?" Roy sadly inquires.

"No, thanks to Cathy's quick thinking. She and I applied for a new business license with her name and my name and dropped the moocher! All the BVI Government is concerned with is making sure their native people are included in business in the British Virgin Islands, and trust me, Cathy is a much better person to deal with."

"I know she's a sweet girl and all, but business is business. I certainly hope you got everything in writing?" Gloria says.

"Yes, we did, Mother Gloria. Billy owns sixty percent of the business, Cathy owns, on paper only, twenty percent, and I own the other twenty percent. It was a little tough getting it through Licensing with Billy owning the majority of the shares, but God is good and the Premier being Cathy's mother's brother certainly did help!" Lisa brags.

"What really helped was the fact that I'm offering a great service to the people. And El Shaddai will soon be operating out of St. Thomas!" Billy throws in with a big smile on his face. Everyone hugs.

"Oh, Billy, we are so proud of you! And just think, Lisa, you were about to walk away from all this over some foolishness!" Gloria chides.

"Can we just get back to the story? Dad, you were telling us about this ghetto fabulous woman Denisha!" Lisa says.

"Yes, well, that was the same night the sewer main broke and the carnival village had to be evacuated and all the people at the hospital had to be moved," Roy explains.

"Okay, Dad, but what does that have to do with this Denisha lady?" Billy asks.

"Fitzroy got a call that there was a woman in the carnival village who had just killed her boyfriend on St. Thomas. When Fitz got down to the village, the stench was unbearable. The raw sewage hadn't reached the village yet, so Fitzroy and his men went in the crowd looking for Denisha. A picture of her was sent to his cellphone from headquarters, and Fitz was shocked to see it was his receptionist, which made it easy to spot her in the crowd. He arrested her and when he tried to take her to the police station, it was already flooded with raw sewage as well as the fire station," Roy explains.

"So why didn't he just take her on the boat over to St. Thomas?" Billy asks.

"The sea was rough and no one wanted to drive the boat over. So, Fitzroy took the policeman who was on duty home with him and Denisha. The officer sat in a chair outside the cottage the remainder of the night and kept watch. However, Denisha cried and prayed, cried and prayed so loudly it woke Faith up, and she begged Fitzroy to let her go in and sit with Denisha. All of us knew the young lady was set up to take the fall for all these murderers and drug dealers, but Fitzroy had to do his job and arrest her."

"Wow, she doesn't look so stinky after all," Lisa says with a sorrowful look on her face.

"Didn't they say the young lady left the island and ran to Hawaii? That might hurt her as a credible witness," Billy says.

"No, not really. She was in contact with Fitzroy the whole time. Denisha said she had to leave or be killed. Fitzroy agreed and put her in a self-imposed witness protection program. They both were just waiting for the right time to bring her back to St. Thomas to testify," Roy explains.

"Is there any word on Lucille and Wally getting back together?" Lisa inquires.

"Wally has been to Atlanta twice this month, pleading with Lucille to come back home to St. Thomas," Roy sadly says.

"And you know how my sister is when she makes her mind up... stubborn as a mule," Gloria interjects.

"But surely their marriage deserves another chance. You can't just throw your marriage away at the first sign of trouble," Billy says with passion in his heart.

"I whole-heartedly agree, son. Way too many 'Christian' marriages are breaking up because couples are not listening to each other or willing to go for counseling to try and work things out," Roy sadly points out.

"Right now, Hope and Lucille are so involved in their project that if it isn't about getting justice for those people who were shot down in cold blood, murdered in the street like animals they don't have time to hear it." Gloria shakes her head in disgust.

"I saw on the news that the police officer who shot the three of them has resigned and now they're asking for the chief of police to step down as well. You know, my dad went to college with the police chief. Daddy couldn't stand him. He said that man was so openly racist he didn't need to put on his white sheet and hood on his head; everyone knew he was a card-toting member of KKK!" Lisa spews out.

"Thank God Hope has Lucille there fighting with her, because my sister knows everybody who's anybody from the Mayor's office to the Governor's office. Trust me, she won't stop until every one of them is held accountable for taking those people's lives."

"What I don't understand is if these police officers have to shoot someone, why don't they just shoot them in the foot or knee to stop them? There is no reason to shoot someone six or seven times like they are a giant monster! Lord soon come!?" Billy prays.

"What's sad is it's always in the black neighborhoods!" Gloria decries.

"Well, now let's tell the truth; sometimes you have to deal with some ignorant ghetto negroes, and talking to them just isn't getting it!" Lisa flippantly says.

"So you kill them?" Billy screams. Roy and Gloria stare at Lisa.

"Hey, I'm just saying. And you know most of them are probably packing guns themselves. Didn't they say Hope's friend Mabel had a gun in her house robe? Now what kind of person walks around carrying a gun in their house robe unless they're looking for trouble?" Lisa points out.

"Sweetie, please don't say this when Hope comes back or you might set yourself up for a lashing!" Roy says.

"Lisa, just about everyone in those Bricks carries guns to protect themselves from each other!" Gloria says.

"That's what the police are for! Hello!" Lisa sarcastically says.

"Do you know how long it takes for a police officer to respond to a call in that neighborhood? Two to three hours or never and that's after repeated calls! Lisa, you have lived a privileged life, and you have no idea of what life in the projects is like, so may I suggest you stay in your lane and talk about topics you're an expert at, like nursing, having babies, shopping for designer clothes and purses, PTA… you know, things you do really well," Gloria says with an attitude.

"Wow, Mother Gloria, you make me sound so shallow," Lisa says with a sad face and voice.

"You're not shallow, honey! You're the best nurse this island has ever had! Why do you think they keep calling, begging you to come back to work? And you're an awesome mother and wife!" Billy kisses Lisa, who smiles.

"I second that! You're the best at what you do, and Gloria and I are so grateful to you and appreciate how you are keeping those babies coming!" Roy hugs Lisa.

"Yeah, 'cause looks like your sister Faith might not ever give us any babies!" Gloria sadly says.

"Don't give up on her just yet!" Roy admonishes.

"The girl has been married almost four years, Roy, and I know they're doing something over there," Gloria says.

"So, I guess y'all didn't hear what happened?" As quickly as Lisa says it, she wishes she could take it back.

"What happened?" Roy and Gloria both yell with much concern in their voice.

"What happened, sweetie?" Billy calmly asks.

"Mother Gloria, just a few minutes ago you were saying I was the Melee Queen, always in gossip, so I think now is a good time to exercise minding my business. Did you guys just hear Sarafina?" Lisa turns to exit and go check on the baby.

"Hold up! Lady, you'd better park you behind right here and tell us what's going on," Gloria yells.

Lisa has a sad look on her face. "It is not my place to be telling you guys Fitzroy and Faith's business. May I suggest you wait until they are back home and talk with them about why they haven't given you guys any babies? Faith is my best friend and I want to keep it that way," Lisa says in a very proper tone.

Roy and Gloria are standing over Lisa like vultures ready to pounce, just staring at her.

"Baby, I think now is a good time to just tell Mother Gloria and Dad what you know," Billy says with a weak smile.

"Okay, okay! The reason Faith has not come back to St. John yet is because Fitzroy is mad at her, and she is over at Wally's trying to talk things out with him! Now, I said it!"

"No, you haven't said it! Tell it all, Miss Lisa," Gloria says through her teeth.

"Yes, tell us the part about why we haven't gotten any grandbabies yet from those guys!" Roy says.

"Oh, that part?" Lisa says.

"Yeah! Spill it, Lisa!" Gloria says.

"Honey, if you know something, just tell us."

"Billy, please." Lisa looks at her husband like she's about to cry.

"Faith is going to kill me… While Faith was in Atlanta, the pharmacist at the apothecary saw Fitzroy on the boat and told him they had been holding Mrs. Faith's birth control pills for several weeks now and that he could come in and pick them up for her if she's off island or they could mail them to her in the States if she was going to be gone a long time. Now, you happy! I just ratted my best friend out!" Lisa screams.

Roy and Gloria take a seat. They both have a relieved look on their faces.

"Lord, I thought the child had some terminal disease!" Gloria sighs.

"Praise God it's only that! I was thinking the boy was shooting blanks!" Roy says with relief in his voice.

"Lisa, sweetie, do you have any idea why Faith is taking birth control pills, knowing Fitzroy wants children?" Billy gently asks.

"Not only Fitzroy; all of us want babies!" Gloria screams.

"She's afraid," Lisa says.

"Afraid of what?" Roy demands.

"She's... she's afraid that with the work Fitzroy does, there is a strong possibility of him getting killed and she would be left alone to raise the children," Lisa painfully says.

"That's crazy! She has us!" Gloria is up and pacing the floor.

"Gloria, my darling, I need you to calm down. The fear that Faith is feeling is a legitimate fear. Now, you and I both, more than anyone in this room, know there is nothing worst then losing your spouse, real or imagined," Roy says.

# Chapter 15
## Faith Explains

"Faith, it was not easy seeing Junior on that stand in court today. Thank God his mom was not alive to witness this or it would have surly killed her quicker than the cancer did. I've been living with a child all these years who was someone other than the young man I thought I raised," Wally shares as he opens the refrigerator to take out something to cook for dinner.

"Wally, you can't blame yourself. Many times, young people these days are influenced by the world more than they are their parents. It's a fight! Spiritual warfare going on! And sometimes it looks like the enemy is winning at every turn. But we can't give up!" Faith cries.

"What do you and Fitz want for dinner, smothered steak or goat?" Wally continues taking food out of the refrigerator.

"Wally, you don't have to cook. We can just go out and eat when Fitzroy finishes at the court," Faith says.

"Cooking is therapy, that and my music collection are the only things that are keeping me sane right now. Speaking of music, what you want to hear?" Wally walks over to his massive music collection, ready to type in Faith's selection.

"I'd like to hear something soft and relaxing," Faith says.

"I've got just the right tune: *'Mozart's Violin and Piano Concerto No. 3.'*" The music comes on and Wally returns to the kitchen.

"Excuse me, a Nevis man who listens to Mozart?" Faith laughs.

"I'll have you know, my dear, that in Nevis, my beautiful little island, we are very cultured people. I used to play piano with the Classical Society of Brown Hill! I bet Fitzroy never told you that, little lady," Wally proudly says.

"Nope, can't say we've discussed the Classical Society of Brown Hill." Faith smiles.

"Well, the next time you are in Nevis, you must insist that my boy take you to one of their recitals, which happen every other month at the Anglican Church. You will be very pleasantly surprised and entertained. So, what will it be, goat or steak?" Wally holds a bag of meat in each hand.

"Let's do the goat. It's one of Fitzroy's favorites and now that the trial is over, it will probably be our last night intruding on you." Faith smiles.

"Intruding! Are you crazy? Can't you recognize a lonely man dying for company when you see one?" Wally chuckles as he pulls out his pressure cooker from his gourmet kitchen pot rack.

"Now you can tell me to back out of your business but I've got to ask… any word from Aunt Lucille?" Faith timidly asks.

"My darling, we are family and if you can't talk about your problems with your family, then who else you got?" Wally shrugs his shoulders and continues preparing their meal.

"Nosy people who just want to be in your business so they can gossip and make you think they really care!" Faith jokes.

"You have a point there! And trust me, there is a whole lot of people like that who call themselves 'friend.'" Wally shakes his head as he seasons the goat meat. "Lucille is being polite, which is a good sign, because you know your auntie has a tongue sharper than a double-edged sword!" Wally chuckles.

"Yeah, she can slay a whole army with that tongue alone!" Faith shakes her head, laughing.

"I messed up, Faith. I'm not going to lie to you! I should never have put my son before my wife! I mean the Bible clearly says; 'A man shall leave his mother and father and cleave to his wife.' And that means your grown children, too! I pray day and night that Lucille will forgive me and come back home. There is such a void here without her! That woman is the craziest person I've ever met, and I love every bit of it. She's wild, adventurous, sexy, daring and beautiful! What more could a man ask for? Faith, hand me those green bananas over there in the basket please." Wally continues cooking.

"Well, even if she didn't say it to you, when you came up to Atlanta to join us in marching for Black Lives Matter, she was so happy you were there. I'll have to show you the picture I took of the two of you walking hand in hand next to the mayor, and Hope with the crowd holding signs and banners and chanting Black Lives Matter!" Faith says with a big smile.

"What a day that was. I am so happy I was there to march for those people who were needlessly shot down like animals being hunted. Faith, my heart just cries for their families. Never would such a thing happen on my Island of Nevis. Our police officers don't even carry guns!"

"Well, I hope the day never comes when they will have to carry guns. But don't be surprised if packing weapons becomes a necessity even in little Nevis. Western ways and values are spreading to even the most remote corners of the world and with that comes drugs and violence. You may find the citizens carrying big guns and the police's little nightsticks will be no match for them," Faith sadly says.

"I heard the police officer who shot Miss Hope's best friend and the other two people has stepped down from the force," Wally says.

"Stepped down? No, he is on administrative leave... with pay, while the investigation is going on. And it's been reported that the officer has shot five black people in the past two years! That's an outrage!" Faith screams.

"Sounds like a ticking time bomb! And they still let him stay on the police force?" Wally shakes his head.

"Don't worry, Uncle Wally, all those racist police officers are about to be exposed! Thank goodness for the video footage that's out there for everyone to see. Hope's friend Mabel's death will not be in vain!" Faith affirms.

"No, sir! The woman will go down as a martyr. I hear there is a federal investigation into the matter and the big boys have come down from Washington D.C.!" Wally excitedly says.

"Yep! Heads a going to roll now! And just think, Auntie Lucille and Hope are right there, not taking 'No' for an answer, making sure everyone is held accountable, including all these hateful and ignorant political leaders who are so disrespectful of anyone who does not look like them. Do you know Hope is working with the housing authority to make sure every single person in those projects are relocated to a better neighborhood! That's my sister!" Wally and Faith high-five each other.

"Lucille says she called on a lot of her real estate friends for favors as well, to make sure that when people are moved out of the projects they are not put in redlined areas. Lucille says she have never seen so many for sale signs going up as the people start moving into the white neighborhoods." Wally shakes his head, laughing.

"Hopefully, the horrible ones will leave and the inclusive ones will stay. My sister had just purchased a home for Mabel and her grandson to move into in a wonderful neighborhood just before she was killed. She took money from her trust fund to do that for her friend. Can you imagine that?" Faith smiles.

"I liked Hope from the first time I met her. She has such a sweet giving spirit," Wally says.

"Yeah! Kind of reminds me of my dad. He would be so happy if he were here," Faith proudly says.

"So, what is she going to do with the house now that Mabel is no longer here on this earth?" Wally asks as he chops up some onions and peppers.

"She's going to let Mabel's grandson and his mother, who had been absent from his life for some years now, move into the house. The mother had been struggling with drugs but has been clean for a couple of years, found Jesus, has a job and the boy wants to be with his mother. Hope says that both of them are in therapy, and she told the mom she can stay there as long as she stays clean, pays the property taxes and one dollar a month for rent. What a saint!" Faith says.

"That she is. Lucille says Hope will soon be bringing a group of young people to St. John to participate in that program she Dot and Marlin got started," Wally says.

"Oh man! You just can't imagine how these young people's lives will be changed forever! Uncle Marlin, Aunt Dot and their farm hand Dominique have been working around the clock building cottages to house the youth and a few parents, as well as getting the farm set up as an agriculture training center for local children and inner city children from abroad. It starts next month and trust me, you don't want to miss it! I know you are having the grand re-opening of your supper club, but you have got to be there, Uncle Wally!" Faith says with excitement in her voice.

"Miss it! Are you crazy? The club opens the week after the camp and besides, I volunteered to be the camp's chef for the first week," Wally says, laughing with joy and pride.

"And they got the right person to do the job! I just love watching you cook, Uncle Wally. What a difference you are going to make in those children's lives as well. Your blessings are just around the corner, you know; you and Auntie Lucille will be back together in no time. You two really do make a great couple. Don't worry, you guys will be able to recognize your dream of turning 'Wally's' into a fine place for dining and good music. I feel it in my heart." Faith smiles and nods.

"Thank you for those words of encouragement, Faith. Did I tell you I'm changing the name of the club to 'Lucille's'? I'm opening the place up under new management with a new name!" Wally does a little waltz to the music as he turns the flame up on the stove.

"That is wonderful! Did you tell Auntie Lucille yet?" Faith asks.

"No, I want to surprise her when she comes for the opening of the Agriculture Center and the Supper Club next month. And not to get into your business, my dear, but I overheard you and Fitz having a few words last night after you settled into bed."

Wally dries his hands on a towel and joins Faith at the kitchen island.

"Oh! Well, looks like you're not the only one who messed up. I made a big mistake, too. I wasn't honest with my husband and he found out." Faith finds it hard to say.

"Ouch! Lying is a biggie!" Wally echoes.

"Well, I didn't exactly lie!" Faith's face is twisted like she's in pain.

"I see." Wally stares at her.

"Don't stare at me like that, Uncle Wally! I feel terrible enough already for not telling Fitzroy I've been taking birth control pills since we've been married. I feel like… like a cheater!" Faith screams.

"Well, if it's any consolation to you, Fitzroy has never been one to hold anything against anyone for too long. I've known people who have taken advantage of him and in no time he's back helping them again. I'm the one who gets mad for him and have to remind him of what that person just did to him, in case he's forgotten. Fitzroy always tells me, 'Wally, we all have issues and must be forgiving, that way the person can see their fault.' And the next time, he will be wise as a serpent but will always remain gentle as a dove. Can you imagine that? Just give him a minute and this too shall pass." Wally pats her hand and gets up to make a salad.

"You make it sound so easy, but trust me, Fitzroy is mad! I mean he's not screaming or calling me names or anything like that. I almost wish he would so I can feel bad and cry and get it all over with. But no, Mr. Always Composed is being kind with less chat. Hell, I think he's giving me the polite silent treatment." Faith stomps her feet and pounds the tabletop.

"Now, you're going to have to let him have his moment, Faith. Something like this is a huge blow to Fitzroy. That man wants some babies and after being celibate until you guys got married, he's been doing everything by the book. I'm sure finding out you were on the pill took a little wind out of his sail." Wally points to Faith with the salad spoon as he tosses the lettuce and tomatoes in a bowl.

"I know, I know. The moment he picked me up at the airport, I could see in his face something was wrong. He kissed me like I was his sister or something and as soon as I climbed into the van there they were sitting on the seat… the birth control pills! My heart hit the floor. It was a quiet ride to town. In a way, I'm glad the trial was going on, because that has given me more time to collect my thoughts and have a civilized conversation with him tonight," Faith says.

"You think tonight is a good time, sweetie?" Wally grinds some fresh pepper over the salad and places it in the industrial-sized stainless refrigerator then moves on to check on the goat and boil bananas.

"Uncle Wally, we need to settle this once and for all. That was me you heard last night trying to have a discussion with him. He just kissed me on the forehead turned over and went to sleep! The man was snoring before my head could hit the pillow! How in the world can someone just go to sleep like that when there are issues that need to be resolved? Well, I'm not trying to let another night go down on anger!" Faith yells.

"All I'm saying is, the man is physically and mentally drained with this trial. Give him a day or two to decompress. That way he'll be able to hear you better and the two of you can have an intelligent conversation and you will have his undivided attention. You ever had breadfruit?" Wally walks out on the veranda and returns with a breadfruit.

"Yes, cooked on an open pit. It's nice," Faith says, not paying attention to the question.

"This little puppy is going to sweeten up the pot nicely!" Wally kisses the breadfruit.

"Maybe I'll stay over here with you for a few more days. I dread going home, because you know I'll have to face the lynching mob when they find out! Oh boy!" Faith cries.

"Now that's who I'd be afraid of! Your mother and your Auntie Lucille are definitely sisters. Gloria has a sharp tongue, too! Only difference is hers has a little Christian coating on it… but it still stings!" Wally laughs.

"My mother doesn't even have to say anything, just the way she looks at you sends you running to your room to read scriptures and pray without ceasing!" Faith shakes her head.

"Gloria is still mad at me for the way I treated Lucille when Junior got shot! I admit, I was not in my right mind and I said some horrible things. Lord, I wish everyone had Fitzroy's forgiving spirit!" Wally says.

"Thank God I have Fitzroy's dad. He'll work on my mom's unforgiving spirit. He's the one person she does listen to! Thank God for my father-in-law." Faith smiles.

"The coconut didn't fall too far from the tree! Fitzroy is just like his father. Two forgiving souls! How about a glass of wine before dinner, sweetie?" Wally says, smiling.

"Sure, but I'm thinking about something a little bit stronger," Faith ponders.

"Like what, me dear?" Wally inquires.

"You have any of that guava berry?" Faith gives Wally a mischievous smile.

"You mean the one that's been fermenting for five years that I bring out every Christmas? The one that had you dancing on the coffee table last New Year's Eve?" Wally sarcastically inquires.

"Yeah, baby! That one! But only one glass this time, now that I know the power it possesses." Faith points her finger at Wally.

"Okay, you've been fairly warned!" Wally chuckles as he goes into the pantry to retrieve the large five-gallon crystal goblet filled with berries and fermented liquor and pours Faith a wine glass full.

"I know you don't think I'm going to drink this by myself? If I'm going to get slightly toasted, I can't think of a better person to do it with than my Uncle Wally. Right now, we are two individuals who messed up with the people we love and I think we should have a forgiveness drink together, calling those things that be not as though they are!" Faith holds her glass up in the air while Wally pours his and they toast together.

After a few wine glasses full of guava berry, both Wally and Faith are a bit inebriated and acting silly. Faith is trying to teach Wally how to line dance to the song "Wobble, Wobble." Wally is turning the wrong way and they are bumping into each other.

"Now look, if you want to learn how to do the darn thing, you first have to put on your listening ears!" Faith admonishes her uncle.

"What wrong with you, girl? You don't see these big ears on the side of me face!" Wally points to his neck.

"Uncle Wally, that's your neck!" Faith bends over with laughter.

"Well, it's close enough," Wally says with a confused look on his face.

"Oooh, Uncle Wally, you're in trouble!" Faith slurs.

"What happened? Did Your Aunt Lucille call? I'm always in trouble with her!" Wally says with bulging eyes, looking frightened.

"No, crazy man, your food is burning in the kitchen!" Faith points toward the kitchen, laughing.

"Oh that." Wally waves his hand toward the kitchen.

"You better go see about the pot on the stove," Faith sings.

"There's a pot on the stove? Who's cooking?" Wally asks without having a clue.

"You, silly! Remember I told you not to cook but you insisted!" Faith sings like it's a song.

"Oh! Then I guess I better go and check it out, huh?" Wally stumbles toward the kitchen, then turns back and faces Faith. "Faith, there's smoke in there!" He points.

"Yep! That's why you're in trouble. I think you should turn the stove off. Now be careful." Faith points her finger at Wally.

Fitzroy walks into the house. The "Wobble, Wobble" music is blasting and the house is filled with smoke. Faith is slouched on the couch, and Wally is looking confused, holding on to the wall, trying to decide if he is going into the kitchen or staying in the living room. Upon seeing Fitzroy enter the house, they both have the expression of children being caught doing something wrong and ready to blame each other.

"Wally, is my wife drunk?" Fitzroy shouts as Faith tries to sit up on the couch, crossing her leg like a proper lady but can't seem to get her legs to cross.

"Now, sir, it would not be appropriate for me to answer such a question like that. I must refer you to the lady, because only she would be in a position to answer such a question as that! Me lady, the gentleman from Nevis is inquiring of your sobriety status and judging from the look on his face, it would suggest he needs an answer sooner than later!" Wally falls on the floor, kicking and laughing.

Faith slides off the couch and crawls over to Wally and they both roll in laughter.

Fitzroy, shaking his head, steps over them and heads into the kitchen to investigate where the smoke is coming from. Barely able to see the stove for all the smoke, Fitzroy finds the stove knobs and turns everything off, opens the doors to the veranda and all the windows in the house. Through the smoke in the kitchen, Fitzroy sees the giant guava berry crystal on the counter. He sighs and returns to the living room where Wally and Faith are up off the floor and trying to sit on the couch in a dignified position, which is not working.

"Let's go!" Fitzroy yells as he opens the front door for them to exit.

"But darling, Uncle Wally has prepared a special dinner for us," Faith slurs.

"Sweetie, I think we should do what the man says. He doesn't look very happy, and you know he's a licensed gun-toting officer." Wally laughs very loudly.

Faith puts her finger up to her mouth, whispering, "Shush! He's a detective working undercover! Don't tell anybody!"

"My dear, I believe we've just been busted!" Wally and Faith roll with laughter as Fitzroy leads them out of the front door to the van without saying a word.

"Just remember, Uncle Wally, we have the right to remain solid!" Faith slurs, pointing her finger in Wally's face.

"Me lady, I believe the word is silent!" Wally and Faith look at each other, pause, and then burst into laughter.

Fitzroy opens the back door of the van and waves them in. Faith stops before getting into the van and stares at Fitzroy, moving close to his face. "You want some babies? Then, buddy, dat's what I'm gonna give ya! And if you die and leave me alone with them little varmints, I'm going to kill you!"

Fitzroy smiles as he helps his drunken wife climb in and closes the door.

# PART FOUR

## *Chapter 16*
## Dreams Do Come True

"Who would ever believe that nine months ago something as simple as a Cuss Jar would be the catalyst for making the Youth Agriculture Farm a reality?" Dot rejoices with her husband Marlin as she hands screws to him.

He is standing on a ladder, hanging the last ceiling fan in the fourth cottage built to house their students arriving from near and far. "Only de Father! Me darling, dis 'ere is going ta be life changing fa so many young people. Me heart is singing wit' joy!" Marlin looks down at his wife, smiling.

"What boat are they coming up on?" Dot inquires.

"Fitzroy, Faith, Dominique and Roy all went over on de barge early dis mornin' wit' we two vehicles and Fitzroy's van to pick up Hope, Lucille and de four chir'in and tree parents from de airport. Dem gon swing pass Emancipation Park an pick up four chir'in an' one parent from St. Thomas, den day coming back up on de 2:30 barge. Wally meetin' dem in de park wit de St. Thomas chir'in, and bring de food and tings over fa de week. On de way up ta de farm, dem gon pick up two chir'in and Sister Claudette from de church waiting in de Cruise Bay Park wit day camping tings."

"What's Sister Claudette coming for? And I hope she's not bringing her daughter. This is supposed to be the boys' turn, isn't it?"

"De woman does say she want ta help Wally wit de cooking an' ta show de chir'in how ta make tarts," Marlin says, not believing a word of it.

"Honey, you know that woman is coming to try and get her hooks into Roy! Didn't I hear her daughter is pregnant?"

"Yeah, de gil is wit child and me ain't tink she coming. Just de mudder."

"Marlin, I don't think I've ever been so excited in my life!" Dot says with joy.

"Me watch you toss all night in we bed." Marlin laughs as he comes down off the ladder and kisses Dot on the cheek.

"It's just that there is so much to do! Debbie, Byron, their five older girls, all with names that start with the letter 'F' and the triplets, two boys and one girl all with names that start with the letter 'B' after their father, Byron, Jr., Brice and Brianna, are coming for the opening and that alone is enough excitement. I haven't seen the babies but once since their unexpected birth in Nevis when Debbie came to be in Faith's wedding!" Dot says with a smile.

"The people dem in Nevis still talking 'bout dat. Dem never had triplets born in dey hospital," Marlin says as he closes up the ladder and heads for the door.

"Well, technically, they were born on George and Zipporah's dining room table if you remember." Dot shakes her head in utter amazement, smiling.

"How you mean, do I remember? Me gill, dat was one day none of we will ever forget!" Marlin chuckles.

"Thank God the Bordeaux house has enough rooms to hold my daughter, her husband and eight children! When God said be fruitful and multiply, you know he was talking about Debbie and Byron. You know Debbie told me that Byron told her you offered to pay everyone's airfare to come down here." Dot lovingly smiles.

"Now dat was s'posed ta between us men folks! You womens just too smart, ya in every-ting! Man ain't got no privacy!" Marlin smiles.

"Now that's why I love my Mango Man so much. You are such a giving man." Dot kisses Marlin.

"Well, me dear, every ting looks good and in order for the chir'in dem. Wah you say we take a little nap before dem reach?" Marlin gives Dot a mischievous wink as he heads out of the door of the cabin, carrying the ladder.

"Now, Marlin, you know ain't no napping gon be going on!" Dot giggles and accompanies him to the little house on the farm walking side by side like newlyweds. A baby goat runs up and follows Dot, looking to be fed.

"Not now, buddie! You best go find you mudder!" Marlin rests the ladder on the porch and chases the goat into the fields.

"You are so bad!" Dot teases as she opens the screen porch door and enters the house.

"So you say! Dis 'ere is me and me woman time and me ain't got time for no goat, pig, cow, chicken or man right now!" Marlin laughs his response.

Marlin closes the front door, locking it just as they hear a car coming up the dirt road, traveling fast and creating a cloud of dust. Dot and Marlin peek out of the kitchen window to see who it is, being careful not to be seen by the unexpected visitor.

"Lord, have mercy, it's Chee Chee!" Dot screams.

"You know, she does come to beg!" Marlin acknowledges.

"Probably need to buy gas for that big tank she's driving." Dot shakes her head in disgust.

"Dat two. She mudder tell me de gil got a big weed habit. I tell she mudder dat she does need to tell Chee Chee who she daddy is. De gil big enough ta know de truth. Well, me ain't got time for she right now. Me got me business ta handle. Darling, you go upstairs and get comfortable for poppa and me gon be right up." Marlin grins as Dot does a little sexy walk toward the stairs, causing Marlin to lick his lips.

"Don't keep me waiting, Mango Man!" Dot teases.

Marlin opens the front door and walks briskly out to the Hummer where Chee Chee is about to climb out. "Don't bother ta get out de tank, gil. If it's money ya come fa, move from 'ere! Money done and me ain't got a ting fa ya! I done tell ya ta sell dis 'ere big ting, get a job and stop wit your begging! Now move from 'ere! Me got me business ta tend ta!"

"How you gon talk ta me like dat! I's ya child and you's me daddy! Now! Who I supposed to ask money from?"

"Chee Chee, I gon turn around and go into me house now! Don't bring you backside up 'ere again until you coming ta tell me you got a job." Marlin turns to leave.

Chee Chee gets out of her truck and follows him at a distance. "I know dat Yankee bitch done tell you not to give me no money! I gon fuck she up!" Chee Chee screams to Marlin just as he reaches the porch.

Dot is looking out the open window and can see and hear what's being said. Marlin turns with a look on his face that sends fear through Chee Chee.

"Tell me wa you say? 'Cause me ain't sure me 'ear ya!" Marlin is so close in her face she can barely talk.

Chee Chee backs away.

"Say it again, Chee Chee!"

The young girl runs to her truck and Marlin follows her.

"Now I want you to go home and ask your mudder who you real daddy is, 'cause me finished wit you. You done crossed de line, young lady. You don't know me a-tall but you will know me very quickly if you ever threaten me wife, 'cause me will kill you! Now move from 'ere!"

Chee Chee is in shock and very afraid of Marlin. She can't turn her hummer around fast enough to get off the farm. From a distance, she gives Marlin the finger.

Marlin shakes his head and walks back toward the house, where Dot meets him at the door.

"You okay?" she asks.

"Better den okay! Now, what you doing down 'ere? Me tink you upstairs waiting for de Mango Man!" Marlin chases giggling Dot up the stairs.

* * *

Later that afternoon, at the airport in St. Thomas, Fitzroy parks his van in the no parking zone, sporting his "Official Business" sign so as not to get towed. He, Faith, Roy and Dominique wait for the arriving passengers to disembark from the plane sitting on the tarmac.

"I see them! There's Auntie Lucille getting off first!" Faith waves, hoping her aunt can see her from the distance.

"Those two boys following behind Lucille must be our next project," Roy acknowledges.

"Are those their underwear showing halfway down their backside?" Dominique inquires.

"And what's up with the big braids all over his head? Are those wannabe dread locks?" Faith says with her nose turned up.

"I don't know what's worse, seeing his underwear or that row of gold teeth in his mouth; the glare from them is trying to compete with our Caribbean sun. Looks like the sun is losing." Fitzroy laughs.

"They're fake, honey. I've seen some boys in a rapper video wearing them. They're slip-on teeth!" Faith reflects with disdain.

"Well, the other young man has his hair neatly cornrowed. Now if he'd just put on a belt," Roy laments.

Behind the sagging-pants boys, who look to be around twelve-years-old, are two young ladies in their early twenties, wearing booty-shorts, laughing and pointing to the mountains in the distance, in awe. One of the young ladies drops her purse and turns sideways to pick it up.

"Oh no! I think I just saw an orange whale tail rising up from the back of those skimpy shorts," Faith screams. "Now that's just nasty."

"Well, at least it matches the orange and burgundy hair." Fitzroy chuckles as Faith pokes him.

"Were you looking at that girl's butt?" Faith teases her husband.

"How could any miss it? I'm sure everyone on the whole plane can identify every detail of that backside in a line up. My girl is leaving nothing to the imagination," Fitzroy says, laughing.

"She looks very sexy!" Dominique says, grinning.

"Dominique, you've been on the farm too long with the pigs! You don't know what sexy is!" Faith teases.

"Put your tongue back in your mouth, young man. Let's stay focused. Now, remember we are on a mission, and we don't want to start judging or we won't be able to minister to these young people. The best thing we can do is embrace them and lead by example," Roy admonishes them all.

"Fitzroy is not embracing the booty-short chicks! I mean her cheeks are hanging out of those skimpy shorts," Faith screams.

Everyone looks at her with a smirk on their faces.

"Okay, okay, I get the message. We must be accepting and loving! Well, I just want to see how *accepting* you'll be when those boys cuss you for telling them to pull up their pants!

This is going to be a bigger project than I imagined," Faith bemoans.

"Well, it looks like two of the boys coming down the stairs now have their pants pulled up and they're actually wearing a belt. Okay, not too bad," Fitzroy says.

"That's probably their mother walking behind them. Looks like she cleaned up for the trip. Probably never been on a plane before in her life; look at those nails! They resemble claws. Dominique, remember to take a video of her feeding the pigs with your cellphone; I'm sure we can make a bunch of money on *America's Funniest Home Videos*." Faith laughs.

"*S'il vous plaît,* no one talk! Look at the beautiful mademoiselle in the white sundress and sun hat. Careful, my darling that you don't trip in those sandals!" Dominique follows her every move, smiling lustfully.

"Calm those French hormones down, son!" Roy pats him on the back.

"Please, I beg you, let that exquisite woman ride in the truck with me. I promise I will carry myself like a perfect gentleman!" Dominique pleads, not taking his eye off the young lady descending the stairs of the airplane.

"No!" Fitzroy and Faith yell at the same time.

"All you see is body, young man. That hat is covering her face. Besides, she might not even be with our group," Roy chides.

"I don't see Hope," Faith nervously says.

"I'm sure she's bringing up the rear." Fitzroy calms her down.

"Well, pinch me, and tell me I'm not dreaming! It can't be!" Dominique screams.

"What!" Faith hollers.

"That's Mademoiselle Hope! I recognize the legs! Going back to America has been a blessing! She looks simply marvelous! I could sop her up with a johnny cake!"

"Okay, enough from you, young man. Dominique, you have managed to surprise the old man. I would have lost my shirt in a bet if someone told me you are so woman crazy!" Roy chuckles.

"Dad, the boy has been locked up on the farm for three years now. We must make sure he gets out more often; he doesn't even have television or internet. It's a wonder he even knows who the President of the United States is," Fitzroy says.

"Hey, I know who the President is… It's George Bush!" Dominique says, smiling. Everyone looks at him in shock.

"Say what? Don't you know we elected our first African-American President who is serving his second term?" Faith asks incredulously.

Dominique laughs. "Of course I know that! I'm just making fun. Oh no, here she comes. My heart is racing so fast!" Everyone laughs at the nervous young man.

Faith runs to the gate to embrace Lucille and Hope. "I missed you guys so much!" Faith is jumping up like a young child with excitement.

"I missed you, too, Faith!" Hope hugs her sister tightly while Fitzroy and Dad embrace Lucille.

"Let's step aside and let the people pass. So who do we have here?" Dad says to Hope, so she can introduce her guest.

"This young lady is Kesha and her son Sean and Sean's friend Mookie," Hope introduces the woman with the two boys wearing belts and their pants up.

"Man! I thought the airplane was going to land in the water!" Sean shouts with excitement.

"Me, too! I mean the plane was just inches above the water! I held on to my seat so tight I think I broke the armrest!" Mookie yells.

"I've never experienced anything like that before and have never said the Lord's Prayer so fast in all my life," Kesha says, laughing and the group joins in.

"I'm so sorry! I should have given you guys a heads up… And I'd like you to meet Shantay and her son Dante." Hope gestures to one of the women wearing booty shorts and one of the boys with the sagging pants, who doesn't look at them when he's introduced. He laughs with his friend, who also is wearing sagging pants.

"Dante! You hear the people say hello to you?" Shantay yells at her son.

"Yeah! I said hi!" the boy yells back at his mother with an attitude.

"My name is Shantay, but everybody calls me Tay. Thank you for allowing us this opportunity."

"You're very welcome, Tay," Fitzroy says, causing the woman to give him a big smile.

Faith has her eye on Tay, watching for any sign of inappropriate behavior.

"And last but not least, meet Rochelle and her son Khalid!" Hope says.

"Y'all got any sharks out there?" Khalid asks with his gold slip-on teeth slipping.

His friend Dante laughs.

"Nigga, what you laughing at! Yo' ass can't even swim!" Khalid yells at his friend.

"Khalid! Watch your mouth! Don't make me have to tell you again." Rochelle is embarrassed about her son's choice of words.

"Let's head over to the baggage claim area," Fitzroy instructs.

Faith, Lucille and Hope walk slowly together so they can talk without the group hearing them.

"Okay, what's up with this elegant, stunning, demanding-attention look, little sister?" Faith teases Hope.

"She looks good, doesn't she?" Lucille brags.

"Yes, she certainly does! And why do I think you had something to do with this transformation?" Faith smiles.

"Because she did. Auntie Lucille made it clear to me when we were selling our Black Lives Matter Project and meeting with business executives, government officials, and people in a position to help make changes in the lives of our people, that I had to dress in a professional manner so they could hear me and not judge me by the clothes I wore. Trust me, it worked! I got the attention I was seeking and was heard loud and clear! We raised more than $1.2 million!" Hope throws her head up in the air with a queen's attitude.

"OMG! You go with your bad self, Miss Attention Grabber! And… let the records show you're just full of grabbing attention. Dominique almost lost his mind when he saw you descend the airplane stairs," Faith teases just as Dominique looks back at Hope, bumping into a woman pushing a stroller.

"Poor thing doesn't he know he's out of his league! Marlin needs to find him a yard girl!" Lucille mocks.

"That's cold, Auntie! Dominique is a fine young man," Hope says as both Faith and Lucille stop in their tracks, holding Hope back to chat before reaching the baggage area.

"Hold up, Miss Thing! I know you are not interested in that farm boy! Haven't I taught you anything?" Lucille puts her hands on her hips with a stern look on her face.

Hope laughs.

"Please say it isn't so! Not the help!" Faith screams.

"You two are snobs and know nothing about Dominique except what you see on the surface," Hope says.

"Well, please enlighten us!" Lucille says.

"Yeah!" Faith says, waiting for clarification.

"Dominique is a graduate from the University of West Indies. His wealthy father was murdered in an uprising and he was rushed out of his native country of Haiti for fear of being killed. Dominique is the heir of his father's fortune," Hope tells the ladies.

"And what fairytale book did you read that in? Don't be so gullible, Hope," Lucille screams.

"All those guys from Africa and the Caribbean come with the same story... My father is a very wealthy man! My father is the chief of my tribe! Then you find out they are nothing but starving students! Besides, the man works on a pig farm!" Faith points out, whispering.

"Well, ladies, in the Bricks you know we don't believe nothing people say out of their mouths, because most of it is a lie, especially if it means they are trying to be better than the rest of us so... I looked him up on Google and Wikipedia, his daddy and his momma! And everything he said is true and then some! Bam!" Hope says and walks away from Lucille and Faith, leaving them looking astonished.

As they turn the corner toward the baggage claim area, they hear a disturbance. Dante and Khalid are arguing with the manager of the duty-free liquor store adjacent to the baggage claim. Fitzroy is walking over to mitigate the situation. The two sagging-pants' mothers race over to defend their sons.

"What's the problem, Red?" Fitzroy asks the appropriately named red-haired Creole man with concern in his voice.

"These thugs, dem just thief from me store. Dem take some cigarettes!" Red points an accusatory finger at them.

"Don't be pointing your finger at my son and calling him a thug!" Tay shouts as she takes the stance of a person ready to fight.

Hope runs to calm the young lady down. "Chill, Tay! Fitzroy will work it out."

"I know I didn't hear this woodpecker head call my son a thief!" Rochelle screams.

"De boys, dem thief the cigarettes! I see dem in de mirror. Check dey pocket! Check dey pockets!" Red yells.

A crowd is starting to form around them.

"Red, give me a minute with the young men. You guys go back over and wait for the luggage," Fitzroy says as he summons the boys to follow him. Both the boys look at their mother and Hope to see if they should go with Fitzroy. The mothers nod their heads in approval.

"You're in good hands, Dante and Khalid," Hope reassures them. The boys follow Fitzroy to his van while the ladies return to the conveyor belt to claim their luggage.

"Don't worry, Red. I'll be right back!" Fitzroy reassures the business owner.

"Me ain't worried, Fitz! Me know you does know how ta handle tings." Red returns to his shop to check out a line of customers waiting to pay.

Roy and Dominique help the ladies lift their overweight bags off the conveyor belt.

"Dominique, I'm going to let you grab the ones that look like they weigh over 100 pounds!" Roy laughs.

"Monsieur Roy that would be all the bags!" The men both laugh in spite of the situation looming with the boys.

Nervous, Rochelle and Tay keep looking outside the terminal where the boys exited with Fitzroy, trying to get a glance of what's going on and hoping they would return quickly.

"You ladies can relax. My husband wouldn't hurt a fly," Faith says, trying to comfort them.

It's your husband we're worried about! Those boys don't respond well to discipline," Tay confesses.

Faith has a look of fear on her face.

"Excuse me, Roy, but I don't know what the seating arrangements are for us getting over to St. John, but I'm going to have to insist that you do not put me in the same car with all these ghetto fabulous people. The plane ride here was more than I can stand," Lucille pleads.

"Lucille, this is an excellent time for you to use your skills to minister to the young ladies. I'm sure you can drop a few wardrobe tips in their direction," Roy says, smiling.

"You must be joking! It's going to take longer than a ride on the barge to St. John to help these chicks! That's more than twenty-years' worth of damage you're asking me to take on during a fifty-five-minute ferry ride. Not to mention the risk of getting cut, cussed or both! No, buddy, I'm going to stay in my lane until after you guys do your job of breaking the wild fillies in first! Now, do I need to hail me a cab and make my way over to the ferry solo?" Lucille stares at Roy.

"You know we're picking up your husband in town before we get on the ferry? He's waiting in Emancipation Park with a group of local youth who will also be participating in the camp," Roy says, smiling.

"What does Wally have to do with this camp thing?" Lucille asks.

"He's volunteered to be our cook for the week. He's going to be teaching a few of the kids how to prepare gourmet meals and encourage them to seek careers in culinary arts. Dominique, catch that bag before it kills Miss Tay! The boy needs to stop gawking at Hope and pay attention," Roy editorializes as he resumes his discussion with Lucille.

"Roy, this isn't some kind of set up to get me and Wally back together, is it?" Lucille asks with an attitude.

"Oh no! You and Wally are grown folks. What business would we have meddling in your affairs?" Roy matter-of-factly says.

"Hmmm! So you say! Sounds like my sister Gloria has her hand in this. She needs to be worrying about paying you more attention so the two of you can get moving with that stalemate fake brother-sister relationship!" Lucille says with a mean tone in her voice.

"Oh, you didn't hear?" Roy slyly says.

"Hear what?" Lucille asks, irritated.

"Gloria is my woman now. We done worked through that brother-sister stuff and moved on to the next level! *And* I'm taking my woman home to Nevis for a few weeks to court her when the camp is finished." Roy smiles, showing all his teeth.

"Well, I'll be damn! How come nobody's told me any of this?" Lucille decries, hands on her hips.

"Like I said, we try not to get in grown folks' business and hope grown folks will stay out of ours. Let me go over here and help Dominique with the trolley." Roy walks off grinning!

"Faith!!!" Lucille screams.

Once outside with the two boys, Fitzroy leads them to his van parked in front of the airport. Before they reach the van, Fitzroy is greeted by a police officer who has papers for him to sign. The boys freeze in their tracks upon seeing the officer approach them, thinking they are going to be arrested and wondering if they should run.

"Should we run?" Dante whispers to Khalid.

"We don't even know where the hell we are and it's hot as hell out here!" Khalid replies, whispering.

"We could run up in those mountains," Dante whispers back.

"And get shot like that man on TV did for running? Chill out," Khalid demands, talking through his teeth.

Fitzroy picks up on this. "Relax yourselves; the officer is here to talk to me. This has nothing to do with the two of you."

"Pardon me, sir, but I have some documents here that require your signature. I was told you were here waiting for a flight to arrive. The Saint Clair boy is ready to be moved to his next location. We were not sure if you wanted him to be shipped to the prison in Kentucky or Virginia. There's also the matter of the former chief of police." The officer hands Fitzroy the papers.

As Fitzroy ponders his questions, the officer stares at the two boys standing next to Fitzroy with his eyes fixing on their sagging pants.

"Request permission to speak freely, sir, on another matter?" the officer says as Fitzroy looks over the paperwork.

"Sure," Fitzroy says, still studying the information in his hand.

"Sir, I don't know who these miscreants are, but I pray they find a belt quickly because that underwear showing shit ain't working here in the Virgin Islands. They will find their asses in jail very quickly for indecent exposure." As the officer speaks with anger, he looks both the boys in the eyes.

"Throw us in jail? You must be kidding! We ain't from here and we can take our black asses back to Atlanta!" Khalid is incensed.

"Not before I lock-up you and your smarty-pants friend where we does have plenty of men waiting to tap that little thug ass!" The officer retorts with a menacing grin.

Fitzroy chuckles as he sees the frightened look on Dante and Khalid's faces as they both reach to pull up their pants that keep falling back down.

"Okay, okay, Sergeant, I think they've got the message. These young men are my friends and my guests for the next two weeks; let's have Walter Saint Clair, Jr. moved to Virginia; he has an uncle there who works with ex-offenders so maybe he can assist in helping him receive some true rehabilitation. I'll take care of moving the former chief myself. Right now, I don't want anyone to know his location or where he is going. I need to make sure his transport is not compromised." Fitzroy signs off on one of the papers and gives them back to the officer.

The young boys are amazed at the authority Fitzroy has over the threatening officer.

"Thank you, sir. I'll take care of it right away." As the officer turns to leave, he points his fingers at his eyes and then to the boys, indicating he's watching them.

They hold their pants up with one hand as Fitzroy escorts them to his van. Once inside, Fitzroy offers them a cool drink from the cooler under the back seat.

"Okay, listen up, men. This is the deal. I know it's going to be a little different for you here in the Virgin Islands and people may try and push your buttons like my officer just did, but I want you to know I have your back."

The boys have a look of surprised on their faces.

"You got our back! You don't even know us!" Dante is perplexed and out of his element.

"True, and you don't know me either. But I'm on a mission to get to know you guys, and I want you to get to know me. We can learn a little something from each other," Fitzroy casually says.

"You a cop! Ain't a damn thing we can learn from you except how to be a snitch, and where we come from snitches get stitches!" Khalid angrily points out.

"Hell, yeah! Or dead!" Dante seconds.

"Actually, I'm not a cop. I'm a detective and I work for the FBI, and I'm not looking for any snitches. I'm looking for real men who are not punks and want to be leaders." Fitzroy faces the boys, challenging them.

The boys are shocked to hear he is a detective with the FBI.

"We men," Dante quickly affirms.

"And … and we ain't no damn punks, neither!" Khalid adds, stumbling over his words.

"Okay, okay. Then let's put our money where our mouths are, shall we? Now, I've got a thousand dollars here saying that you guys can't last a week without cussing someone out, fighting, or showing the world and anybody looking the crack of your behinds," Fitzroy shrewdly proffers while pulling out a roll of money from his pocket.

The boys' eyes get real big.

"Hold up! Let me understand something. You saying you gon give us a thousand dollars to pull our pants up, don't fight nobody and not cuss for one week?" Khalid is incredulous.

"A thousand dollars *apiece*?" Dante presses for clarification.

"That's right, a thousand dollars *each*," Fitzroy calmly says.

"Oh, *hell* naw! Why you gon do something like dat for us? Man, you full of shi… I mean … full of stuff!" Dante corrects himself, just in case Fitzroy is true to his word.

"And what we got to give you if we don't do it, 'cause ain't nothing free!" Khalid wonders what's at risk.

"Well, you don't have any money, so what do you think is fair?" Fitzroy grins.

"Man, this is some bull… stuff!" Dante says.

"I'll put it in writing," Fitzroy calmly says.

"Okay, okay. But why you doing this for us?" Khalid asks.

"Because I'll be rewarded," Fitzroy says.

"Aw, man, this is the craziest … mess I ever heard of!" Overwhelmed Dante is nearly lost for words.

"Okay, are you men in or not?" Fitzroy gets to the point.

"A thousand dollars? Hell, yeah, I'm in!" Dante says with excitement.

"But you still ain't said what we have to give you if we lose?" Khalid agonizes as he takes a swig from the cold bottle of water in his hand.

"I'll tell you what. First of all, I don't think you guys are going to lose and if you do, your punishment will be that you will have to stay an extra week here on the island and shadow me everywhere I go, and you will have to buy me lunch and keep a daily journal of everything that goes on during that week," Fitzroy says.

"Oh hell yeah! I'm in, too! But wait, is saying 'damn' and 'ass' considered cuss words, 'cause I know we gon see some fine-ass women with some big asses and I just can't help myself if those words come out I know I'm going to say damn!!!" Khalid says, laughing and Dante high-fives him.

Fitzroy laughs with the boys.

"Okay. We'll make that exception. However, you must do it with respect. You don't have to be loud where everybody hears you. Agreed?"

"Agreed!" Dante says.

"Hell yeah! Now we ain't gone have no problem getting our money, are we?" Khalid reverts to his thug voice.

"No, man. My word is my bond. Let's shake." Fitzroy reaches out to shake the young men's hands and they tussle with each other to shake first.

"We gon get *paid*!" Dante shrieks with delight.

"Oh, one more thing. I ain't no journal writer. My spelling sucks! Writing in journals is for homos and chicks," Khalid worries.

"I don't know about that. I keep a journal and my beautiful wife can tell you without hesitation I'm not a homo," Fitzroy casually says.

"No doubt, but we ain't the journal-keeping type!" Khalid says.

"Hey, I ain't worried about keeping no journal 'cause I'm gonna get paid and leave this place in two weeks. What he's asking us to do is no sweat! I'm getting off that plane in Atlanta one thousand dollars richer, Bro!" Dante brags.

"You sound like a determined young man!" Fitzroy pats Dante on the back.

"Oh, yeah! I ain't never had that much money in my life!" Dante shakes his head.

"Now listen up before we go back in the terminal to join the group, I need you to give me the stuff you stole from my boy Red's store," Fitzroy matter-of-factly says.

The boys look at him with fear in their faces.

"Man, we…"

Fitzroy cuts Dante off. "We men or punks? Give me the stuff and let's move on. Your character is at risk."

"What that mean?" Dante asks.

"If you can't be trusted in little things, then how can you be trusted with bigger things? I need to be able to know I am dealing with men of character." Fitzroy looks at the boys.

"I got character!" Khalid says.

"Man, you ain't got shi.. nothing! You the one stole them cigarettes!" Dante exposes his friend.

"I can't believe you ratting me out!" Khalid punches Dante.

"Look, starting right now, everything you did before doesn't have a thing to do with us moving forward! Khalid, give me the cigarettes and let's go inside and help the men load the luggage!" Fitzroy says as Khalid reaches in the back of his sagging pants and pulls out a bent-up carton of cigarettes.

Fitzroy and Dante look at the carton with disgust on their faces.

"Dang, man! You suit-cased that! I bet it stink! You had it all down in yo ass!" Dante yells.

"It's still good!" Khalid defends.

"I don't know, dude. I think we might want to just throw that away and pay the man," Fitzroy says.

"How much?" Khalid says.

"I don't smoke but probably around fifty bucks," Fitzroy says.

"And where I'm supposed to get fifty bucks? Will he take EBT?" Khalid is apprehensive.

"EBT?" Fitzroy has no idea what Khalid is talking about.

"His Eat Better Tomorrow card. You know, food stamps! Y'all don't have that down here?" Dante is amused.

"Well, Red sells liquor and cigarettes in his store, not food, so I know the man isn't going to risk losing his license by taking your food stamp card for these cigarettes. I'll tell you what. I'll take them back inside and pay for them and trash them. Then I'm going to deduct fifty from your thousand so your payout will be $950 should you win our bet. How's that sound?" Fitzroy suggests a solution.

"That's cool! I'm gon win!" Khalid says.

"Okay, looks like my dad, Dominique and the ladies are loading the truck. Go help them and put some of the bags in this van. Take a couple bottles of water and offer it to the ladies," Fitzroy instructs them.

The boys climb out of the van.

"Say, Mr. Fitzroy. You got a pin or something we can use to hold our pants up?" Dante asks, motivated to keep his end of their deal.

"Here, take my belt." Fitzroy gives the young man his belt.

"What about me?" Khalid says.

Fitzroy opens his glove compartment and finds a latch that goes on a key ring. "This should work. Hook it on to a couple of your belt loops and clamp it." Fitzroy gives the boy the latch and hands him a small plastic bag.

"Thanks. What is the bag for?" Khalid is at a loss.

"This bag is for you to put the cigarettes in. I know you don't think I'm going to touch that package after it's been all down in your butt!" Fitzroy declares.

Dante bursts out laughing. From a distance, the boys' mothers can see them, and they are totally confused when they see Dante and Fitzroy laughing and high-fiving and Dante putting on a belt.

"Oh, one more thing, men. This bet is between you and me. If you tell anyone, the bet is off," Fitzroy seriously says.

"No problem!" Khalid confirms.

"Cool!" Dante voices his agreement.

After all the luggage is loaded into the vehicles, Fitzroy assigns everyone their seats. Faith, Hope, Tay, and Rochelle ride with a grinning Dominique, who is delighted that Hope will be in the same car with him on the ride to St. John.

Lucille and Roy ride together to pick up Wally, a camper and a parent, along with some of Wally's cooking supplies. Lucille pouts but quickly realizes it's better than riding with her airplane companions.

Fitzroy takes Kesha, Mookie, Sean, Dante and Khalid with him as he follows behind Roy. He, too, will pick up campers from the park where Wally is holding down the fort until they arrive to be transported on the barge to St. John.

Upon pulling up to the curb at the park, Lucille's eyes zero-in on Wally, who along with two teenage boys, is carrying large pots to Fitzroy's van parked behind them. A local Caucasian woman of French decent follows closely behind Wally, carrying a sewing machine. A teenage boy, who is very handsome and looks to be the product of a mixed marriage, appears to be her son and is carrying several bolts of material and a metal case with a strap on his shoulder that probably holds a movie camera. Lucille is watching all this from the car window, sizing up the situation.

"He's lost a lot of weight," Lucille comments sadly.

"Yeah, his son's trial was hard on him and not having you around didn't help much either," Roy casually replies.

"I know you're not blaming me, Roy! The man walked out on me!" Lucille bristles.

"You both walked out on each other," Roy says, still maintaining a low voice as he prepares to get out of the car.

"Well, I'll be damn. I can't believe you're blaming me," Lucille lowers her voice and talks through her teeth.

"No, I'm not Lucille, but you need to check with the Good Lord and see what He has to say about it, 'cause what keeps ringing in my ear is 'to have and to hold until death do us part,' and it don't look to me like neither one of you is dead."

"But, Roy!" Lucille readies to mount her self-defense.

Roy cuts her off. "Lucille, I'm going to help load these campers and their stuff in Fitzroy's van. And like I said, we grown folks, and grown folks handle their business. Now handle yours!"

Roy gets out of the car, leaving Lucille pointing her finger at him with her mouth opened. He turns away from Lucille with a big grin on his face, giving Wally, who is a few feet away, a wink and a veiled thumbs up.

Wally greets Lucille with a kiss on the cheek as he climbs into the backseat of the car along with the French woman named Lizette and her son.

Once everyone is loaded in their respective vehicles, they head toward Red Hook to load their cars onto the barge for a fifty-five-minute ride across the sea from St. Thomas to St. John.

"I want to thank you for allowing my son to participate in this program. Charles, tell the man thank you." Lizette nudges her son, who is sitting between her and Wally on the backseat.

"Thank you, sir. If it's okay with everyone, I'd like to video tape this experience and create a documentary for my class project," Charles asks.

"Sounds like a great idea. I'll have to run it by the others and get releases from the children and their parents first," Roy responds.

"But of course!" Lizette seconds.

"Charles attends a local private school on this island and they have made some very interesting films that have been entered into competitions and won several awards," Wally brags.

"Maybe you can teach some of the other campers a few things about videography," Roy gives the young man something to consider.

"Sure! No problem," Charles is excited about the opportunity.

"Not so fast, honey. That camera cost a lot of money and we have to make sure everyone is properly trained and that it's secured when not in use," Lizette is unsure of the situation.

"Uncle Wally and I already discussed that, Mom!" Charles cuts her off before she can say anything else.

Lucille's ears perk up at the boy calling Wally 'Uncle.'

"Uncle Wally? Is this your nephew, Wally?" Lucille expects Wally to answer but the young man blurts out his response.

"Mom says I should call him Uncle Wally. You know how nosey people are when they see a man coming to your house a lot. So to keep the people out of my mother's business, Mom thought it would be good if I called him Uncle Wally," Charles naively says.

Lucille unfastens her seatbelt and turns around to face her husband, who looks like he ate a rat.

"And just how often does Uncle Wally come over to your house, young man?" Lucille calmly asks.

"Lucille, this is not the time nor place," Wally interjects.

"Wally, is there a problem? Who is this woman?" Lizette asks.

"Lucille is my wife." Stuttering Wally finally manages to say.

"Were you having trouble saying I'm you wife, Wally? Young man, cover your ears… Wally, are you fucking this woman!" Vexed Lucille screams and Roy gasps.

"That is none of your business! And please don't talk like that around my son!" Lizette yells back at Lucille.

"Okay, okay, everyone calm down. Lucille, please turn around in your seat and put your seatbelt back on. Please," Roy sternly but calmly asks.

Lucille turns around but not before she reaches into the back seat and smacks Wally across the face. Roy pulls over to the side of the road to try and calm the situation down. Fitzroy's van is following them, and he pulls over, too.

"It's nothing like that, Lucille!" Wally insists before Lucille can smack him again.

Roy exits the car and opens the door for Lucille to get out just as Fitzroy approaches the car to see what the problem is.

"Son, give me one of your passengers and take Lucille, please."

Fitzroy sees the frustrated look on his dad's face and decides not to ask any questions but to just do as he says. Lucille slides out of the car, giving Wally a look that could kill.

Lucille climbs into Fitzroy's van, and Kesha changes places with her sliding into the front seat next to Roy. Wally attempts to say something to Roy, but he is having none of it.

"We'll talk later, my brother," Roy calmly says and Wally respects his wishes.

They continue the drive to the barge in silence.

However, Fitzroy's van is another story. Lucille is fuming mad and she doesn't care who knows it.

"Fitz! The man has been cheating! 'Grieving' my behind. And had the nerve to bring that woman and her son up in my face! All three of them are lucky Roy got me out of that car, 'cause I wasn't stopping at just smacking Wally; Miss Thing was next! Lucille's hands are flapping as she speaks. Khalid, Dante and Dante's mom Tay are asleep in the back of the van; traveling since early morning has caught up with them.

Mookie and Sean are busy looking out the window at all the coconut trees and people selling provisions on the side of the road and trying to adjust to the fact that people drive their cars on the wrong side of the road. They both marvel at the sight of a man pulling two goats by a rope as the van passes them around a bend in the road. The young boys are used to people fussing and confusion, so they don't even hear Lucille or anything she says. Mookie and Sean are professionals at tuning out and staying out of grown peoples' confusion, knowing you can be killed if you say the wrong thing.

"Calm down, Lucille. You don't know if Wally is seeing that woman. The boy just said he comes over to their house," Fitzroy reflects what he's just heard.

"See, now you think I'm stupid, too. That woman was all up in my husband's grill...hell, she damn near was holding his hand in the backseat," Lucille says.

Fitzroy laughs and this really makes her mad.

"What the hell you laughing at?" Lucille is annoyed by Fitzroy's response.

"You! I thought you didn't want the man anymore," Fitzroy teases.

"I never said that!" Lucille counters.

"Hmm!" Fitzroy says, smiling.

"Hmm! Is that all you have to say?" Lucille stares at him.

Fitzroy keeps his eyes on the road with a smile on his face.

"Okay, okay, I get it. You're just like your daddy! You both think it's my fault that Wally and I split up. Well, you two can think whatever you want, but God is my witness, Wally left me!" Lucille turns away from Fitzroy and stares quietly out the window the rest of the ride to the barge with tear-filled eyes.

As Fitzroy maneuvers the van onto the barge, the Atlanta visitors wake up to the sound of the men directing Fitzroy where to place the sixteen-passenger van on the deck of the transport boat.

"Where the hell are we?" Dante queries, half asleep.

"This looks like a war ship!" Khalid speculates.

"It's a car ferry. I've seen them in movies," Tay says.

"Wow! Will we see any sharks?" Sean betrays his fears.

"Long as day don't come up on dis here boat, I'm cool," Mookie says.

"Once we park and the barge takes off, we can get out," Fitzroy informs his passengers.

"We not going to fall in the water, are we?" Mookie asks.

"No. There are railings all around the barge, and you can go on the upper deck and get a good look at all the surrounding little islands," Fitzroy says.

"Do you see my mom?" Sean asks.

"She's right there in my dad's vehicle. See, they're backing up on the barge in front of us." Fitzroy points out.

"Well, when we get out, Mookie and I are going to need to stand with her, 'cause I know she going to be scared and we might have to calm her down," frightened Sean says.

"I understand, tiger! I'll get you to your mom right away." Fitzroy uses the rearview mirror to look directly into the child's smiling face.

"Anybody ever jump off this boat?" Khalid wonders aloud.

"If they did, they didn't live to tell anyone about it," Fitzroy says as he positions the van in its resting position and turns the engine off. "You guys go ahead and get out."

Sean and Mookie race to grab Kesha's hand. Roy leads them to the upper deck to get a better view. Lizette and her son Charles go below to the ship's air-conditioned lounge. Lucille shoots fiery darts in the direction of the woman, who quickly moves out of her view.

Fitzroy gently grabs Lucille's hand as she attempts to exit the van. "Let's talk," he says.

"Let's talk about what, Fitzroy? You guys are the judge and jury, what more is there to say?" Lucille asks, hurt.

"Look, Lucille, this is what I know. Wally is not intimately involved with Lizette. You went back to Atlanta and Wally went up there to try and make a go of you guys' relationship. When he came back to St. Thomas, feeling defeated, he started volunteering his time at this school where he's been mentoring a few of the guys in cooking. Lizette's son Charles is one of his mentees. Between Wally Junior, going to jail, he himself running you back to Atlanta with the horrible things he said, and trying to reopen the Supper Club without any help, mentoring has been a great outlet for Wally. You know, he's just one thought from falling back into depression."

"Well, where is this boy's father?" Lucille bluntly asks.

"Charles' dad died last year of AIDS," Fitzroy sadly says.

"AIDS! Like HIV-AIDS?" Lucille has a look of terror on her face.

"Yes. Charlesworth was a long-term standing senator here in the Virgin Islands. Everyone knew he was gay except his parents."

"And obviously his wife!" Lucille frankly adds.

"Oh, she knew. Lizette was a cover girl. Her job was to conceal his penchant for men to throw his parents, homophobic voters and fellow politicians off the track; a job she did very well," Fitzroy says, reminiscing of the couple's cloistered relationship.

"Well, he must have swung his thing in the other direction at least once, 'cause the woman has a son. And if Wally was tapping that... all I can say is he better get tested!" Lucille crassly says.

"The woman was artificially inseminated! Charlesworth was not about to lose the admiration of his life-long lover by impregnating Lizette," Fitzroy discloses.

"So what was she getting out of this *arrangement*?" Lucille is mystified.

"This is the really sad part," Fitzroy laments. "Lizette loved Charlesworth from the very first time she laid eyes on him. He was kind to her, a gentleman's gentleman, and the ladies considered him quite handsome. She adored being seen on his arm at official events; taking his lover out in public like that was certainly not an option. Somehow, all the pretense seemed real to her, and she deluded herself with the belief he would one day give up his wayward lifestyle and become a true husband to her. Having a son was the crown jewel of the masquerade for the both of them. She was elated with the pregnancy and when he suggested naming the boy after himself she was sure her prayers were being answered. Mind you now, he desperately wanted a son and he was a great dad; sporting events, recitals, spelling bees, graduations, trips abroad, you name it – that boy knew his daddy loved him. And Charlesworth protected the boy from any chatter on the island that might trouble his mind. You know there was plenty of that when word got out about is *'little illness,'* as he called it. Only he and God know the whole truth about who was doing who and how he contracted the AIDS virus. Lizette tried to conduct her own inquisition on the down-low, but he derailed that, and true to form, even when he was on his death bed, it was his lover – not her – he wanted by his side."

"And just how the hell do you know all this, Fitzroy? Your ass needs to be one of the television writers for *'Days of Our Lives!'*" Lucille says, laughing.

"You know the business I'm in. It's my job to know what's going on in these islands. Besides, people have a way of telling me all of their business whether I want to know it or not," Fitzroy reflects.

"I guess it's kind of like being a hairdresser. There is something about when a stylist works on your hair, you just start telling her everything that's on your mind," Lucille says in a daze.

"Maybe it's the chemicals, the heat from the hot comb or the weave thread resting too close to the brain?" Fitzroy teases and Lucille punches him.

"Okay, so the daddy was gay; now I guess you gone tell me the mother is a lesbian?" Lucille says with a smirk on her face.

"Actually, no. Lizette is one of the sweetest, most giving, women you'll ever meet. She comes from old money; and whatever anyone asks of her, she makes it happen. Her family originated from a little French island near St. Marten called St. Barts. From what I understand, she is so grateful for Wally taking time with her son that she offered to help with all his advertisement for the club. The woman is well respected around town, and she's just the right person to help Wally with his public relations and interior design. What that woman can do with a sewing machine and a bolt of fabric is amazing."

Lucille makes a rude noise.

"Lucille, Wally only has eyes for you. So I'm begging you, don't go out there and make a fool of yourself. Okay?" Fitzroy stares into Lucille's eyes, pleading with her to do the right thing.

"You mean, don't make a fool of myself again? The reason I'm in your ugly van is because Roy put me out of the car for slapping the shit out of Wally. Thank God I changed rides before I got arrested for beating down everyone on the backseat, including the young man." Lucille hangs her head in shame.

"You and Wally need to go home and work your differences out," Fitzroy urges.

"Then why am I on this barge? We don't live in St. John," Lucille takes Fitzroy's suggestion to heart.

"Well, I guess you're going to have to wait until the camp is over. Wally made a commitment to help out, and I don't think he's going to renege. And if I'm not mistaken, I believe you're listed on the program to teach one day this week."

"Yeah! I'm supposed to teach these ghetto mommas about etiquette." Lucille and Fitzroy laugh.

"Well, thank God for forgiveness and sins being washed away! From this moment going forward, you're a new creature in Christ," Fitzroy celebrates.

"Whatever!" Lucille laughs.

"All right now, don't dismiss your blessings," Fitzroy teases as he opens the van door to get out.

"Wait! Don't leave me, I feel like the two little boys who got out of the van. I need you to hold my hand! I'm scared and embarrassed!"

Fitzroy goes around and opens Lucille's door and they walk hand in hand to the air-conditioned section of the boat for her to apologize.

# Chapter 17
## Who Said It Can't Be Done?

Fitzroy, Dot, Marlin, Faith, Lucille and Wally are all sitting around Dot and Marlin's farmhouse kitchen table, having their morning briefing meeting. Several portable fans are blowing to cool the kitchen off. Faith passes a notepad and a pen to each of them.

"Thank you, sweetie," Roy says and Faith gives her father-in-law a smile.

Lucille is uncomfortable and takes the note pad to fan with. "Marlin, when the hell y'all gon get some air conditioning up in here? I can't believe you're a millionaire living like this! And you got my sister down on this farm sweating like one of your pigs, when she got her fabulous house up in the nose-bleed section of the island with amenities that will rival the royal family!"

"Who tell ya me's a millionaire!" Marlin looks at Dot, who shakes her head no.

"Can we just have our meeting? Besides, everything all of us have belongs to God! Now, is Khalid still having trouble going into the pigpen to help clean the stalls?" Roy asks.

"He's shooting the water hose over the wall with a lot of pressure but he's not going in," Fitzroy tells the group.

"The young man is afraid of the pigs. One of the boars chased that poor child clear across the farm! Marlin had to get a ladder to get him out the Tamarind tree!" Dot chuckles.

"De boy never should have messed wit de boar when him mating wit he woman; him get vexed! De boy been harassing de pig since him got 'ere. Just mischievous, now him lucky de boar ain't throw he down and give him serious licks!" Marlin says, laughing.

"Farm life might not be for Khalid," Faith says.

"Maybe not, but it certainly has taught him how to care about more than himself. I wish you could have seen him helping Dominique when the lamb gave birth to five little ones. That boy was fascinated beyond belief; he even had tears in his eyes. Now, he'll deny it, but the young man was crying! Dominique let him pick one of the baby sheep out and he named him after him. Every night and the first thing in the morning, Khalid goes to check on the baby lamb," Fitzroy proudly reports.

"There is no way you can spend time on the farm and not get an up-close view of life in its simplest form," Wally adds.

"I feel like Sza Sza Gábor in that old television show *Green Acres* where her husband gave up on New York and moved them to a broken down farm and him singing, 'Farm living is the life for me,' sitting on a tractor wearing business suit pants and a vest! His wife wearing her fancy gowns in their broken down farmhouse singing, 'I get allergic smelling hay…I just adore a penthouse view, darling. I love you, but give me Park Avenue!'" Lucille bellows out a laugh.

"Well, I certainly don't feel that way. Living on the farm is the best thing that ever happened to me! Who would ever have predicted I'd find my life purpose at this age? Only God knew!" Dot shares.

Marlin gives her a kiss on the cheek and Dot beams.

"All right, you two, can't you see we're in a meeting?" Lucille chides her sister and brother-in-law.

"Well, how's it going with you and your three mentee young ladies Auntie?" Faith quickly changes the subject before Dot and Lucille start fussing.

"Well, I'm very happy to inform you that I've managed to get those skunk and calico color weaves out of their heads! We're no longer *ghetto fabulous*, but simply fabulous. Now that young girl, Kesha, decided she wants to go natural. So if you see someone walking around here looking like Bush Momma gone wild, I had nothing to do with the Angela Davis-throwback-from-the-seventies-afro-look!" Lucille reports.

"Yes, I saw Tay coming out of one of the cabins and I hardly recognized her," Fitzroy says, smiling.

"Well, I'm sure she recognized you! All that girl talks about is you. I'm constantly reminding her you're a married man! Then she rolls her eyes at me and flips me off. Thank God, Faith, you're not an insecure woman or you might have to borrow my gun and shoot that broad!" Lucille laughs.

"No, I won't be needing your gun, Auntie. I thank God my husband only has eyes for me! Now, *that's* what's keeping me from shooting her." Faith laughs.

"I'm amazed at the transformation I've seen in both Khalid and Dante. They are almost... gentlemen," Dot says with astonishment.

"Well, I wouldn't go that far! But there has been a drastic improvement. Most notable is we are not being subjected to looking at sagging pants, their dirty-behind underwear, or the crack of their butts!" Lucille takes a breath, preparing to continue.

"Yep, God is good!" Fitzroy interjects quickly, hoping to change the subject.

"Wally, have you heard from Lizette or Charles since they left the farm?" Roy inquires, picking up on Fitzroy's intervention. Everyone is quiet and holds their breath to hear what he has to say.

Wally lowers his head and speaks in a sad voice. "Well, Lizette is still angry and says Charles will not be coming back to the camp as long as Dante is here. She won't even let me talk to the boy."

"Look, the woman must have known the child was a little sweet! Mothers are the first ones to know when their children are gay. Now, they might not want to 'fess up to it, but they know! Besides, Fitzroy told me the boy's daddy was a big sissy!" Lucille blurbs out.

"I don't think I quite said it like that! And I certainly didn't tell you that so you could tell everybody else, Lucille!" Fitzroy firmly says.

"My bad! I'm so sorry, Fitz! I should never have said that, knowing you shared confidential information with me. But you did say the whole town knew the man was gay and Lizette was his cover girl." Lucille tries to cover up her mistake.

"Anything else you want to share, Miss Blabbermouth!" Fitzroy asks, annoyed.

"Sorry!" Lucille takes her finger and pretends she's zipping her mouth.

Unable to contain herself, Lucille abruptly resumes her painful diatribe. "But, can you imagine Lizette walking into the boys' cabin and seeing another boy hugging her child? That's just weird, especially knowing the child's family history!" Lucille's distress has her face is contorted.

"Okay, Lucille, I'm going to have to ask you to let someone else talk unless you have more to report about your classes," Roy insists.

"They were just hugging!" Fitzroy interjects.

"Teenage boys don't hug!" Lucille screams.

"Lucille!" Roy gives Lucille the eye not to say another word.

"Thank you, Roy!" Dot screams.

"Thank you, Roy? Oh no, you're not going to go there, sister! Don't let me start talking about your closet queen." Lucille points her finger at Dot.

"Go where? What closet queen? Lucille, you just have a little too much to say about people. And the way you say it is so ugly!" Dot whines.

"Ugly? I'm just honest! And if maybe you were a little more honest instead of trying to hide the fact that your son Noah is gay; hell, he's probably hugging another man right now as we speak! And I won't call no names, but if one of us were honest about Noah's sexuality, he might not feel like he has to live in another country instead of around his own family for fear we will condemn him to hell for being gay!" Lucille rebukes.

"How dare you! My child is not gay!" Dot is almost in tears, screaming.

"The man is gayer than Peter Pan in a tutu!" Lucille shouts back.

"Enough! This is not getting us anywhere! Enough!" Wally exclaims in pain.

"Who do you think you're screaming at?" Lucille attacks Wally.

"I am screaming at you, Lucille, my wife who I love dearly. My beautiful wife who can sometimes be brutal with her words and hurt other people! My wife who has the kindest heart and will do anything for the people she loves but at the same time will rip your head off if you do or say something she doesn't like. I'm talking to my wife, who saved my life, when I was at the end of my rope, my awesome wife who gave me a reason to live. My wife who I too was rough with my words and I hurt with the ugly things I said when Junior got shot. Ugly words I will live to regret for the rest of my life because they hurt you! I don't want to ever be that vicious hurtful person! I never ever want to hurt you with ugly words and I pray that you will try to stop hurting people with your words! They cut to the very core, Lucille! Please, stop! I'm so sorry!" Wally cries like a baby.

Lucille is shocked and timidly walks over to her husband to comfort him.

Roy, Dot, Marlin, Faith and Fitzroy get up slowly and walk out of the kitchen, leaving Lucille and Wally crying in each other's arms.

Once on the porch, they find a seats and continue their meeting until Billy, Lisa and Cathy pull up in a pickup truck and greet them. Cathy is wearing her airline stewardess uniform.

"Me peas! Would you look at dees beautiful people dem!" Marlin walks off the porch and shakes Billy's hand and embraces Lisa.

"What, I don't get a hug? You know I'm officially in the family now!" Cathy cries.

Dot runs over and hugs Cathy.

"Now that's what I'm talking about!" Cathy says, smiling.

"Hey, Dad, Fitzroy, Faith, Dot! Looks like you guys having a serious meeting! Are my two recruits ready? Flight 22 to St. Croix departs in 90 minutes," Billy says, smiling.

"And I understand I have a future stewardess who will be shadowing me," Cathy says in a professional voice.

"Yes! And trust me, they are hippopotamus happy!" Faith says, laughing.

As if on cue, Mookie, Sean and Kesha make their way across the nearby field, running and waving.

"We're coming! We're coming!" Kesha yells, making sure they are not left behind.

"I'd say someone is excited," Fitzroy says, laughing.

Kesha, out of breath, stares at Cathy from head to toe in awe.

"Hi, I'm Cathy. Is something wrong?" Cathy inquires.

"No, just that you look so beautiful. Your uniform is pretty too. I'm Kesha," Kesha says, shaking Cathy's hand.

"It's so nice to meet you, Kesha. I'm glad you like my uniform, because I have one for you in the truck. You know us girls have to represent!"

"Oh my Lord!" Kesha doesn't know what else to say so she keeps repeating, "Oh my Lord!"

Sean and Mookie laugh at her.

"Climb in the truck, Co-pilots, your hats are on the backseat."

Mookie and Sean pull each other back to be the first one in the truck. "Man, let go! No, you let go!"

All the adults are so tickled at watching the boys and Kesha. Billy kisses Lisa and leaves her there with the family as he takes off with Cathy, Mookie, Sean and Kesha. He blows the horn as they speed down the dirt road, heading to catch the boat to St. Thomas where Billy's plane is waiting to take his new recruits and paying passengers over to St. Croix.

Hope, Dominique, and Khalid walk across the farm at a distance, waving to the honking car.

Marlin notices that Dante is not with them. "Me wonder were de boy Dante is? Me ain't see he. I hope dem no leave he der by he self!"

"Yeah, I certainly hope he's not being isolated," Roy seconds.

"I think his mother is punishing him for what he got caught doing. I heard she tried to beat the hell out of him. His best friend Khalid been calling him a homo ever since," Faith shares.

"I don't see either of the boys' mothers," Dot observes.

"They got stuck in Coral Bay last night. For some reason, they thought the bus runs all night," Fitzroy explains.

"What were Tay and Rochelle doing in Coral Bay, honey?" Faith asks.

"They wanted to explore the other side of the island before it was time to head back to Atlanta," Fitzroy explains.

"So where did they sleep last night? I certainly hope they didn't have to sleep on the side of the road. You know they have wild donkeys that come out at night in Coral Bay! Oh my Lord!" Dot is worried.

"Relax, Dot, they didn't have to sleep on the side of the road. I called some friends, the Matthaises who live in Coral Bay; they recused them from the road and put them up for the night. Thank God for church family. They'll put them on the bus back to the camp this afternoon."

"Praise God!" Dot says.

"So, they called you, honey?" Faith questions.

"Yeah. Tay called me just before we were about to turn in for the night," Fitzroy casually says.

"Hmm!" Faith mumbles.

"Hmm what?" Fitzroy naively asks.

"I sure hope I don't have to borrow Aunt Lucille's gun!"

Fitzroy hugs his wife and laughs.

"I ain't laughing!" Faith hits her husband.

"Baby, you look so cute acting jealous!" Fitzroy continues laughing.

Hope, Khalid and Dominique reach where everyone is standing.

"Where is Dante?" Roy asks.

"The homo is in the cabin feeling sorry for his-self!" Khalid's response is venomous.

"Khalid! Calling Dante a homo is not cool and it's not working for me!" Fitzroy says in a very serious voice, causing Khalid to check himself.

"Sorry, man!" Khalid says with his head lowered.

"I go get de truck and drive over to de cottage and get he. Me gon take de boy for a ride," Marlin says as he kisses Dot and heads for his truck.

"Wait up, Marlin. I'm coming with you." Roy races to catch up.

"Walk with me, Khalid," Fitzroy says to the young man as they walk toward the porch.

"Lisa, how come the girls aren't with you?" Faith asks.

"You think they want to come with me with all Aunt Dot's grandkids and those triplets there at the house! They aren't even paying their daddy any attention! Oh Aunt Dot, Mother Gloria said you need to bring your butt to your other house and help cook. Debbie and Byron want a break. I think they're going to hike Reef Bay Trail," Lisa says.

"Oh my goodness, with all this camp stuff going on, I totally forget I'm supposed to watch the kids. Lisa, are you coming?" Dot asks as she opens the door to get in her truck.

"Are you crazy? No! I have a break! Me and my main girl here are going to hang out! Right, Faith?"

"Soon as I get my purse out Fitzroy's van. Baby, what you gon do?" Faith asks her husband.

"I'm going to go over to St. Thomas and I'm taking Khalid, Wally and Lucille. We're going to go over and talk to Lizette and Charles," Fitzroy shares.

"I thought Wally said she doesn't want to talk to anybody!" Faith says as she grabs her purse.

"Yeah, that's what she said, but we're going over there anyway! Wally, Lucille, y'all come on out of there. We got places to go and people to see!" Fitzroy opens the porch screen door and hollers inside.

"Why I got to go? I didn't do anything!" Khalid pouts.

"That's the point, you didn't do anything. A real friend speaks up for his boy, especially when you know Dante isn't of that persuasion."

"What?" Khalid doesn't understand a word Fitzroy said.

"Get in the van, son. We'll discuss it on the way over to St. Thomas." Fitzroy is authoritative.

Khalid obeys Fitzroy as he would obey the good father he never had and climbs into the truck.

"Monsieur Wally is the camp cook, sir. If we let him go, who will prepare the meals for the campers?" Dominique says with concern in his voice.

"You will. Keep it simple… hotdogs, beans and a salad. Oh and make some Kool-Aid; those Atlanta folks love Kool-Aid!" Fitzroy says as Wally and Lucille exit the house, holding hands and pecking each other on the lips.

Faith and Lisa giggle at seeing this as they jump into Faith's jeep and drive off.

"Where are we going?" Lucille says in a giddy voice.

"To save a young man's life! Get in the van," Fitzroy instructs them as he opens the driver's door and climbs in.

"Don't worry, sir, I have everything under control." Dominique waves as everyone pulls off, leaving him standing alone.

"I know! See you tonight, son!" Fitzroy yells out of the van.

# Chapter 18
# Dot's Family

As soon as Dot pulls up to the Bordeaux house in her truck, she finds her daughter Debbie and son-in-law Byron dressed in shorts, sun hat and sneakers, looking like American tourists, waiting for her so they can leave.

"Mom, did you forget we were here in St. John visiting you? You've hardly spent any time with the kids," Debbie says in a whining angry voice.

"Now, Mother Dot, if we're a burden, just let us know and we can make arrangements to come at another time," Byron chimes in.

"The two of you need to stop complaining and saying dumb stuff like that. No you didn't come at a bad time and you'd better not think about leaving before I get to spend time with my grandbabies. Besides, you just got here yesterday and there has been so much unexpected stuff going on at the camp that required my attention this morning," Dot says as she stands on the porch ready to relieve the parents of eight, the last three being triplets.

"Mom, you have Marlin, Fitzroy, Faith, Auntie Lucille and Uncle Wally there to help. Maybe you're doing too much; I mean, you're not twenty-years-old anymore." Debbie feels the need to stress this point.

Dot is surprised at her daughter. "No, I'm sixty-five, for the record, and just what does my age have to do with me being one of the camp directors?" Dot waits for a response and clarification.

"Mother Dot, I'm sure Debbie didn't mean anything by it. It's just that..." Byron stops talking.

"It's just that what?" Dot puts her hands on her hips, waiting for a reply.

"Mother, it's just that you seem silly to us trying to recapture your youth when you should be at home relaxing and cooking, baking, scrapbooking, knitting... whatever people your age do. Not working on a farm with pigs, goats, chickens, cows and sheep!" Byron ventures.

"What sixty-five-year-old woman climbs a ladder and picks mangos?" Debbie says, flapping her arms in frustration.

Byron hugs her to calm her down.

"You guys go ahead and enjoy your hike. We'll talk later."

Debbie kisses her mother as she and Byron take Dot's truck to go hiking. As they pull out of the parking space, Dot calls out to them. "Byron and Debbie, I'm going to need the two of you at the camp tomorrow to help out!"

Debbie hollers out the window of the truck. "And what about the kids! Mother, we can't bring the children down to that farm!"

"Yes, you can and you will! This conversation is over. Go and enjoy yourself." Dot walks into the house where Gloria, who is chasing one of the triplets and trying to put him back on the potty, greets her.

"Girl, now I know why the good Lord closes a woman's womb at a certain age! You see, all this chasing kids and lifting them is for young women! Dot, we have gotten old! Thank God that your teenage granddaughters are here to help, 'cause even Debbie and Byron can't handle these little ones alone."

Gloria catches the toddler and sits him on the potty. "Now if you move from here before you drop some business in this potty, you won't get a cookie!"

"Okay!" the little one sadly says as one of Dot's teenage granddaughters comes out of the room to greet her.

"Hi, Nana! You look tired." Farren kisses her grandmother on the cheek and flops on the couch with a book.

"I'm fine, thank you. Let your sisters know they're coming down to the farm tomorrow," Dot says as she bends over to kiss the little boy on the potty.

"What's up with you, Dot? Looks like you lost your best friend," Gloria says as her sister passes her to go in the kitchen to get a cold bottle of water from the refrigerator.

"Nana, Mom says it stinks on the farm and she doesn't want us down there because we might catch something," Farren says from the couch, loud enough for her grandmother to hear her in the kitchen.

Dot's surprise shows on her face, but she manages to respond calmly. "You'll be fine, darling. Your mother hasn't been on the farm to know if it stinks or not."

"Nana, I think Brice pooped. You want me to wipe him?" the young lady asks.

"Would you please and then come in here and get him a cookie when you're finished," Dot instructs her.

Gloria and Dot sit at the island in the kitchen. Noticing that Dot seems depressed, Gloria watches her with concern. She waits for Farren to get the cookie for the toddler and leave the kitchen before she speaks.

"Nana, is it okay if Brice watches *Veggie Tales* with Byron, Brianna and Kamari?" Farren looks in the kitchen, holding the little boys hand who is chomping down on his cookie.

"Sure. And would you please dump the potty for Nana? Are your sisters in their rooms?" Dot asks as Farren removes the bowl from the potty to dump in the toilet.

"I dropped them at Trunk Bay a little while ago. Debbie and Byron will pick them up after their hike or if they get bored they'll call one of us to come and get them," Gloria informs.

"Why didn't you go with them, Farren?" Dot asks.

Farren pauses.

"She has her monthly and her sister told her she might draw sharks to them if she got in the water," Gloria whispers as Farren takes her little brother's hand and potty bowl and goes into the media room to join the other children.

"That's crazy! And just when did she get her period? The child was just born! How can she have her period already? I guess Debbie and Byron are right. I am old!" Dot shakes her head in grief.

"Old? No, they didn't go there! If we listen to their dumb butts, we'd be rocking on the porch, knitting and taking care of grandbabies!" Gloria angrily says.

"That's just what she said I should be doing and not trying to act young living on a farm picking mangos and dealing with animals. Gloria, I wanted to shake her until her brain locked into place," Dot shares.

"Don't take this the wrong way, Dot, but Debbie was never the smartest bulb in the lamp. The good Lord created Debbie for one purpose and that was to breed babies!" Gloria says, laughing.

"Actually, for two purposes and the other is to be a submissive wife to Byron," Dot says, smiling.

"Well, at least she knows her purpose in life. Some people never find theirs," Gloria says.

"You know, I'm happy to see my grandchildren and all but Debbie and her judgmental ways are starting to get on my nerves. After Marlin and I picked them up from the airport, she had the nerve to pull me to the side and ask me how come I haven't taught him proper English yet."

"Oh no! What did you say to that?" Gloria waits patiently to hear the answer.

"I asked her if she was talking about the same man who paid to fly her, her husband and all their children to the Virgin Islands first class," Dot casually says.

"You're good, because if Faith had ever talked to me like that, she'd be wearing dentures! How dare that ungrateful woman say something like that? Remind her that when in Rome, you speak like the Romans!" Gloria points out.

"Or you take your behind back to Athens before Cesar kicks your butt out!" Dot yells. The ladies roll with laughter.

"Dot, Debbie's your only daughter!" Gloria teases.

"And I'm her only mother! Tomorrow, I'm having all of them, including the three-year-olds, bring their uppity behinds down to the farm. I'm going to have Byron lead a noon Bible study and the girls are going to learn a little about the animals on the farm, starting at the pigpen! And if they don't like it, they can let the door to the plane hit them in the back! Gloria, you know I put up with George's lying and cheating for more than thirty years, so I'll be damn if I'm going to let his daughter push me around! She doesn't know me, honey. Momma is not the same timid Momma she knew in Atlanta." Dot is upset and talking fast.

"Slow down, killer! I think you have a great plan and just tell me what you want me to do, 'cause I've got your back." Gloria pats Dot on the back.

"Speaking of killer! Girl, I was about to kill Lucille. That woman pushed my last button today! In front of God and everybody, she announced that Noah was 'gayer than Peter Pan in a tutu' and I was in denial. Now, where in the hell did she get the notion in her head that Noah is gay?"

Dot's face is contorted and her hands are on her hips. Gloria is quiet.

"What you think about that? The nerve of her, huh?" Dot presses her point. Gloria is still quiet.

"And when did you get so quiet!" Dot inquires of her sister just as Kamari walks in the kitchen.

"Hi, Auntie Dot! Grammy, Sarafina is awake. She's crying in her crib. You want me to tell Farren to get off the computer and get her?"

"I'll get her, sweetie," Gloria says.

As Gloria turns to leave Dot grabs her by the arm and issues new orders. "Honey, ask your cousin to get the baby and change her diaper. I need to speak with your Grammy."

Kamari obeys her Aunt Dot, smiles and leaves the kitchen.

"Now, Gloria, you have never ever been lost for words! Is there something you need to say to me?" Dot stares her in the eyes.

"Well, Dot, it's just that... It's just that... Hell, I'm going to say this as gently as I can. I believe Noah is gay. Now he didn't come and tell me, but I've had that inkling about him since the child was about three years-old. Surely you must have noticed something different about him yourself?" Gloria says, being extra careful not to hurt Dot's feelings.

"Noticed something different about him like what?" Dot asks as if she doesn't have a clue.

"Well... let's start with the fact that he was always styling your wigs and sometimes wearing them around the house," Gloria points out.

"The boy wanted to be a hair stylist, that's all," Dot defends.

"Okay, then let's look at the fact that he enjoyed playing with Debbie's dolls more than she did. The boy had names for each of the dolls and held regular tea parties when George wasn't home, for fear of being beaten." Gloria stares at her sister.

"Oh, please, don't tell me anything about George! That man didn't know any of his sons! He barely spent time with them!" Dot dismisses.

"Now you have a point there. So, can I get you something to eat? I'm fixing sandwiches for the children and a nice garden salad." Gloria clearly wants to change the subject.

"Why are you doing that?" Dot sadly asks.

"Doing what?" Gloria knows what she's talking about.

"Trying to brush me off. We have not finished our conversation about Noah." Dot raises her voice.

"Listen, Dot, we love Noah and his being gay or straight won't change that. Now if you need to know for sure whether your son is bent that way, then I'd suggest you call him and the two of you have a conversation. Noah might be ready to talk about his sexuality; I mean everyone these days is coming out of the closet like it's the fashionable thing to do. I myself liked 'Don't Ask, Don't Tell!' Who really needs to know your business anyway except you, your partner and God? You don't see straight couples on television announcing, 'I'm straight!' How you do it and whom you love just isn't everybody's business! Besides, does it really matter to you if Noah is gay?" Gloria asks.

"Of course it does! How would you react if you found out Faith was a lesbian?" Dot throws at Gloria.

"Okay, you have a point there. I'd probably be angry, might not want to see her, but if she showed signs of being a lesbian since childhood, I think I might be the first to know it. Now, I might be in denial and constant prayer for a different outcome, but if I'm to be honest with myself then… then it might be a hard bullet to bite but eventually I'd have to accept my child as that," Gloria acknowledges.

"No one wants to accept their child as gay!" Dot screams.

"Like I said, that's a hard bullet to bite. But what are you going to do, lie to yourself and others? I've known some pastors and politicians who married women to hide their sexuality. You remember Grace Hightower, the first lady over at Beulah Tabernacle?" Gloria asks.

"Oh yeah! The woman could dress to the hilt! You and Rev invited George and me to a few of their Christmas parties at their fabulous mansion, one of the only times George and I did something as a couple. Now Grace had one fine behind husband. I ain't gon lie; if he even looked like he would give me the slightest and I mean the slightest attention, I would have stabbed Grace in the back and taken that man!"
Dot says, laughing.

"And you would have been wasting your time. Pastor Hightower was not interested in women!" Gloria shares.

"Gloria, bite you tongue! That man was married to Grace for over twenty-five years! She was his First Lady sitting there on the front row every Sunday morning giving the congregation her million-dollar smile, supporting her man!" Dot exclaims.

"Million-dollar fake smile! Grace was his cover girl and she knew it!" Gloria snaps her fingers.

"And just how do you know this? Did he get busted like that pastor in California taking pictures of his self in the bathroom and sending it to young boys he was having an affair with?" Dot shakes her head in disgust.

"No, my girl went into the relationship knowing the situation. Pastor Hightower asked her to be his wife under the condition that he would take good care of her, build her the house of her dreams and give her whatever her heart desired except his love. Dot she sold her self for a material life," Gloria shares.

"You still haven't told me how you know all this this!" Dot is intrigued.

"After Rev died, one of the ladies in the church gave me a brochure about this Retreat for Grievers. Dot, I was hurting so bad I decided to go on the weekend retreat, praying for some relief. When I got on the bus that was taking us to the retreat in the mountains, the first person I spotted was Grace Hightower! I immediately thought her husband had gone home to be with the Lord just as Rev had. When we got to the hotel, the hostess paired us up as roommates for the weekend. Well, Sweet Jesus, please forgive me if what I'm saying is gossip, but my girl finally had an epiphany and decided to walk out on her fake marriage of over twenty-five years. She said the Lord spoke to her one morning and said, 'What are you doing here and how is that you could be brought for silver and gold?'"

"Dot, I have to say that was one powerful workshop weekend. Captives were set free; there was so much crying and praising going on in that hotel! Deliverance was on everyone's face.

"The last night Grace and I shared our room together, she confessed to me how she had sold herself out to her husband and was ashamed. She said she was going to confront him the second she got back home and tell him she wanted him out of her paid-for house, half of his pension, and he had one month to step down as pastor or she would expose him!" Gloria shares.

"Oh my goodness! Did he do it?" Dot waits for an answer.

"Pastor Hightower did exactly as she instructed him. The man told his congregation he was diagnosed with a rare disease that showed a promise of a cure in people living in the remote country of Siberia. He asked that the church look after his wife during his long absence and to show the new pastor who was appointed by Grace the same love they had shown him over the years," Gloria says, laughing.

"Good for Grace!" Dot says, joining Gloria in laughter.

"Oh, it got even better! The new pastor Grace appointed was a widowed gentleman that Grace had been friends with since college days, and he said the Lord had told him many years ago even before he married his deceased wife that Grace would be his wife!" Gloria relates.

"Stop lying! This sounds like some fairy tale!" Dot hollers.

"Well, Dot, it's no more a fairy tale than what the Lord did for Marlin and you, me and Roy, George and Zipporah, Lisa and Billy, Faith and Fitzroy. You know He's in that kind of business! All we have to do is be obedient and willing to step out of our comfort zone!" Gloria smiles.

"Wow! I feel so loved right now. Would you look at God? He has given all of us with broken wings the ability to fly again!" Dot rejoices.

"Honey, why don't you give Noah a call when you get a chance and have a heart-to-heart talk with your son? Let him know he is loved by all of us." Gloria embraces her sister just as Kamari leads the triplets into the kitchen, holding diapers and wipes.

"Grammy and Aunt Dot, one of them made boo-boo and Farren says she needs help! I'm not allowed to clean poop yet, here!" Kamari gives Aunt Dot the diaper.

"I did not boo-boo," the triplet girl Brianna says.

"Well, if it's not boo-boo then something has gone wrong in your Pamper or one of your brothers'!" Kamari tells the defensive little girl as the ladies bellow out a big laugh, causing Kamari to join in.

"You guys are too big not to be getting on the potty! Nana is going to have to get you trained before you go back to Georgia," Dot says as Farren walks in the kitchen carrying Sarafina and her soiled diaper to put in the trash.

"Good luck! Fushia, Faith, Farrah, Freda and I have been trying and they just won't use the toilet. Now Brianna will do number one and two in the potty, but she's afraid something will eat her bum if she tries to do number two in the toilet. It makes no sense, but that's what she says! Brice will do number one and two in the potty, if you say you're going to give him a treat. But Byron... that boy doesn't have a clue!" Farren is exasperated.

Farren gives Sarafina to Gloria on her way to the trashcan to get rid of the wet diaper.

"Monster in toilet, Nana! Monster bite my bum!" Brianna says. Everyone laughs and Brianna looks like she is going to cry.

The triplet boy Brice hugs his sister and pats her back to make her feel better. "Don't cry sister... Don't cry!"

"How sweet," Dot is proud of her grandson.

"Brice loves her so much and will hurt anyone who tries to do anything to her," Farren tells her grandmother.

"What about Byron Jr.? Does he protect his sister too?" Gloria inquires.

"Now that's another story! Junior marches to the beat of another drummer, as Farrah would say."

Byron looks at Farren, not sure if she's talking about him.

"And just what does that mean?" Dot is anxious for details.

"I don't know, but something is not exactly right with him. Don't tell Mom or Dad I said this but… Byron, Jr. is slow! It's like his brain is in another zip code. Most of the time he doesn't hear anything you say to him. I'm not sure he even knows his name, because he will not respond. You have to take him by the hand and talk directly in his face to get his attention. Byron, Jr. is always the last one to get up in the morning and won't go to sleep unless he bangs his head like a crazy person. Junior has broken five headboards and knocked the plaster out of the wall twice in their bedroom." Farren shakes her head hopelessly.

"Have your parents taken him to the doctor? Maybe he has a hearing problem," Gloria shares Dot's concern.

"Byron, Jr. can hear the cartoons he watches. The boy laughs right on cue when something stupid happens. Dad says there is nothing wrong with him that a butt whooping won't take care of and all those doctors will do is try and tag his son as special and put him on a bunch of medications he doesn't need."

"Well, have the butt whoopings helped?" Dot anticipates the response.

"Of course not! Dad is in denial that his namesake might have issues," Farren flippantly says.

"Well, surely your mother has spoken up on the child's behalf," Gloria inquires.

"Please! If you know my mother, then you know she is Dad's puppet. He pulls all the strings and she moves in whatever direction he leads her," Farren says with disgust.

"Well, you certainly are very opinionated young lady!" Dot raises her voice.

"I'm sorry, Nana, it's just that... never mind! Come on, Byron, I'll change you." Farren turns to leave the kitchen, holding the little boy's hand.

"Hold up, young lady. I'm not finished talking to you," Dot insists.

"Listen, I'll change the little tyke while you and Farren take some time to talk." Gloria rounds everyone up and leaves the kitchen.

"Sit down, young lady, we need to talk," Dot says to her second-eldest granddaughter.

"Nana, I don't want to get in trouble with my dad. He's made it clear that family business stays in the family!" Farren says.

"Well, Farren, I am family! So, let's talk and I promise you what you say will be between you and me." Dot holds up her left hand in a scout's honor position.

Farren smiles. "Nana, I think it's your right hand you're supposed to raise." They laugh together as Dot changes hands.

"So, what's going on?" Dot calmly asks.

"Where should I start, Nana?"

"Start with you." Dot gently takes Farren's face into her hands and kisses her on the forehead.

"Okay, you know I turned eighteen last month, and my prom was the same week," Farren sadly shares.

"Didn't you get my gift?" Dot quickly inquires.

"Yes, Nana! And thank you for the hundred dollars. Of course I had to tithe ten percent, save fifty percent, give an offering of ten percent and that left me with thirty percent for myself," Farren points out.

"What? I already tithed on that money! That's crazy!" Dot is surprised and disappointed.

"There are a lot of things that are crazy at our house," Farren sighs.

"Go ahead, honey, tell Nana," Dot prompts the young lady to continue.

"Oh, I was telling you about my prom and my eighteenth birthday. Well, first of all, I went to the prom by myself," Farren makes a smirk on her face.

"As fine as you are? I know there were boys lined up to take you to the prom!" Dot is not understanding.

"Yep! Until they hear what my daddy's rules are," Farren sarcastically says.

"Rules? What rules?" Dot cannot imagine.

"Oh, there is a whole list of them. The biggest turn-off is we are not allowed to go out with any boys unless it's going to lead to marriage! My dad has to meet them and the first question he asks them is, 'What are your intentions with my daughter?' Nana, we don't even know what major we are going to select for college and Dad's asking what intentions we have for marriage! Hello! I stopped bringing anybody home to be subjected to his primitive caveman ways! It's embarrassing!" Farren throws her hand up in the air.

"What about your older sister Faith?" Dot inquires.

"Since Faith is living away from home in the dormitory at Spellman, she is not under the microscope like Farrah, Freda, Fuchia and me. Faith has figured out how to play the game," Farren says, smiling.

"Play the game? What does that mean?" Dot waits for an answer.

"Faith has a college cellphone that she leaves at school when she comes home and a home cellphone number that she does not give out. So when she's home, no boys or friends call her; that way Dad and Mom are not in her business. She helps out at church, around the house and spends a lot of time on mission trips. Faith says she's just biding her time until she graduates and lands a job, then she's moving as far away from

Mom and Dad as possible, maybe even out of the country! I told her I'm coming with her," Farren says with an animated face.

"Wow! I'm sorry you girls have to live such a strict life," Dot voices her regret.

"I mean, Nana, we all love Jesus but Dad is taking religion to another level. Soon, we'll be wearing sack cloth and bonnets!" Farren is at the end of her wits.

"What about the other girls?" Dot asks.

"Farrah is depressed, Freda has run away twice and Fuchsia… well, let's just say Fuchsia does her own thing," Farren tells her Nana.

"Fuchsia does her own thing? She's not doing drugs or anything like that is she?" Dot has a look of fear on her face.

"Nana, the girl is a serious weed head. She tried to hide her stash in between my pads when we were packing! I told her she must be crazy! I was not going to jail for her or nobody! It wasn't until we landed that I figured out why she insisted on carrying the babies' diaper bag. Lord Jesus, thank God she didn't get busted!" Farren shakes her head, and Dot is lost for words.

"Nana, you have to promise me you're not going to tell anyone what I just shared with you!" Farren has a look of regret and terror on her face.

"No… I said I wouldn't and now I regret I did. Farren, this is deep! I surely have to do something to save my granddaughters!" Dot frets.

"But you promised! You can't say a thing! You promised, Nana!" Farren cries.

"Okay, okay, calm down. I'm not going to get you in trouble." Dot hugs and comforts her.

"Thank you, Nana, because I don't know who else to talk to. I can't trust any of my friends because they will blabber my family business all over Atlanta!" Farren sighs.

"What about the youth pastor at the church? Can't you talk to him in confidence?"

"The youth department at our church sucks! Hardly anyone comes because it's so boring! Besides, the youth pastor's son is the one Fuchsia gets her weed from. Nana, everyone is so fake, pretending they're all holy and when they're outside of church it's another story! If you get on Facebook, everybody is talking about *Scandal, Empire* and *How to Get Away with Murder*! If you post something about Jesus, you don't get any likes, but post something about *Scandal* and you not only get at least fifty likes, you get comments that keep coming for days! It's like nobody cares about church or Jesus or any of the things we grew up believing and they make you sound so stupid if you bring it up. Nana, I'm confused and feel so lost!" Farren buries her head against her grandmother's neck. Dot hugs her.

"I know, I know! I was feeling that way for almost sixty years, and I'm going to make sure my granddaughters don't have to wait that long for deliverance. It's time we have a 'Come to Jesus' moment!" Dot vows.

"You mean like a baptism?" Farren doesn't understand.

"We can throw that in, too, but more like a moment where we all confess things that are bothering us without being judged. We're just going to lay it all before the Lord," Dot boldly says.

"Well, just don't make me the first one to come forward whatever you do!" Farren pleads.

"No, sweetie, you come forward as the Spirit leads you. Yep, before you and your family leave the Virgin Islands, the 'captives will be set free!'"

# Chapter 19
## Life Has Its Challenges

Dot, Marlin and all the camp counselors really went out of their way to make the campgrounds look very festive for their closing ceremony. A giant tent with a stage is erected in the center of the grounds with chairs to accommodate speakers and guests, as well as round tables covered with beautiful cloth, floral arrangements, stemware and china adjacent to what will become the buffet table.

Dot has been watching what's been going on from a distance under the tent, but shakes her head in disgust and decides to let George deal with their daughter Debbie, since he was the one who created the horrible attitude she has of thinking she's better than everybody else. Yep, George did that and now let him fix it! Dot continues what she is doing with a smile on her face.

Gloria, Dot, Lucille, Lisa, Faith and Zipporah are under the large tent, busy putting on table cloths and setting floral arrangements on the guest tables as they get ready for the big closing ceremony for the campers tomorrow. Everything looks so beautiful. Each of the ladies is making sure they put their special touches on everything. Lucille insisted on using china and silverware along with stemmed crystal glasses. Gloria thought it was a bit much for an event being held outside on a pig farm but decided to pick her battles and go along with it. Today is a special day for Hope, who had the vision to bring inner city children to the Virgin Islands and work on a farm as a way of transforming their lives, as well as Dot and Marlin, who built the facility to house the young people. The last thing Gloria wants to do is upset Lucille by argue with her about china and crystal goblets; besides, this is a fight she would not win.

Dot and Zipporah certainly do have a lot to say! Lucille notices as she watches them sitting at a table, cutting fresh flowers and making arrangements for Faith and Lisa to put on the tables. Whatever they are talking about looks pretty serious.

"I wonder what the two of them are talking about. Who would ever have thought that the new wife and ex-wife of that dirty dog, lying, cheating George would be sitting in the Virgin Islands chatting like old buddies!" Lucille hopes for some insight from Gloria.

"Nobody but God! You know He's a healing God and He and only He is in the miracle working business. I say you mind your business and let's finish setting these tables," Gloria teases.

"And miss an opportunity to be in their business? Not gonna happen! Hold the fort down while I go over there and see what the hell is going on!"

Lucille sashays over to investigate. Gloria shakes her head, smiling, and continues setting the tables alone.

Dot and Zipporah stop talking abruptly when Lucille arrives in their area.

"Is there something you need, Lucille?" Dot asks.

"No! I just came over here to see what the hell the two of you are talking about. Judging from the look on you guys' faces from across the tent, it looked very serious." Lucille puts her hands on her hips, waiting for a response.

"Uh… Mrs. Nosey, I know you have better things to do than worry about what it looks like over here! We got this, so you can sashay your behind right back over there and finish what you were working on," Dot says, just as Faith comes over to pick up another arrangement for the table.

"It's looking so good, Aunt Dot and Auntie Zip! You ladies really outdid yourselves with these floral arrangements! And Auntie Lucille, what a brilliant and classy idea to use china! Everything is looking so beautiful!" Faith picks up an arrangement, whistling and turns to leave.

"Thanks, darling!" Zipporah says with a big smile.

"Yes, sweetie, everything is looking so lovely," Dot chimes in.

Both Dot and Zipporah look at Lucille, waiting for her to go back to working on her table setting.

"What?" Lucille says.

"What? Take you behind back over there with Gloria and finish setting those tables!" Dot is impatient.

"So, y'all got secrets over here?" Lucille pries.

"Yeah," Dot casually says, not giving up any information.

"So that means you not going to tell me what's up?" Lucille presses.

"Correct!" Dot replies.

"Oh, Dot, she's family and maybe able to help. I mean, Lucille has been with quite a few men in her life, unlike you and I," Zipporah says.

"Is that a compliment or a put down? Now I'm not sure if I even want to get in you heifers' conversation." Lucille turns her face up.

"Good!" Dot retorts, waiting for Lucille to leave.

Lucille takes a seat at the table. "Okay, I'm in. What's going on?"

"I see it's hard to hurt your feelings." Dot smiles.

"I'm a strong woman and your little comments only make me stronger... so what's up?" Lucille leans forward toward the women, waiting for the juicy gossip.

"You tell her, Zip, since you agreed to let her in the business!" Dot suggests.

"Just get to the point, one of you guys! What's up?" Lucille whispers, like she's being let in on a secret.

"It's Georgie," Zipporah sadly says.

"He's not dying, is he?" Lucille blares.

"No, no, no! Nut-ting like dat!" Zipporah calms Lucille down. "It's just dat..."

"What!?" Lucille can't stand the suspense.

"He ting ain't working properly and him is sad," Zipporah slowly reveals.

"His 'ting?'" Lucille struggles to understand.

"He man ting," Zipporah whispers, pointing down to the private area.

Lucille bursts out into non-stop rolling laughter.

Dot and Zipporah watch Lucille cracking up, with serious looks of regret on their faces for letting her in on their conversation.

"Zipporah, I told you it was a bad idea to mention anything to her. Look at her acting like a childish fool. Go on back over there with Gloria and get out of us grown women's conversation." Dot points her finger at Lucille.

"No, no, I'm sorry. It's just that you guys caught me off guard. I mean George was 'King Stud,' swinging that thing all around Atlanta, had the women going wild for it and now you saying it's gone south is just… hell, it's funny, okay?" Lucille whispers.

"Ain't nobody laughing, Lucille. It took a lot for Zipporah to open up about George's erectile dysfunction and the last thing she needs is for you to laugh," Dot says and Zipporah nods in agreement.

"You're both right, and I apologize. Tell me how long has this been going on? I see you two have the little boy, so it couldn't have been all that long since he's been able to get it up," Lucille gingerly says.

"Nehemiah gon be makin' tree years in December. Him six months younger dan de triplets. George been having trouble since we get married. De Viagra was working but now nutting happening; me just lay der waiting and waiting. Me wait so long me just fall asleep and next ting me know it's morning and me husband looking sad at de breakfast table," Zipporah regrets.

"You just lay there? What you doing laying there?" Lucille questions Zipporah.

"Me waiting for he to climb on top of me. Dat's wat me sposed to do, right?" Zipporah whispers like a lost girl.

"Wrong! Zip, there is more than one way to skin a cat! Girl, you jump on top and ride it!" Lucille quietly counsels.

"What the hell is she going to ride if the thing is limp!? That's the craziest advice I ever heard!" Dot brushes Lucille off.

"Lord, help me! I forgot I'm talking to two of George's virgins. You do 'nasty' things before you hop on top. Things that drive the man crazy!" Lucille explains.

Dot and Zipporah look at her like they don't have a clue as to what she's talking about.

"Me darling, we does kiss, and might I add we put our tongues in each other's mouth when we kiss. Now when me first do it, me tink it was the nastiest ting ever, but me get used to it," Zipporah says, shaking her head.

"Well, that was good for a start but you need to take that tongue and move it all around that man's body. I mean get all up in every crack and crevice! Girl, you have got to work that tongue… no place is forbidden!" Lucille says, pointing her finger at Dot and Zipporah as she speaks.

Dot and Zipporah are stunned and lost for words.

Dot finally says, "That sounds like... like something a whore would do. No decent woman is going to put her tongue in places God just didn't create it to go. What other suggestions do you have, because that's just too nasty to even think about." Dot shakes her head in disgust.

"You might be able to learn a little something from a woman of the night! They always have customers and I bet most of them are returning customers!" Lucille conjectures.

"Now me must confess..." Zipporah begins.

"Confess that you used your tongue? Go, girl! Then what's the problem?" Lucille looks confused.

"No, no, me ain't do dat! Oh no. Me want ta confess dat me once watched de sex video when George an me first get married so me would know what ta do but me didn't like watching dem women wearing maid's clothes and carrying whips an tings! Dem just look nasty and fake. And dem men wasn't even dey husband! Me pray for forgiveness den burn de tape."

"Who cares if they were married? You wasn't going to marry them! If you had not burned the tapes, I'd suggest you watch them with George when you get back home. Remind me to see if I still have some of my old tapes I can give you before you go back home to Nevis. And you better watch them," Lucille admonishes.

"Watching pornography is an abomination! God frowns upon that!" Dot yells.

"Now, you see, that's why Sadie took your man from you. I heard that woman's nickname was Deep Throat Sadie!" Lucille whispers.

Dot is furious and it shows on her face. "Lucille, if you don't have anything concrete to offer then may I suggest you take your butt back over there and help Gloria set the tables? I have had enough of your condescending opinions!" Dot sternly says.

"My bad! I'm sorry. Certainly didn't mean to step on any toes. Okay, here's a nugget I'm going to share. Now, this wasn't my situation but let's just say I had a friend who had the same problem you are having, Zipporah, and she and I used to talk. She and her husband tried everything short of her having sex outside of their marriage." Lucille is interrupted before she can make her point.

"Oh, that will never happen. I love Georgie, even if we never have sex again in me life! Sex ain't every ting!" Zipporah makes clear.

"I don't know about that! If it ain't first, then it's a very close second to food and water!" Lucille says, laughing.

"Can you finish the story, Lucille?" Dot jumps in.

"Oh yeah. Anyway, they had tried everything, then my friend got this nasty magazine in the mail and when no one was home, she went through it out of curiosity and lo and behold, she saw this device that looked like a hard plastic tube with a hose and hand pump on it and this thing; kind of look like a bong... you know, the clear water pipe we used to smoke weed out of in college."

Both Dot and Zipporah shake their heads, bewildered.

"Okay, work with me here. So, my girl orders the thing and trust me, she was a nervous wreck waiting for it to come. She wondered if the mailman would know what was in the package... suppose it went to the wrong address and her neighbor got it... what if her church members found out. This woman worried me every day with her concerns about this thing; I was one happy camper when it finally came! Then there was another problem," Lucille says, sounding exhausted.

"Wa happen? De neighbors dem find out?" Zipporah asks with anticipation.

"I bet they sent the thing without instructions!" Dot counters.

"None of that. The thing came with great directions, pictures and everything! The problem was her husband thought she had lost her mind if she thought he was about to stick his crown jewels in some plastic pipe," Lucille animatedly says.

This time, Dot and Zipporah burst out in laughter.

Gloria hollers from across the room, "I don't know what's so funny, but Lucille you'd better get back over here and tend to your project."

"Hold your horses, I'm coming! So you ladies think that's funny?"

Zipporah and Dot both answer at the same time. "Yes!"

"Me not sure if George would want to put he ting in dat tube either," Zipporah says.

"Don't worry about that, Zipporah. If he's anything like the George I was married to, trust me, he would put his whole body in the tube and squeeze the pump at the same time if he thought it would help his sex life," Dot says with conviction.

"I tink you have a point dere!" Zipporah says, after pondering what Dot says.

"So did the pump thing work?" Dot asks.

"After about a year of trying to get him to use it, he finally decided to try it on their anniversary. Well, honey, the thing worked so good, Rev had the hardest time getting his manhood out of the tube! The thing blew up so fat!" Lucille explains.

"Did you say, 'Rev?' As in our sister's deceased husband?" Dot inquires, puzzled.

"Girl, I don't know what you're talking about. I know you didn't hear me say, 'Rev!'" Lucille nervously tries to cover up her slip of the tongue.

"Me does 'ear you say, 'Rev,' just as clear!" Zipporah innocently says.

"Just shut up, the both of you! And if I ever hear either of you repeat what you *think* I just said, I will hire some very bad men to come and rough you up!" Lucille walks away quickly to go and help Gloria.

Zipporah and Dot laugh so hard Gloria wants to know what's going on.

"I gon ask Sister Gloria if she can tell me how ta purchase one of dem penis pipes," Zipporah says in between laughter.

"And have some very bad men come and rough you up?" Dot asks, rolling with laughter. The woman are now hugging each other and laughing together.

"Maybe I'd better go over there and see what's so funny! Now they've got me interested," Gloria says as Lucille picks up a beautiful china plate out of a very well-packed box.

"Just mind your business and let's finish dressing these tables!" Lucille dismisses her sister's curiosity.

Dot and Zipporah continue talking and sharing their experiences while working on their centerpieces.

"Dot, why Debbie all lockup on de porch wit de chiren like dat? She need to let dem run around in de yard," Zipporah puzzles.

"Now, that is one special child. George created a monster in Debbie. From the day I brought that child home from the hospital, her daddy has spoiled her reckless! And being married to Byron hasn't help one bit. Debbie went straight from her daddy to her husband and both guard and protect her like she's their trophy prize. The girl has never had a chance to use her own brain or experience life outside of those two men's protection. Now she hovers over her children and protects them from everything ranging from a terrorist attack to a mosquito bite!"

Dot shakes her head in disgust as she watches her daughter sitting on the porch fanning from the heat.

"Looks like Georgie goin over dere ta say some ting ta she," Zipporah observes.

"This should be interesting. Oh, look at little Nehemiah following his daddy! Zipporah, he is the sweetest boy. Do you know he came up to me and gave me the biggest hug and he called me Nana just like my grandchildren? He definitely has your sweet spirit!" Dot comments.

"Him is such a blessing in Georgie and me lives. I don't know what we would do wit out he. He daddy is so proud. God is good, my friend... God is good!" Zipporah rejoices with a big smile on her face.

"Apparently George is confronting her about sitting on the porch... he's moving that board that has the children on lock down," Dot says.

"Debbie, why are you sitting here all locked up on this porch with these babies? Let these kids run in the yard!" George yells.

"No, Daddy! Put that board back. We don't want the babies in the yard. There are too many animals out there and they might catch something," Debbie whines.

"Catch what?" George looks at her like she's crazy as Brianna, Brice and Byron, Jr. take off running toward the animals grazing in the yard by the side of the house.

"I don't know, Bird Flu or Ebola, I don't know!" Debbie cries.

"Debbie, there is no Bird Flu or Ebola on this farm."

"Daddy! Daddy! Byron doesn't want..."

"De gil look like she gon have a heart attack! Maybe you should go and help, Dot," Zipporah suggests.

"Not me! I'm going to sit right here with you and finish these centerpieces and watch what promises to be great entertainment," Dot laughs.

"Okay! Me gon watch, too. Dis 'ere might be better dan watching me favorite television show!" Zipporah snickers.

George ignores Debbie and keeps walking toward the area where the sheep and goats are grazing, following his son and excited grandchildren. Debbie has a look of fear on her face she races to keep up with her dad and the toddlers. Just as she is about to reach the area where George is allowing the kids to pet the baby lambs, Debbie sees her older daughters on a horse being led by Marlin and Roy. Debbie is in shock. The girls are laughing and begging the men to let go of the reins.

"Now she's distracted by seeing her daughters on the horses. I'm so glad they are finally getting to enjoy something on the farm," Dot says, smiling.

"Let go, Uncle Roy! We can do it!" Little Faith screams with excitement.

Just as Roy is about to let go of the reins, Debbie screams, "Get my children off those damn horses before they fall! Now!"

"Me tink ya speak too fast! De mudder bout ta make dem get off de horses! Aw, too bad, dem look so happy," Zipporah sadly says as Lisa comes up and takes a group of floral arrangements from the table.

George is shocked at what he is hearing; he approaches the men and the girls on the horses. Little Faith's smile turns to a frown. Farrah and Fuchsia are pouting and refuse to get off the horse.

"We are fine, Mother! Please!" Farrah screams.

"Are you crazy? If you fall and crack your neck, who do think is going to save you?" Debbie screams.

"Jesus!" Freda yells. "Don't spoil it for us, Mother!"

"Debbie, we're not going to let the girls fall. Relax!" Roy says.

"The only way I'm going to be relaxed is when my girls are on this ground and not sitting on top of a million-pound horse! Get down now!"

"Sweetie! The men are not going to let anything happen to the girls. Calm down." George intercedes on behalf of his granddaughters.

"Daddy, all of this is too much for me. Byron is not going to be happy! Please just let me go back on the porch with my babies and you girls go over there under the tent and participate in the Bible study your dad is leading with the other teenagers. Now!" Debbie asserts.

"I don't think so, Mother. I'm going to ride this horse and when I'm finished, we can talk. Uncle Roy, you can let go of my reins. I know how to ride a horse. I've done it in Peru, Venezuela, and at school in Georgia. Mother, I suggest you calm yourself down and try and have a good time today." Little Faith takes the reins from surprised Roy and rides off.

"So I guess you guys are going to be defiant like your older sister too?" Debbie screams at the remaining three girls.

"No, Mother," Freda says as she attempts to get off the horse but is stopped by her grandfather.

"Would you men please continue showing the girls how to ride?" George boldly disregards Debbie.

"Daddy! I'm their mother!" Debbie is stunned.

"And I'm *your* father! Let's walk!" George leads Debbie back to the porch. They notice Nehemiah, Brice and Brianna talking to the baby goats and Byron, Jr. giggling, kissing and hugging the baby lamb along the way.

"Get my children now!" Debbie screams and heads back to the porch.

"Did me 'ear she say she their mother!" Zipporah asks Dot.

"That's what I hear. And I also heard George pull rank and say he's her father! You go, George! Looks like things might be changing."

Dot and Zipporah high-five each other.

"Oh me God, de little triplet is kissing de sheep and trying ta climb on he back." Zipporah laughs.

"Well, would you look at that? I have never seen that child so happy. He's even talking! Isn't it amazing the effect that animal is having on the child?" Dot excitedly says.

"Now, Dot, me ain't want ta say nut ting but we is family... wa wong wit de child? Me does see he banging he head an him just look like him dere but de lights ain't on. Please forgive me if me over stepping me boundaries," Zipporah gingerly states.

"No, no, you're right in your observation. I see the same thing and when I tried to talk about it with Debbie, she brushed me off. Farren says her father is in denial and doesn't want to get help for the child because he's afraid the doctors will try and medicate the little boy and give him a label. Can you believe that?"

"Pride comes before de fall!" Zipporah reflects.

"Oooh, look, the daddy is coming from his Bible study over by the stage area to get the child off the sheep. He doesn't look happy!"

Dot and Zipporah watch with excitement.

Byron steps quickly to remove his son Byron, Jr. from the baby sheep he is trying to climb on. Junior is having the time of his life until his dad grabs him up in his arms in one swoop.

"What is wrong with you? Don't you know those animals carry germs that can kill you?" Byron screams at his son as he approaches the house where George and Debbie are settling down on the porch with the other children. Byron puts the child on the porch and slides the board across the steps so he can't leave the restricted area.

"Honey, you have to watch him. Didn't we agree the children would not be allowed to roam on this farm?" Byron reprimands his wife.

"I know, Byron, but my dad thinks it's a good idea to let the children run in the yard," Debbie explains.

"Byron, you can't keep these kids confined to the porch. There is so much for them to see on the farm," George continues.

"George, you handle your son and let me handle my children. Now I don't want them out there mingling with the animals and that's that! So please respect my rules!"

Byron takes off back toward the stage area where his students are waiting for him to continue their Bible study.

"George doesn't look happy. I guess Byron had the last word," Dot says. Zipporah sadly shakes her head.

Faith and Lisa approach the table where Zipporah and Dot are.

"Why are Debbie and the kids sitting on the porch?" Faith asks.

"It's a long story! You know how special your cousin is," Dot replies.

"Yep! Sounds like dictator Bryan has her and the kids on lockdown!" Faith sighs.

"That's a grown woman! Since when do we women have to do everything our husbands tell us to do? Now you know Billy would never have me and my kids sitting on a porch!" Lisa protests.

"Well, all-you does know de woman is de first lady at she church, and in dat position, de wife must be submissive ta de husband," Zipporah explains.

Everyone looks at Zipporah like she's speaking Greek.

"Uh, Auntie Zip, things have changed a bit since the last century! Woman are allowed to vote, go to college, hold jobs and tell their husbands, 'No!'" Lisa high-fives Faith.

"Me know all dat, but me just saying dat dis is de life dem does live and who are we ta criticize?" Zipporah shrugs her shoulders.

"Lord, I'm so happy my husband doesn't think like they did before the days of woman suffrage!" Faith says.

"Maybe you ladies could take Debbie out and have a chat with her?" Dot pleads.

"Been there, done that and trust me this is no small problem. Debbie didn't just get like that overnight, and it's going to take a lot of prayer and counseling to break that stronghold on her. Besides, who says she's not happy?" Faith explains.

"De girl don't look happy ta me. Look dere!" Zipporah points to the porch.

Everyone looks at Debbie looking miserable and George patting her hand trying to console her.

"You have a point, Auntie Zip," Faith agrees.

"From here, it definitely looks like depression. Been there!" Lisa exclaims.

"We only have about ten more tables, ladies, then we can work on decorating the stage," Faith reminds the ladies of the task at hand.

"I think your Aunt Lucille made a skirt for the stage. Check with her, sweetie," Dot says.

"Okay. Everything looks so elegant! We did good!" Lisa brags as she and Faith pick up more flower arrangements and leave.

"Looks like the girls are back with the horses," Dot observes.

"So soon! Dem just leave," Zipporah says as she wraps a bunch of flowers together with a beautiful ribbon.

"They don't look happy," Dot notices.

The girls are helped off the horses by Marlin, Roy and Wally. Byron sees his daughters getting off the horses and once again excuses himself from his Bible study to deal with his family issues.

Zipporah and Dot watch as Byron races from the stage area toward the farmhouse to have a few words with his girls. The girls walk toward the farmhouse with their heads hung down.

Debbie greets them with a sour face. "And what are my disobedient daughters doing back here so soon?"

"I know I didn't see you girls getting off those horses! What did we say about mingling with these nasty animals on this farm? Debbie, didn't you remind them?" Byron sternly asks his wife.

"Calm down, Byron, I'm sure all these animals have had their shots. You're overreacting, son."

"Like I said before, George, I have my rules!" Byron says.

"I told them not to ride the horses and they blatantly disobeyed me!" Debbie cries.

"Hey, we're right here," Freda quietly says!

"Young lady, have you lost your mind talking to your mother like that!" Byron grabs Freda by the arm and reprimands her.

"Ouch, Dad! You're hurting me," Freda screams.

"Byron! You're hurting the child," George interjects.

"George, with all due respect, this is my family and if I need your advice, I will ask for it."

Byron lets go of Freda's arm. George shakes his head in disbelief.

"Dad, do you think we all should stop for a moment and pray?" Younger Faith asks.

"No, you guys go inside and I will talk to you girls later." Byron dismisses them.

"No, I need them here!" Debbie asserts, surprising Byron.

"Okay, find a spot on the porch.

Debbie, tell Byron what you told me," George encourages.

"I'm your puppet," Debbie sadly states.

"My puppet? Where on earth did you get that foolishness from?! You're my Godly wife."

"I overheard the girls talking last night and one of them said, 'It's like Mommy doesn't have a brain,' and the other one said maybe they should take me to OZ and see if the wizard could give me a brain. Then I heard Farren say, 'Mommy's just Daddy's puppet... he pulls all the strings and she moves in whatever direction he tells her to go!' Byron, they are right!" Debbie sobs.

Byron turns toward his daughters, who are sitting on the porch with their backs leaning against the banister, looking surprised.

"Hey, I just agreed. Freda was the one who started the conversation," Farren defends herself.

"Wow! You guys are just going to throw me under the bus like that when you know all of us hate the way… never mind," Freda feels betrayed.

"Never mind what, Freda? Darling, please don't be afraid to talk. We desperately need to hear what you have to say," George encourages.

"Not really! These are children, George, and until they start paying bills up in my house, I don't really care what they think. Now you guys need to apologize to your mother and ask God to forgive you for saying such awful things. Apologize now!" Byron demands.

The girls are quiet.

"Byron, I think we should defer this conversation until when we get up to Gloria's house this evening. This is really not the time or place. Besides, it looks like there are more immediate issues that need to be addressed." George offers guidance.

"Like what? There is nothing more important than my family!" Byron counters.

"True. However, you have those young people waiting for you under the tent to finish their Bible study," George points out.

"Right, right! You girls come and join us in the Bible study and we will continue our family conversation at your grandmother's house later. Is that all right with you, honey?"

"Sure. I'll just stay here with the little ones until you're finished," Debbie resigns.

"Okay, sweetie. Please try and feel better. Don't worry, God is in the working-out business," Byron says.

Byron kisses his wife as he and his daughters head toward the tent to continue Bible study, leaving George to comfort Debbie.

As the Bible study resumes, Khalid poses a question in response to Byron's previous comment. "But, dude, how you gon say we shouldn't have sex until we get married when preachers be getting it at home *and* on the down-low!"

"First of all, young man, I prefer you call me, 'Pastor' and not, 'Dude.' Now to answer your question, yes, even people of the faith mess up, but thank God for forgiveness. No one is perfect, but we must strive every day to be more like Jesus. He's the only one who's perfect and a true friend who will stick closer to you than a brother," Byron explains.

"Camille and I are close friends who stick together in any kind of weather, right, girl?" Denisha says to her best friend.

"You know that's right! Had me following your behind all the way to Hawaii when I couldn't even spell it!" The two ladies burst out laughing and high-five each other.

Byron shakes his head at their ignorance.

"I sure could have used Jesus the other day when everybody turned against me, even my best friend who I called my brother!" Dante says, looking in Khalid's direction.

"I'm sure Jesus was there all the time, young man, sending intercessors to act on your behalf," Byron says in a comforting tone.

"Intercessors? What's that?" Dante is confused.

"Your guardian angel!" Denisha speaks up.

"Intercessors are people who stand in the gap and protect you, validate your character, protect you in times of trouble," Byron explains.

"Oh, you mean like Mr. Fitzroy, Mr. Roy, Mr. Wally and Mr. Marlon… men who believed in me and didn't listen to a bunch of wack mess! Yeah, they were truly my intercessors." Dante affirms.

"You got that right! Mr. Fitzroy saved my life!" Denisha testifies.

"And don't forget made us a little bit richer in the process!" Camille hollers and high-fives Denisha again.

Byron cuts them off. "See, son, you just named four men who allowed God to use them on your behalf."

"My Nana is my intercessor. She listens to me and doesn't judge me. I can tell her my deepest secrets and know that they are safe with her," Farren blurts out.

Byron is surprised but does not acknowledge his daughter's input.

Khalid moves on to another subject. "What about all those churches on every corner collecting money and ain't nobody doing nothing for the people in the neighborhood! They running a business, pimping the poor folks and then they go back to their big-behind houses in their fresh new cars that the poor people bought for them. That's messed up!" Khalid is moving his hands like a rapper.

"You know you right, brother! Me lights were cut off, de water bill had a turn off notice and de gas in me cylinder was empty! Me go to de pastor of me church and de man tell me him would be praying for me. I asked he how was dat going to help turn me lights back on and get de water bill paid before Friday when dem come ta cut me off? He tell me dat me had to have the faith of a mustard seed! A mustard seed? Da man almost get cussed but me realized me was in de church so me just tell he ta go to hell and me leave." Camille relates a difficult experience in her life.

Everyone laughs except Byron.

"That's messed up!" Freda screams, laughing at Camille's story.

"So, did your utilities get cut off?" Byron asks.

"No, but only because me girl here does give me de money ta pay de bill and me pay she back when me get paid!" Camille proudly brags.

"So, seems like you did have the faith and you were sent an intercessor from God," Byron resolves.

"Me ain't know 'bout dat! 'Cause when me go to the house of God, de pastor turn me away wit not even a dollar for me troubles. It's me sinner friend dat help me!" Camille contests.

"Yep! Me help she, but me girl ain't never pay me back! And don't be calling me no sinner!" Denisha says, laughing.

"Now that sounds like a real friend," Dante says to Camille and Denisha.

"So going back to your question Dante, the Bible teaches that you don't need to worry son, because whatsoever a man sows, that he shall reap!" Byron points out loudly.

"Can you please explain that, Pastor Byron?" Charles asks.

"You mean, Mr. Intelligent, camera operator, honor roll student doesn't know what the pastor is saying?" Khalid teases and this irritates Dante but he doesn't say anything.

"I'm very aware of the words he is using, but I've never heard them used in that context and that's what I'm having difficulty understanding," Charles explains.

"'I'm having difficulty understanding!' Nigga, please!" Khalid taunts, flapping his hands.

"Young man, we don't use the word 'Nigger' here, so please refrain from using it again. Now if you have something meaningful to contribute we're open, but if name-calling and using degrading words is all you want to do, I'm going to have to ask you to excuse yourself from the Bible study."

"Pastor, his vocabulary is very limited, so forgive him," Dante interjects.

"What, Nig... Man! Who you talking about? You done got with you little half-breed homo friend and now you think you better than me?" Khalid confronts, moving close up in Dante's face.

"All right, all right, stand down! Back it up, young man." Byron stands in between the two boys.

"Naw! He's been riding my butt ever since me and Charles became friends and I'm sick of it!" Dante is defiant.

"You mean Charlesetta!" Khalid says, laughing.

This really angers Dante.

"Excuse me, but please allow me to put these ugly rumors to rest once and for all. I am not gay, I have never had any thoughts of being with a man. I admire Dante because he is a very caring friend who really appreciates me teaching him how to operate a camera and do editing. The same skills I offered to teach you, but you refused. Dante has shared with me music that he's written that's close to his heart and tells the story of the community he lives in; stories I can only imagine because they are not part of the world I live in. I find the lyrics very interesting and would like to help him create a video to go them. So, if you would kindly stop calling me names, I would appreciate it! I am an artist!" Charles defends himself and Dante.

"Some of my best friends are gay and I don't think name-calling is cool. You should not judge a person by their sexual orientation," Little Faith states her point of view.

"Excuse me, young lady! God does not approve of homosexual lifestyles!" Byron chastises his daughter Little Faith for her statement.

"God also doesn't approve of people lying and stealing either! So what's your point, Dad?" Fuchsia counters.

"I don't need to hear from you girls, okay?" Byron admonishes his daughters.

"You invited us to this Bible study and now you don't want us to talk?" Freda questions her dad, who gives her an angry look.

"Well, as I said, I'm not a homosexual and really don't care what you think, Khalid," Charles stresses his point.

"Yeah, right, homo!" Khalid yells, and turns to walk away just as Dante punches him in the face.

"Help!" Byron screams as the boys tussle on the ground, causing many of the chairs and tables with glass vases holding the beautiful centerpieces the ladies made to turn over and crash to the ground along with much of the stemware and china. Camille and Denisha, who are sitting close to the brawl, barely manage to jump out of the way.

"What the heck!" Fuchsia screams as she backs away from the fight just before they move in her direction.

"Stop it! Stop it now! Please stop it!" Little Faith is in tears as the boys continue fighting like enemies, thrashing the place. Byron tries to break them up but is mistakenly kicked in the face and his mouth is bleeding as he screams for help again.

Dot, Lucille, Gloria, Zipporah, Faith and Lisa are in shock. They can't believe what they are seeing. All their hard work goes crashing to the floor.

Marlin and Roy see what is going on from across the yard where they just finished putting the horses back in the barn. They run to help, as does George, who quickly removes the board from the porch. The men manage to help break up the boys. Byron has blood running out of his mouth and spits on the ground where he sees part of his broken tooth lying in the blood. Marlin and George hold Dante back while Wally and Roy hold Khalid.

"What is going on here, guys?" Roy demands just as Fitzroy pulls up to the farm in his van with the two boys' mothers, Rochelle and Tae, along with Kesha, Sean and Mookie. They are all wearing their bathing suits. Sean and Mookie are carrying rubber inner tubes and wearing snorkel masks. Their smiles quickly turn to frowns. Rochelle and Tay race over to where their sons are being restrained by the men.

"This is not part of the plan!" Roy scolds as he turns to notice Gloria crying and holding a large floral arrangement and broken vase that she picked up off the ground. Lucille, who is in shock, picks up a broken china plate and just stares at it. Gloria cries and Roy walks over and takes her in his arms and comforts her.

"It looks like a hurricane came through here!" Fitzroy is dismayed!

"I can't believe what I'm seeing! We worked so hard!" Faith says.

"Now you see, this is how Atlanta ghetto folks roll!" Lisa accuses.

Faith gives her a look that dares her to say another word.

"Oh me God, looks like de tent is leaning! Somebody needs to knock de stake down in de ground or it's gon fall," Zipporah yells.

"It's nothing but the devil! I don't know how you guys thought these hooligans could be helped in a few weeks!" Byron says as he wipes the blood from his mouth and picks up his broken tooth from the ground.

"That's a terrible thing to say, Byron! These boys have come a very long way!" Dot sets the record straight.

"Me just glad dem didn't have a gun or we all could be dead!" Camille screams.

"Explain to me right now what happened here or I'm going to haul the two of you off to jail!" Fitzroy sternly says.

Marlin secures the tent, shaking his head in disbelief.

"He pissed because I talked about him and his little homo boyfriend!" Khalid fumes.

Dante tries to start fighting again but Fitzroy jumps in front of him.

"Have I made myself clear? Fight again and I'm going to have to take you into town and book you. Don't say another word!" Fitzroy says.

Dante mutters unintelligibly under his breath, then finally speaks aloud with tears rolling down his face.. "Khalid, tell everybody who the real homo is! Tell them, man!"

"I don't know what you talking about!" Khalid has an obvious attitude.

"Yeah! Tell them how Day-Day used to tap your ass! And don't lie, because I saw him doing it to you in the alley around by Teaka and them's back porch! You was hollering like a little bitch! Tell them, Khalid! Tell them!" Dante is crying and ready to fight.

"Oh me God, dis 'ere is better den going shopping or watching *Empire*!" Camille says, popping her finger in excitement.

"Gil, dis 'ere is sad! Look at de boy mudder in shock! De woman is hurting from hearing such tings bout she son. Me feel like crying!" Denisha sadly says.

"Yeah, tell them who the real homo is, Khalid!" Dante screams.

Fitzroy grabs Dante by the arm and leads him away from the campground to the van with his mother Tae running to keep up.

Khalid runs toward the cabin with his mother sprinting behind, screaming his name!

"My God, we only went to the beach and we come back to this confusion! It's confirmed; I know I'm not going back to Atlanta – there's too much craziness there for me!" Kesha announces as her son and his friend look sadly on.

"Oh Lord, soon come!" Gloria prays after hearing what Dante has disclosed.

# Chapter 20
## Healing

Dot, Marlin, Debbie, Byron and their children are sitting around in the kitchen and living room, talking loudly about the events that happened at the farm. Byron is holding an ice pack on his badly swollen face and his broken tooth sits on the counter in a sandwich bag.

"Dad, you really should put that broken tooth in a glass of milk until you get to a dentist," Little Faith suggests.

"Honey, that milk will be sour before I get to a dentist, because you know I'm not letting any of these backward people come anywhere close to my mouth."

"I'm sure they have some okay dentists here on the island. Fitzroy and Faith can recommend one," Debbie says, comforting her husband.

"They probably got their degrees from Kmart or some no name online college! No sir, just everyone start packing, because I've had enough and we are going home! I'll email my dentist and see how soon he can squeeze me in."

"Leaving? Dad we haven't spent any time with Nana!" Little Faith cries.

"I guess when I get to heaven, God will tell me why I was born into this family!" Freda screams and runs to the bedroom.

"Are you serious, Dad?" Fuchsia cries.

"I'm staying!" Farren defiantly declares and runs out of the room.

"Get back here, Farren and Freda, now!" Byron yells to the girls who have left the room.

"Dad, think about what you're saying," Little Faith pleads as Freda and Farren return, standing in the doorway leading to the bedroom and crying.

"Byron, Dot has been looking forward ta spend time wit de chirin. Maybe dem could stay an we put dem on de plane back home later?" Marlin suggests.

Dot doesn't say a word, but the sadness she is feeling shows in her face.

"No way! And the word is 'children' not 'chirin!' I can see my *children* staying here and when they get back to Atlanta, they will be talking like some ignorant bush people! Debbie, start packing the little ones up and you girls, I don't want to hear another word from you! This has been the trip from hell; so round up you stuff and do as I say. We're leaving here on the first thing flying tomorrow morning!" Byron lays down the law.

"Byron! Are you hearing yourself? You just insulted my mother's husband, who was so kind to pay for all nine of us to fly here First Class on vacation, open their house up to us and have shown us nothing but love since we arrived and you talk to them like that! You have managed to terrorize our daughters and completely make their vacation the real vacation from hell. What are you thinking? This is not right. We are people of God and look at how we're acting," Debbie says, shaking her head in disbelief.

"Don't trouble your head, me daughter. Me just grateful me sweetie Dot get ta see she grands for de time she have," Marlin humbly says.

Debbie pats his hand and continues speaking her mind. Come over here, Freda."

Debbie calmly summons her daughter who approaches her mother with her head down. Debbie hugs her. Freda is surprised.

"I love you and I want you to know you didn't pick the wrong family. God knew exactly where he wanted you to be placed. Nobody is perfect and I'm talking about your father and me as well. Farren, Fuchsia, Freda and Little Faith, I need you guys to know that what you all said about me being you daddy's puppet and not having a brain really hurt, but God knew it was exactly what I needed to hear," Debbie reveals.

"They were out of place saying that, honey, and they will be punished!" Byron retorts.

"No, they won't. Byron, we need to ask God to forgive us for not being the parents He called us to be. We have been so consumed with our ministry that we just put our children into a one-size-fits-all box, ignoring their different personalities and gifts. I don't want my girls in a box anymore. I lived all my life in a pretty little box with a bow on it wrapped up so nicely for everyone to admire. Byron, I want out of that box! I need to find out who I am. The girls were right and I thank them for bring to light the fact that their mother needs to find out exactly who she is." Debbie smiles and hugs her daughters.

"You're being silly! You're my wife… the mother of my children… the First Lady of my church! Isn't that enough?"

Dot and Marlin look on as Byron doesn't have a clue.

"Did you just hear yourself, Byron? Everything is about you – *your* wife, *your* children, *your* church – there's no *me* in the picture at all. It's high time you realized there is a 'you' and a 'me,' and the two will have to work together in order for there to be balance in our lives."

"Honey, we can discuss this once we're back in Atlanta. What do you say?" Byron pleads.

"We came here to spend two weeks with Mother and Marlin and that's exactly what we are going to do," Debbie calmly says.

"Debbie, are you being defiant?" Byron asks.

"No, I'm exercising my first example of the '*me*' principle. I love you but we're staying because it's the right thing to do. Now, honey, if you want to go home, then we'll see you when we get back."

"Yes!" Freda celebrates.

"You see, you're teaching them to be disrespectful! Do the 'yes' thing again, Freda, and you'll find yourself in trouble," Byron reprimands his daughter.

"Sorry, Dad. I'm just excited we're getting to stay," Freda humbly says.

"Well, that's not settled yet. Your mother and I still have to talk this over," Byron confidently says.

"Marlin, let's go out on the veranda and let them talk," Dot says, taking Marlin by the hand and turning to leave.

"No, Mother, I'd like you and my stepdad to stay. You guys are our family and weather Byron knows it or not, we need you guy's wisdom and guidance." Debbie looks at her husband.

"Fine, fine, fine! If that's what you want. I don't understand what guidance you will get from them that I can't provide for my family." Byron shrugs his shoulders.

"Are you sure, Debbie?" Dot questions.

"Yes! Why don't we all move to the living room. This is a good time to talk, while the little ones are napping."

Everyone follows Debbie into the adjacent living room, taking a seat.

"I can't think of a better place for healing to take place than here in the Virgin Islands. I think it will be symbolic to starting over again... like being a born-again virgin, for the lack of a better phrase. Now I'm going to start with my first born, Little Faith. Mommy knows about your boyfriend Yusef."

Faith's mouth is wide-open, ready to defend herself.

Debbie continues, "Stop! Just close your mouth before you say something that is not true!"

"Busted!" Freda whispers.

"As-salamu alaykum!" Fuchisa quietly teases and Debbie gives her a stern look.

"Yusef! As in a Muslim name?" Byron is alarmed.

"Yes, and he's just a friend!" Faith cries.

"That's not what he said to me," Debbie casually counters.

"First of all, young lady, who gave you permission to have a... a boyfriend or whatever you want to call it and especially a Muslim! You're coming out of that school right away! Debbie, I told you we never should have let her stay in the dorms!" Byron is pacing and talking loud.

"Honey, sit down and relax. The only way I see this family moving forward is for us to bring our skeletons out of the closet," Debbie responds.

"Mom, is that you?" Fuchsia has a puzzled look on her face.

"It's a new day, sweetie. You mother has been living in a bubble way too long and you guys popped that bubble! It's time for a change!" Debbie boldly shares.

"But there is absolutely nothing wrong with our lives! We are one big happy Christian family," Byron says, feeling frustrated.

"Who said we were happy? I'm not happy! All I see is fake, fake, fake!" Farren says in a low voice.

"What are you talking about, little lady? And let's back it up; I'm still stuck on my oldest daughter dating a Muslim! Debbie, please tell me it isn't so. Where did you get this foolish information from?" Byron queries.

Little Faith is quiet.

"The young man called me. He said he's been calling Faith's cellphone and it's just going to voicemail. He was concerned that something might have happened to her, so he white-paged us; that's the computer version of directory assistance and got our church and home phone numbers. I talked to him just before we left to come here and he sounds like a very caring, nice young man who is looking forward to meeting us," Debbie matter-of-factly says.

"And polar bears will be wearing coats in hell first! Okay, I'm having trouble here and I need you to confirm that this boy a Muslim-Muslim or just has one of those modern day names, Faith? Answer me now!" Byron demands.

"Yes, Dad, he is a Muslim," Faith confesses.

"Then you must know whatever this is the two of you think you have going on ends right here and right now! Do you understand me, young lady!?"

"Byron, you're upsetting her. Let's drop it down a notch. Please," Dot says.

"Excuse me? I am a Christian! My family is Christian and my daughters and sons will not date Muslims! This boy could be a future Jihadist!"

"Daddy! He's nothing like that!" Faith clarifies.

"You don't know that. Every time one of these crazy people comes out of the closet and kills a bunch of folks, when they interview their neighbors the first thing they say is 'he was such a nice person... I never would have thought he was capable of doing something like that!' Young lady, we believe in the Word of God; that is in the Holy Bible not the Koran! This is a slap in the face. It ends now!" Byron points his finger at Faith and heads toward the front door to go outside and cool off.

Marlin jumps in front of him, blocking his way. "Me don't tink you need to leave just yet. All de skeletons ain't out de closet yet."

"Bushman, you need to move out of my way! I need to go for a walk. This is too much for me right now!" Byron says.

"Marlin's right, Byron. Don't leave. We need you here… your family needs you here," Dot entreats.

"Me know you vexed, but please stay, me friend," Marlin says.

Byron returns back to the living room and Debbie continues.

"Freda, the gig is up… I know you're smoking weed and that has to stop! Don't look around at your sisters, because they didn't rat you out. I've smelled it on your clothes. Now I know young people smoke this stuff and most of them often experiment with harder drugs sooner or later, so I'm nipping this in the bud!"

Freda is shocked. Dot is shaking her head.

"Did I just hear you say my little girl smokes weed?" Byron can't believe what he's hearing, and he falls down on the couch, holding his head.

"Mom, you have the wrong person," Freda squirms!

"Don't lie to me, Freda! Didn't I say this is the time for healing? If we confess our sins, God will be gracious to forgive us of them… so now is the time healing can start!" Debbie sternly says.

"But, Mom!" Freda tries to defend herself but is cut off by her sister Fuchsia.

"Mom, you probably smelled smoke on her because she was standing close to me when I was smoking."

"Well, I'm glad you didn't let your sister take the blame! Oh, you were next, young lady, because I found a pipe in your jeans when I was doing the laundry! Seeing that thing broke my heart! The smoking stops, Fuchsia!" Debbie says to her daughter.

"It's not like I have a habit or anything... I can stop whenever I want to. It's just when things aren't going right with our family, it's a soothing escape," Freda explains.

"Lord Jesus! What else? First I find out that my daughter is dating a future terrorist and now I'm learning that my middle child is on drugs! Lord, where have I failed you!" Byron cries out.

"Dad, please relax yourself before you send your blood pressure up," Faith says to her father.

"Yes, honey, please," Debbie seconds.

"Relax? We're not exactly talking about our children having problems with math or science; this is some serious stuff, Debbie!" Byron continues to cup his head in his hands, trying to understand and find relief.

"Moving on. Byron, I met with the counselors at Farren's school the other day and they are concerned that..."

"That what!" Byron screams.

"Please let me finish. They are concerned that Farren is suffering from depression, and we should look into getting help for her," Debbie discloses.

"Mom! You said we would handle this and you would not bring Dad into it! You know how he feels about doctors putting labels on us! Mom, you promised!" Farren cries.

"Oh, sweetie. I can't keep something like this from your dad, and trust me, we are going to get help for you just like we planned. Come here and give your momma a hug."

Debbie hugs and kisses her daughter to reassure her that she is there standing by her side.

"Debbie, you know those doctors are just going to load Farren down with medication and… and give her some crazy diagnosis and title that will follow her for the rest of her life! Jesus will fix it! Honey, think about it, please!" Byron begs.

"I've thought about if long and hard, Byron. Not only will we seek help for Farren's depression, but we are going to get help for Byron, Jr. We are doing a disservice to our children by not dealing with their physical as well as mental health. God gave us wisdom to know when it's time to seek help, and we will continue to seek His guidance through much prayer and research. We owe it to our children. Don't worry, darling, we will get through this. God did not bring us this far to leave us or forsake us and remember, He never said life would be easy," Debbie calmly says.

"I wholeheartedly agree. Your father and I are living proof that God is a God of second chances. Look at what He's done for George and Zipporah and Marlin and me," Dot says, smiling and offering words of encouragement.

"Oh no, you don't!" Byron points his finger at Dot and Marlin, who are standing next to each other.

"Oh no, you don't what?" Dot asks with a puzzled look on her face.

"Do not use your situation, because God is nowhere up in you guy's relationship! God makes it clear in the Bible that he is against divorce and any man who marries a divorced woman is committing adultery. You two are adulterers! So don't try and sugar coat your union together! You should have stayed with your husband George!" Byron says without hesitation.

"Oh my God! You need to apologize, Byron!" Debbie says, shocked at the words that just came out of her husband's mouth.

"Dad! That was so mean," Farren cries.

"Say one more word against me and me sweetie and me gon throw your ignorant behind over de balcony! Just say one more word!" Marlin approaches Byron.

"Marlin! Don't give what he said any attention. God knows our hearts and if we are living an adulterers' life then I thank God for forgiveness and grace!" Dot calmly says.

Farren starts to cry. "Why is daddy being so mean?"

"Okay! Enough! The enemy is alive and he in here attacking us like a hungry roaring lion trying to destroy this family! Everybody just stop and be quiet for a moment and recognize!

"Lord, your word clearly says where two or more are gathered in your name, there you are in the mist. Lord, we welcome you here and we call out the name Aba Father! We are under attack by the enemy who comes to rob, steal and destroy! The enemy is a liar and the truth is not in him! Satan, we rebuke you in the name of Jesus and we command you flee from here! We are the children of the Most High God, we are a royal priesthood, we are heirs to the throne and you are a defeated foe! We will not act like we are not God's children, we will not insult one another, we will not wear blinders over our eyes and close our ears so we may not see or hear each other's cry! Lord, please give us patience, teach us to love, not when it is easy but when it is difficult. God, you are love and please teach us to have humble and contrite spirits that we may be a representation of you. Father, this is my family, the ones you have counted and know every single hair on their heads. Please, Lord, forgive us of our sins and remove anything from us that is not like you. In the precious and powerful name of your son who died for our sins, Jesus the Christ, I pray," Faith prays.

"Me ain't tink we does have ta worry bout dis child going Muslim and leaving Jesus," Marlin whispers to Dot.

Farren, Fuchsia, Freda, Debbie and Dot are all embracing each other and weeping. Marlin and Byron look at each other and slowly find their way into the group, embracing their family.

"Lord, please forgive me! Lord, please forgive me!" Byron falls to the floor, crying, where his wife and daughters join him in weeping and crying out to the Lord.

Dot and Marlin leave the room, holding hands, walking with an extra bounce in their step and smiling.

# Chapter 21
## Closing Ceremony Hits A Snag

The damage was too extensive to the china, stemware and centerpieces for the ladies to recover and replace in such a short period of time, so the event had to be moved to another venue.

When Hope and Dominique returned to the farm that afternoon after going to St. Thomas to pick up beautiful trophies for the campers, they were devastated to see the damage that was done to the area designated for the ceremony.

Hope cried, not necessarily because of the damage to the tables and decorations, but because she felt like she had failed the project. Hope felt like the boys, Khalid and Dante, were no better than when they left Atlanta four weeks ago. She prayed that all their hard work would make a difference in their lives by giving them a chance to experience something different and surround them with loving and caring people who wanted them to succeed.

Dominique quickly knocked down any doubt she was feeling about the boys being a failure by recounting all the accomplishments they made since they arrived on the farm. This brought a smile to Hope's heart.

Dominique didn't stop there. He knew he had to make the closing ceremony a success, not only for the young people, but for the beautiful strong women from a place called Atlanta he had come to admire and love, so he walked across the road to the beautiful five-star hotel and begged them to allow the campers to use their ballroom for the closing ceremonies.

Never in his wildest thoughts could Dominique have imagined what would happen. Once he told the manager of the hotel the mission of the camp, he was so moved and praised them for helping inner city children and offered to decorate and provide a buffet for the youths and their guests, free of charge.

Dominique returned to the farm to find Hope, Dot and Marlin sitting on the porch trying to figure out how to rearrange everything and just have chairs set up for the ceremony, because the tent was still leaning.

"If we take the tent down, the people will burn up in this hot sun!" Dot complains.

"If we don't take de ting down, den de people dem might be wearing de ting on dey heads. De tent gon fall!" Marlin explains.

"Maybe we can pass out umbrellas for them to hold to keep the sun off of their heads," Hope suggests.

Dominique walks up to them, smiling like he just won the lottery.

"And what are you grinning about?" Hope questions him.

"You are going to be grinning as well when I share the good news!" Dominique says with his chest pushed out, beaming with pride.

"Well, we certainly can use some good news right about now!" Dot says in an exhausted voice, tired from trying to figure out a workable solution for their dilemma.

"I just left the Palm Hotel and the manager is so impressed with everything we are doing here on the farm with the campers that they are going to host the closing ceremony!

And… they will take care of the decorations and the food…for FREE!" Dominique proudly exclaims.

"No way, Dominique! Stop playing!" Hope yells.

Dominique nods his confirmation; Hope is beside herself jumping up and down.

"Oh my Lord! Would you look at God?" Dot is overjoyed.

"Me tink me gon cry!" Marlin says, smiling.

"I'll go call Lucille and Gloria and tell them the good news, then I'll round the campers up and head them over to the hotel," Dot says.

"I'll send out an email, Facebook, Instagram and Twitter blast to all of our guests to let them know the venue has changed," Hope says with excitement.

"Don't forget to call Fitzroy and Faith, so they can let their shuttle drivers know when our guests get off the boat they should bring them to the hotel," Dot points out.

"Good idea, sweetie. Me gon move de trophies over to de hotel and go an tank me good friend Linton George for being so generous in letting we use de facilities," Marlin adds.

"You are the best, Dominique!" Hope says and gives him a big kiss on the cheek.

Dominique is surprised and holds his cheek; he doesn't want the feeling of being kissed by Hope to go away.

Marlin laughs. "Get used to it, son, 'cause me does believe der will be more kisses coming to ya from de beautiful lady! You done good, young man! You done *real* good!"

Everyone disburses in different directions.

Only five hours ago, the camp counselors were trying to figure out how they would hold their closing ceremonies and now here they are all dressed up with their campers and their guests sitting at beautifully decorated tables inside the Palm's Coconut Ballroom under crystal chandeliers.

Faith and Fitzroy, Lisa and Billy, Gloria and Roy, Debbie and Byron, Marlin and Dot are sitting together at one of the round tables in the ballroom dressed to impress. Marlin is even is wearing a tuxedo for the first time in his life; he keeps tugging at the too-tight bow tie.

Lisa spots Cathy entering the ballroom and is surprised to see she has a very handsome man with her.

"Oh my God! Would you look at Cathy? She looks like Miss America," Faith shouts.

"Correction, I think you mean, 'Miss British Virgin Islands,' and who is that fine specimen with her? He is gorgeous!" Lisa lustfully says.

"I've never seen him around here before," Dot says, staring at the couple.

"That's Jean Paul; he's the new principal at the church school. Seems like he and Cathy met a few years ago during one of her trips to St. Martin. We hired him last week to start in the fall," Roy informs.

"Damn, I wish I wasn't married, I'd give him a run for the money!" Lisa whispers in Faith's ear.

"Married and pregnant with a fine husband of your own! Girl, don't make me have to insist Billy make you take a blood test when this baby comes!" Faith counters.

"Girl, I'm just looking! Okay? You know I'm completely satisfied with my blessings!" Lisa whispers to her friend.

"So you say! Don't forget I know all your secrets!" Faith reminds her.

"And I know all yours too, as boring as they are!" Lisa rejoins.

The ladies laugh.

Everyone waves to Cathy and Jean Paul, who takes a seat at the table next to where Faith and Lisa are sitting.

"Girl! You look good and that man looks better!" Lisa jokes.

"Yeah, I started not to bring him, thinking he might upstage me, but the man doesn't even know he's fine. Not a vain bone in his body," Cathy keeps the laugh going.

"So, how come I didn't know about this man? You've been keeping secrets!" Lisa whispers.

"Jean Paul is just a friend. When he called me to say he was going to be working in Cruz Bay and wanted to get together for lunch, I was shocked! What's the likelihood of that, and to be working at Roy's church school?" Cathy shakes her head in amazement.

"And just think about all the time you were wasting with that good for nothing man in Tortola, and you could have been with Jean Paul! What were you thinking, girl?" Lisa chastises.

"Lisa, turn your nosy behind around and pay attention. Hope is about to talk!" Cathy redirects.

"Wait, just one more question… Did you get 'little boy' cut? I don't want you to scare the man away with that thing!" Lisa asks with a serious face.

"Yes! Now turn around and get out of my business!" Cathy turns Lisa's body around.

"Praise the Lord! Praise the Lord!" Lisa loudly says.

"Praise the Lord, what?" Billy inquires.

"It's a girl thing, honey," Lisa tells her husband.

"Hey, Cathy! So glad you and Jean Paul could come. Hey, Jean Paul! Good to see you." Billy reaches over and shakes his hand.

Everyone at Faith's table waves to the new couple.

On stage is a large projection screen highlighting moments the campers shared during their four-week stay. A wild boar chasing Khalid across the farm and him climbing into a tree screaming for help. The audience roars with laughter. The next clip shows Khalid holding the newly born lamb, feeding him with a bottle, smiling like he just helped birth his own child. Aws are heard from the guests. Rochelle listens to instructions on how to mount and ride a horse, then suddenly the horse turns his head and nibbles on her blond weave hair. Rochelle screams as Marlin gets the horse to let go of her hair.

All the campers standing by Rochelle are rolling on the ground laughing. Then we see Tae in the pig pen, wearing rubber gloves, crying as one of the mother pigs gives birth and she helps the little one find its mother's nipple to nurse. The mother pig turns her head and looks at Tae as if to say 'thank you,' mother to mother. Sean gets his pilot wings from Billy and the look of jubilance on his face, then Cathy gives Kesha her flight attendant's uniform and she jumps up and down excited. In the barn, Dante learns how to milk a cow while being extra cautious that the heifer's tail doesn't smack him. His eyes dart from the tail to the udder and as much as he tries, the tail still smacks him. He throws his hands up in surrender. The guests roll with laughter.

In another clip, Dante tries to teach Charles how to sing rap music. Charles is off beat and horrible. Dante laughs and tells him to stick to producing videos. The boys shake hands in agreement, laughing. Dante, Charles and Khalid sneak into sleeping Dominique's cabin and the boys stand over his bed, dripping water from a cup on his face slowly. Dominique slaps his face, continuing to sleep until the boys increase the amount of water and he wakes up, thinking a bug is on him. He spots the boys hiding on the floor and chases them out of the cabin wearing just his boxer shorts and no shirt. Dominique manages to catch two of them and wrestles them to the ground, laughing.

The next clip shows Hope standing at a whiteboard drawing a picture of a check and all the campers intensely watching as she teaches them how to fill in a check properly. Then she passes out copies of utility bills and grocery receipts. Each person is given a calculator and the campers add up the bills. Hope draws a line on the board with the headers "Debt" and "Income."

There is a clip of Lucille showing the girls and guys how to set a table. The boys are clumsy. Dante tips a wine glass over, shrugging his shoulders he picks it up and tries again. Khalid looks bored but the ladies are paying close attention.

Next is a scene of Roy and Gloria leading a Bible study with the campers; Rochelle's hand goes up and she asks a question about marriage; Kesha's hand goes up and she asks a question about forgiveness; Khalid is seen falling asleep but is quickly nudged by Sean, who tells him to pay attention. Mookie high-fives him.

Another clip shows Dot and Marlin walking hand-in-hand toward the farmhouse and a baaing goat pushes Marlin out of the way and nestles up next to smiling Dot. Marlin yells "Dat's me woman!"

The guests laugh hard. Someone yells out, "Marlin, you got competition!"

The videos end as Hope steps out onto the stage, smiling and applauding all the campers, who are sitting at a table close to the stage. The campers stand up and applaud Hope.

"Well, looks like my sister's vision came to fruition. Look at her up there on the stage beaming with pride. Take a bow, girl! I know your mother and our father are smiling from heaven at all you've managed to accomplish," Faith says, smiling.

"Just think, it all started with a 'Cuss Jar!'" Lisa says, laughing!

"All of you guys need to take a bow! Hope couldn't have done it without the help of her newly found family," Roy points out.

"It was definitely a family affair," Fitzroy agrees.

"Speaking of family, where are Aunt Lucille and Uncle Wally? The ceremony is about to start," Debbie inquires.

"She and Wally missed the boat waiting for Lucille's hairdresser to finish doing her hair. They should be here any minute. I think Wally hired a Water Taxi." Fitzroy give the update.

"Say, Fitzroy, thanks for the dental referral! That brother really knows his stuff. You can't even see the place where the tooth broke," Byron says, showing his teeth.

"Yeah, my boy Sylvester is the best dentist around. He used to be a dentist in the military. We are so blessed to have him here on the island," Fitzroy shares.

"Speaking of blessed... did you tell him, Faith?" Lisa inquires.

"No! This is the first time I've seen him since I found out two hours ago!" Faith whispers as Hope is standing at the microphone welcoming everyone while glaring at her best friend.

Fitzroy overhears.

"Tell me what, honey?" Fitzroy casually inquires while his attention is on Hope.

"Ladies and Gentlemen, I stand before you to let you know that miracles do happen!" Hope starts out her speech.

"Faith's pregnant!" Lisa announces.

Fitzroy jumps up out of his seat, totally oblivious to the fact that Hope is speaking and yells, "Faith is pregnant!"

Everyone in the ballroom claps.

"See, just as I said, miracles do happen! Congratulations to my sister Faith and my brother-in-law Fitzroy. We'll celebrate that later, you guys. But right now I'm talking about a different miracle... I'm talking about a group of people brought here to these beautiful Virgin Islands from the worst part of Atlanta you could imagine and given a chance to see something different. These campers were given a chance to live on a farm with animals, and a group of caring and loving people. Please allow me to introduce to you to one of our campers, Rochelle Mint. Rochelle, please share with us how this experience has made a difference in your life."

Rochelle walks out onto the stage a little nervous but standing proud and ready to give her testimony. Hope walks into the wings.

"I'm a little nervous but that doesn't matter because what I need to say is more important. My name is Rochelle, and I'm the mother of a teenage son. We live in a section of Atlanta called 'The Bricks.' The Bricks will be torn down any day now, the last of the projects in our city. The Bricks were a place where many of us lived all our lives; second and third generations. So seeing the Bricks torn down is bittersweet. Bitter because it's the only home we knew; sweet because it's a dangerous place to live and raise your children. If you want to buy drugs, you can find it in the Bricks. Just ask any man, woman or even child and they can direct you to several dealers. The Bricks is a place where gunshots instead of lullabies are the sounds your children hear at bedtime. The Bricks are a place where it is a given that your boy child will be incarcerated before his sixteenth birthday, get shot or even be killed and your daughters will become pregnant before they finish high school.

"In the Bricks, the highlight of your existence is waiting for your welfare check and food stamps to come around the first of the month so you can pay a few bills, purchase groceries and I do mean pay just a few bills. Then you struggle the rest of the month to make ends meet.

"You might say, 'Well, hell, why don't you get a job and leave that life!' I hear you loud and clear but... for a lot of us it's not that easy. The unemployment rate in our neighborhood is eighteen percent, when the national average is around seven percent at its worst, and then there's discrimination; oh yes, it's alive and popping in Atlanta! To just get an interview at Walmart is an accomplishment. I mean just to be thought worthy enough to be called for an interview, even if you don't get the job, gives you something to brag about to those who never made it past the application process.

"Ninety percent of those who live in the Bricks have criminal records. Mostly petty crime like stealing from the local grocery store, smoking weed on the Boulevard, joyriding in a stolen car that your friend told you was his. When you face the judge for these small infractions, you are given time that far exceeds the crime. Your children are placed in foster care and the cycle starts all over again.

"When I was fourteen years old, I got pregnant and I was too afraid to tell my mother, who was already raising six of us without my father, who was running from the child support people. Not because he didn't love us, but because he didn't have a job and no one would hire him because of his felony record. My mother didn't discover I was pregnant until I was almost six months, and she tried to beat it out of me. But I survived, and when I turned eighteen, I got my own apartment in the Bricks a few doors down from her and my own welfare check. That was the happiest day of my life, until I came here and I thank God for a beautiful lady named Hope, who gave hope to me and my son.

"On Monday, when my son Khalid and I go back to Atlanta, we are going with a new outlook on life. My counselors here have taught me how to look online for college classes that the government will pay for, as well as housing allowances and trust me, it won't be anywhere near my old neighborhood!

"Before I sit my butt down, I have two requests of you good people. The first is, pray for my son and me; you see it took us to come all the way here from Atlanta for me to find out that a very terrible man violated my son, but with counseling and much prayers we will heal. And the second is, don't be quick to judge people who may not live the comfortable lifestyle you have been afforded because maybe all they need is a hand up and not a hand out! Thank you for listening and I will never forget this moment in my life."

Rochelle leaves the stage as Hope meets her with a big embrace. Over at the table where Faith and Fitzroy are sitting, Fitzroy embraces his wife like he's afraid to let go of her. After Rochelle finishes talking, Byron stands up and starts a standing ovation for Rochelle. Debbie beams with pride at seeing him be the first one to stand up, as well as his girls, who are sitting at another table with other teenagers.

"Me tink me gon cry!" Marlin says and Dot hugs him. Lucille and Wally enter and join Zipporah and George at an adjacent table. Lucille look fabulous, and Wally is glowing all over with pride as he pulls a chair out for his beautiful wife. Charles, who is close to the stage videotaping the event, gives Wally a thumbs up.

"Faith is pregnant!" Fitzroy hollers over to Lucille's table, like a proud poppa.

"Say what?" Lucille screams back.

"It's true! Finally!" Gloria teases.

"Okay, ladies, Hope is about to speak. Let's show respect," Roy admonishes the excited ladies.

"Congratulations, Fitzroy! I didn't know you had it in you!" Wally whispers, teasing his joyful friend.

"Now it's moments like this that make you say, 'Yeah!' This is what it's all about... helping others to help themselves. Thank you, Rochelle, for being so transparent and sharing your story with us. Hope beams as she speaks.

"This next lady I want to introduce you to I call my quiet storm. Months ago, when I was having a yard sell to get rid of all my worldly possessions, a young lady by the name of Kesha and her son Sean came by and wanted to know if I had a blender to sell. Her son asked me why I wanted to go to the islands when they have sharks down there. Little did the two of them know, they would be in the Virgin Islands attending this camp less than a year later. Friends and family, allow me to introduce you to Kesha."

Kesha takes the stage with her big Afro hairdo, hugging Hope, who exits.

"Hi, everybody! I know Rochelle said she was shy but I don't think so by the way she said all those heart-touching things so easily. Well, when I tell you I'm shy, trust me, I'm shy. But no matter how shy I am, I have to come up here and thank Miss Hope and all the counselors who are now my family because... because me and my son Sean... we ain't going back to Atlanta! We are staying right here!"

The crowd is clapping wildly. Kesha continues talking.

"I was blessed to meet Mr. Billy and his wife Lisa, who own the airline company El Shaddai. Mr. Billy, along with his stewardess Miss Cathy, are training me to run the ticket counter, so I'm staying and making the Virgin Islands me and Sean's new home! Glory! Glory! Glory!"

Kesha does a little dance like she's in church. Everyone stands and claps as Hope returns to the stage and embraces her. Kesha takes her seat.

"Now you see why I call her the quiet storm!" Everyone laughs.

Sean hugs his mother just as she is about to take her seat. "Mommy, I left my wings in the cabin and I wanted to wear them when we get our award!" Sean cries.

"Sean, you look fine without them," Kesha tries to calm him down.

"But, Mom!" Sean gives Kesha the pitiful look.

"See if one of the big boys will go with you. I don't want you crossing that road and going up in the bush by yourself," Kesha says.

"Mom, I'm not a baby!" Sean whines.

"Look, you heard what I said! Now don't bother me. I want to hear the next speaker."

Kesha smiles as Hope calls on Tae. Sean begs Khalid to go with him to the camp. Khalid realizes Sean is not going to stop asking, so he rushes the little boy out of the hotel so they can get back quickly.

Tae takes the mic and Hope leaves the stage.

"My story is a lot like Rochelle's, so I'll keep this short. What I'd like to share is for the young girls who are here. So many times our parents are the last people we listen to because for some strange reason we think they don't know anything. After we royally mess up, doing all the things they warned us about then the lightbulb turns on… wow, I should have listened to my parents! You see, I'm a victim of hardheadedness! I couldn't wait to be out on my own, get my own apartment, and find a man who I thought would complete me. Isn't that funny, I thought having a man would complete me! Wrong! After the first man I allowed into my life walked out and left me with my son, Dante, denying he was his child,

"I kicked the dust from my feet, opened my door and let another man in. Every time life beat up on him, he would beat up on me until one night he woke up to my big black frying pan banging him all over his mean bad-minded head and his clothes in trash bags on the front lawn. He decided to leave, but not before calling me every name except the child of God in front of my son.

"Now you think I would learn my lesson after all these men coming into my life like a revolving door! Nope! I still believed that my life would not be complete without a man. So my next quest was to not just find a man but to find the right man. So, I went to all the strip clubs, happy hours, and parties my limited funds would allow me to attend. It never dawned on me there were two problems; one, I was looking in the wrong places for a good man and the other was I didn't know who I was. My self-esteem was so low that I was accepting people into me and my son's life who were not worthy.

"It took me coming here to your beautiful Virgin Islands to see clearly. Living and working on the farm, I've watched how the sheep and goat take care and protect their babies. I watched how they wean them from nursing and guide them on how to look for food so they too will be good parents. I was telling my son Dante everything you need to know about life you can learn from the animals on the farm. Thank you, Hope, and all the beautiful counselors for affording me this opportunity. I have truly learned that if I don't respect myself first, no one else will."

Hope embraces Tae. "Are these beautiful stories or what?" Hope stirs up the guests, who whistle and clap.

"Now we could go on all night telling different stories, but I'd like to take this opportunity to tell you about a lady who inspired me to start the camp. Her name was Mabel and Mabel was a very special lady to me. She was my deceased mother's best friend. Mabel was strong! Strong as the Bricks, where she lived in all her life. Mabel didn't take any mess off of anyone and she would fight for you, even be willing to die for you, if someone did an injustice against you."

Kesha, Rochelle, and Tae nod their heads in agreement as Hope continues.

"Mabel is no longer with us… she died a violent death at the hands of a police officer who repeatedly shot her while she was trying to get to her son who was lying in the street murdered.

"Because of the strength of this courageous woman, I would like to name our camp Mabel's Kids. I think she would like that!"

Everyone stands, applauding. Mr. Atkins, Faith's friend and boss, come to the stage and walks up to the mic.

"Hope, your sister has been raving about you and this project since the children arrived. When she announced she was taking a month vacation from work to help, she shocked me, being that she's such a workaholic. But I know Faith; where there is a good cause, you will find her and her husband Fitzroy. Hope, on behalf of my wife and all our employees, I'd like to present you with this check to help with Mabel's Kids. It is my prayer that it will help you to reach out to children in inner cities around the world."

Hope takes the check and embraces Mr. Atkins. Hope opens the check and almost faints. Mr. Atkins holds her up.

"Oh my God, Oh my God! It's for one million dollars!" Hope is jumping up and down.

Mr. Atkins laughs at Hope's jubilance. The guests are whistling and clapping until Khalid and Sean run in screaming for help.

"The farm is on fire! The farm is on fire!" Sean and Khalid run into the ballroom shouting, putting an end to Hope's bliss.

"Did he just say the farm is on fire?" Hope says into the microphone.

"Yes! The farm is on fire! Somebody help!" Khalid cries.

"Me tink me 'ear de boy say me farm on fire!" Marlin jumps up from the table, followed by Fitzroy, Wally, Billy, Jean Paul and Roy.

"Darling, I need you to call the fire department and you ladies stay here while we go and see what's going on," Fitzroy says.

"I'd like to help!" Byron says, getting up to follow the men out of the hotel. Dominique is already across the street as soon as he heard the boys say the farm is on fire.

"There seems to be a problem over at the farm and it's being investigated. If everyone would continue to enjoy their dinner, we will be back shortly with an update," Hope says in the microphone then quickly dashes out of the hotel.

"Mom, I should go and help!" Khalid says to Rochelle. "I can help save the animals."

"Khalid, I think we should let the men handle it," Rochelle says, afraid her son might get hurt.

"Mom, what kind of man would I be if I don't help at a time like this? Besides, I have to make sure baby Khalid, the lamb named after me, is safe!" the boy pleads.

"I'm sure he's fine!" Rochelle says, trying to comfort her son.

"You don't know that, Mom! I'm responsible for him and I need to make sure. Please, Mom... I need to do this!"

"He's right, Miss Rochelle. We should go and make sure all the animals are safe; they were our responsibilities," Dante says.

"I'm in, too!" Charles says.

"Tae, are you okay with this?"

Tae nods her head. "Okay! But just be careful."

Khalid kisses his mom and the young men run to help.

The farm is burning fast, and the men are doing everything they can to get the animals off the farm. Dominique is herding the pigs across the road to the beach; Byron is leading two horses across the street and tying them up to a coconut tree on the sand. Marlin and Roy are herding a family of goats and sheep across the road. Hope, still wearing her formal dress, carries two baby kids in her arms, crying out to the boys to grab some of the animals. Khalid sees his namesake sheep crying for his mother by the side of the barn and runs and swoops him up in his arms, reassuring him that everything is going to be okay. Dante jumps on the backs of one of the horses and rides him to safety on the beach.

Byron runs back across the road to the farm, ties a rope around the neck of a cow and leads her away from the fire. Marlin is standing next to him, trying to steer the baby calves to follow.

"Me proud of you, son!" Marlin says to Byron.

"Well, Pops, I'd be lying if I didn't tell you I'm operating outside of my comfort zone, but somehow it feels so good! Come on… let's move it! Move it!" Byron yells to the cow as he pulls the rope.

Dot, unable to sit in the hotel knowing there is a fire crosses the road, leaves, only to find their house is engulfed in flames. Dot stands at the side of the dirt road in tears.

"My darling, please go back to de hotel! Please, my sweetie. Me would not want to live if some ting happens to you!" Marlin begs his wife as he ushers the animals to safety.

"Who would do something like this? I don't understand! Who would do this?" Dot falls to the ground in her grown, weeping. Marlin picks his wife up and exhorts her to the safety of the hotel.

"My darling, we are safe and de house we can build again. No need to trouble your head. Me promise you de farm will come back better dan before. Now I does need you to trust me and go back inside wit de ladies and dry your tears. Your Mango Man gon make every ting good."

Marlin kisses Dot, who goes back inside the hotel. The firemen are fighting the flames with a vengeance as the older men and younger men watch the charred cabins fall to the ground under the pressure of the powerful water hose.

Local people who are trying to pass the road in their cars pull over to the side, getting out and asking how they can help.

"Tank you so much, me friend! Please help save de animals," Marlin begs.

Several men and women race up the dirt road to help guide the animals across the street to the beach.

"Say, Mango Man! Put some of the animals on my truck and I will take them out to my farm in Coral Bay for safety. I'll even drop some by me brother's place near the clinic!" says a fellow farmer who pulls over to the side of the road with his large trailer truck.

"Tank you, my friend! Tank you so much!" Marlin cries as the truck driver gets out of the large truck and lowers the automatic lift. Police officers and everyday citizens help herd the animals into the truck.

Just when Marlin didn't think it could get any better, he sees other neighbors pull up with their trucks, some small and some large, and help herd the animals into their vehicles.

"Everything is gone! Everything is gone!" Hope cries and Dominique holds her in his arms.

"Everything is not gone! We are here, and we will not be defeated! We will rebuild this camp bigger and stronger than ever! You will see! Dry your tears, my lady, because I promise you this wrong will be made right! Look, look at all the people who have come to help!"

"Wow! Would you look at that? Now I'm crying tears of joy! Just look at all these people, Dominique! Where did they all come from? Thank, thank you!" Hope hollers out to everyone who passes her.

Hope and Dominique walk across the road together, their clothes dirty and their faces covered in soot, but they walk hand-in-hand into the ballroom with confidence, passing Khalid, who is holding on to his baby sheep like it's his first born.

"Khalid, you think you should be bringing the animal in here?" Hope asks

"Miss Hope, I just need to know he's going to be safe! I'm all he has now," Khalid sadly says.

"Young man, I believe his mother is being loaded onto one of the trucks outside. Go and find her. She'll be so grateful to you." Dominique advises the smiling young boy, who races outside to find the crying lamb's mother.

Lucille and Gloria comfort their sister Dot, who is still trying to understand what's happening.

Farren, who is sitting at her grandmother's side, speaks words of comfort. "Nana, don't cry. Remember the man just gave the camp a million dollars. Do you think that might be enough to rebuild the camp?"

"You know, I think she has a point there, Dot!" Lucille says, laughing.

"I didn't think of that!" Dot says, feeling somewhat better.

"What someone met for evil… God met for good!" Gloria chimes in.

Many of the guests stop by her table to offer their symphony and leave checks on the table for donations to the camp as they exit the hotel.

Linda Peters, Marlin's great-niece, stops at the table and embraces Faith and kisses Dot. "Don't worry the truth will come to light sooner than later and expose the wicked people who did this. You know I'm still in college and working part-time at the television studio, but I'd be so happy if you would accept my check. It's not much, but it might help replace a table or cabinet or something small," Linda says with sincerity.

"Aw, Linda, that's so thoughtful of you!" Dot says, hugging the young girl.

"You're the best, Linda!" Faith joins in the group hug as Linda leaves smiling and so happy she could help in some way.

"Don't forget what that young lady Hope said... 'God is in the miracle business.'" a lady says to Dot as she puts a check on the table and exits with her husband.

"Now when you catch whoever did dis 'ere ting, me could call me cousin ta take care of de situation. Him don't mind going back ta jail, it's he second home," Camille says to Faith.

"Gil, de lady married to a detective, you can't be saying tings like dat!" Denisha admonishes her best friend.

Faith laughs. "Thank you, Camille, but I'm going to just trust God that we won't need to hurt anyone. But thank you so much for your thoughtfulness." Faith hugs Camille and Denisha.

"Now, Mrs. Faith, you does know we come into some reward money and we can't tink of a better situation dan dis ta part wit some of we money. So we like ta give de camp dis 'ere small token." Denisha reaches in her bra and pulls out a wad of cash. "Now me ain't sure if you little breast can hold dis 'ere five thousand dollars, so you might want ta see if Mrs. Dot can hold it fa ya!"

The ladies all laugh. Faith and Dot are in tears. Denisha and Camille hug everyone as they leave. Once at the exit, Camille looks back and gives Faith the "call me" sign, indicating that if she needs her cousin he's available. Denisha grabs her friend and pulls her out of the hotel.

"All of you are in Rosalinda and my prayers. Don't fret, my dear, we are just a phone call away, Dot. And, Faith, congratulations to you and my boy Fitzroy, what a blessing! Oh, by the way... I look forward to seeing you back at work next week." Mr. Atkins gives Faith a kiss on the cheek.

"Mr. Atkins, I just don't know how to thank you for your generous gift!" Faith says, hugging him.

"Thank you so much, Mr. Atkins," Gloria says.

"You really went above and beyond, old Georgie Boy!" Lucille teases.

"I can't think of a better project to spend God's money on. You know it's been a while since you guys have been over to St. Croix to visit us. What do you say after we finish rebuilding this camp, we all get together?" Mr. Atkins urges.

"Sounds like a plan to me," Lucille eagerly agrees.

"I might have to take a rain check; Roy and I will be in Nevis for a few months," Gloria says smiling.

"Well, I guess I lost the bet to my wife," Mr. Atkins confesses.

"Bet? What bet?" Gloria wants to know.

"Well, several months ago when Rosalinda and I were over to meet Faith's new sister Hope for the celebration you guys had for her, Rosalinda said she could see how much Roy loved you, Gloria, and I told her no way! Now, of course I had no business betting her, because you women have radar for these things but it just seemed so farfetched." Mr. Atkins laughs.

"How much did you bet?" Farren asks.

"Farren! That's none of your business!" Dot admonishes her.

"Well, hell, I want to know. How much, Georgie Boy!" Lucille inquires. Everyone waits to hear.

"Oh, Just two," Mr. Atkins casually says.

"Come on, Georgie, only two hundred dollars! You're slipping. For a man of your means that's Cracker Jack money!" Lucille teases.

"Actually it was two million!" Mr. Atkins hugs Lucille and exits the hotel laughing.

Zipporah and George, who have just come from outside, approach the table.

"Me tank God de fire out and no one was hurt. Me just keep praying and praying as me watch all de people come and help," Zipporah shares.

"I'm going to go ride with one of the truckers and help him unload the animals. I just came in to let you know there is no need to worry, Dot. You guys have offered a great program here for these young people and no matter how bleak things look, it's going to be okay." George kisses Dot on the cheek and exits.

"Now that's one bet I would have lost if someone told me I would live to see the day George talked to Dot like that. Honey, I would have bet four million!" Lucille says, laughing and everyone joins in.

Jean Paul enters the hotel, dirty and sweaty. "Cathy, you think you can get one of the ladies to drop you to the boat? I'd like to continue helping with the animals. I know you're on duty and have a flight to catch shortly?"

"No problem, Jean Paul. I'll get to the boat okay." Cathy gives him a peck on the cheek with all eyes looking.

"I'm going to round the girls up and take them up to the house, Mother. You want to go with us?" Debbie asks.

"You guys go ahead. I'm going to hang around here and wait for Marlin," Dot says.

"All of the men have gone out to Coral Bay to help with de animals," Zipporah says.

"In that case, then us women can just collect all these checks and head up to Bordeaux!" Lucille suggests.

"We haven't thought about what we are going to do with the campers," Faith says.

"They can all just go to my Chocolate Hole house!" Lisa offers.

"That's so thoughtful of you, Lisa." Dot hugs her.

"Please. I'm so happy to have someone using the house," Lisa says, smiling.

"I'll go with you, Lisa, to take them over to the house. Charles's mom will probably want us to put him on the ferryboat to St. Thomas," Faith says.

"I'm surprised her over-protective behind isn't here standing over her precious Charles with a microscope, making sure every strand of hair is just the way it was when he left home," Lisa says, laughing.

"Since that whole episode with her thinking Dante and Charles were gay happened and how she exploded and took the boy out of the camp, only to find out none of it was true, may have left her a little embarrassed to show her face around here."

"Besides, there is no way Charles is going to miss the closing ceremony! No way! Charles probably will not go home until the last child has boarded the airplane tomorrow," Hope adds.

"You know that's right. That young man is joined at the hip with these kids," Dot adds.

"I don't think the poor child has ever had any friends. And I blame it on his over-protective momma! Thank God for Wally stepping in and saving that boy!" Lucille chimes in.

"Make sure you check everyone's luggage just before they board the plane because you might find Charles hiding inside!" Dot teases.

"The girls and I will go up to the house and sort through our clothes and give them to the young ladies. I think the boys are about the same size as Byron. I'll gather up some of his clothes. I don't know about Charles; he's a little small," Debbie says.

"Some of Billy's clothes are at the house and they should fit Charles. There are plenty of extra toothbrushes and hygiene stuff at the house, so that's taken care of as well," Lisa says.

"What do you say we all meet at the Chocolate Hole house around seven for dinner?" Lisa proposes.

"So, we'll finish the closing the closing ceremony at Lisa's place, but what are we going to do about all this food the guests didn't eat?" Hope wonders.

"We will just ask if the hotel will offer delivery service to the Chocolate Hole house, the hospital, the fire station, the police station and then the celebration will continue at the house! Now that we solved that, let's move on to the next problem… rebuilding the camp!" Lucille hollers.

"Yes, rebuilding the camp!" Dot says in a weak voice.

Everyone laughs and starts to exit the hotel but not before the hotel manager, who is holding a video camera in his hand, stops them.

"Ladies, I am so sorry to hear about your loss and if there is anything we can do at the hotel to make your transition to your next place a smooth one, please don't hesitate to call on us, after all we are sitting on the land your husband owns, Mrs. Dot."

"Thank you so much. How kind," Dot replies.

"As a matter-of-fact, we were just about to call on you to see if you would have all this leftover food delivered so it would not go to waste," Hope inquires.

"No problem, but, ladies, there is something I need to share with you; please allow me to connect my video camera to your projector on stage. Have a seat."

Hope follows the hotel manager to the stage area while the other ladies take a seat close to the stage, waiting with anticipation to see what is so important.

"What do you think it is, Nana?" Farren asks.

"I'm not sure, honey. I just hope it's not any more bad news; I don't think my heart could take anything else today," Dot sadly says.

"Don't worry, Dot, we're here with you." Gloria squeezes her sister's hand.

"That's right, Aunt Dot!" Faith chimes in.

"I think I'm going to fix me a plate before the show starts. You know I'm eating for two. You want to join me, Faith?" Lisa gets up to fix a plate.

"You go ahead. I'm having trouble holding food down." Faith sits in anticipation of what's about to come on the video screen.

On the video screen, Chee-Chee's big yellow Hummer is parked in front of the farm. Then Chee-Chee walks up the road toward the Hummer with a gas can; she puts some gas in the vehicle then climbs up the grassy embankment with the gas can and pours gas all around the property and sets it on fire. The flames almost catch her; running, she jumps into her vehicle and drives up the road to the house, where she pours gas on the house and the nearby barn. She runs and jumps into the vehicle once again, taking off toward town.

Everyone is quiet and in shock. Dot sobs uncontrollably. Lisa pushes her plate of food away. Faith is sick and runs to the ladies' room to throw up. Gloria follows her.

"That wicked girl!" Cathy cries.

"Nothing but the devil! After all Marlin did for her and she isn't even his child!" Dot screams.

"This hurts! And I know it's going to kill Marlin when he sees this. How low can a person go?" Lucille says with anger.

"Please can you keep this video on the screen until the men return?" Dot asks the manager.

"But of course! You ladies go ahead and I'll see that my staff delivers the food to the destinations of your choice. And again, I am so sorry for your loss."

Everyone leaves the ballroom, quietly reflecting on what they just saw. They split up into different cars and head over to Chocolate Hole.

Faith sends a text message telling Fitzroy and the men to go to the hotel as soon as they finish to see the video. She didn't give too much details in her text because she knew seeing the video would be enough pain for the men.

It didn't take long for the campers to get comfortable at Lisa's house. Tae and Rochelle had to beg their sons to get out of the pool and eat. Sean and Mookie were exhausted and knocked out on the living room couch with one of them holding the remote control in his hand.

Debbie and her oldest daughter, Little Faith, arrive with clothes for the campers; Dot, Gloria and Faith decided to head back to the house with them. Everyone was exhausted. Lisa said she would come up after she dropped Cathy and Kesha to the boat to go to work and pick up the little ones from the babysitter. Lisa left Tae and Rochelle in charge of managing the house and the two ladies beamed with pride to be given such a responsibility of taking care of what in their eyes was a palace.

The men arrived at the hotel, beat down and extremely tired. They watched the video in silence until it ended.

"I'll go and arrest her; is she still living by Mrs. Caldwell?" Fitzroy inquires.

"She dere! Me gon go wit you, Fitz! De child done lost she mind an me does need ta be dere ta see she face when you take she fa justice." Marlin rises up out of his chair.

"Me want ta tank you mens for all your help! Me gon go wit me friend 'ere and take care of de matter. Please keep me and me family in your prayers."

The men fist bump and hug as they exit.

"Hold up, I'm going with you!" Roy hollers out to his son and Marlin.

The men find Chee-Chee's big yellow vehicle parked in front of her little cottage, littered with debris. A trail of empty Guinness stout bottles lead them to the front door, where Fitzroy knocks with Marlin and Roy standing next to him. Chee-Chee pulls back the tattered curtains and looks out of the window to see who it is.

"We know you're in there, Chee-Chee, so come on out. We need to talk to you," Fitzroy says.

"Yeah bring ya backside out 'ere! Me know you does burn down me farm," Marlin yells.

"Calm down, Marlin, we don't want to scare her. We need her to open the door," Roy admonishes him.

"Open de door? Me goin kick de raggedy door in if she don't come out! De girl bad-minded!"

"Marlin, just let me handle this," Fitzroy calmly says as the door slowly opens.

"Chee-Chee, I need you to step outside," Fitzroy says just as Chee-Chee points a small revolver out the door and shoots it, hitting Fitzroy in the shoulder.

Marlin is out of his mind and rushes the door open, tackling Chee-Chee to the floor. He kicks the revolver away and smacks her repeatedly in the face. Roy rushes to his son, who is bleeding, takes off his dress shirt and applies pressure to the wound. Fitzroy is sitting on the ground.

A neighbor calls the for police help. When they are told Detective Fitzroy has been shot, every police officer in town arrives, as well as the fire department and an ambulance. Chee-Chee is pretty banged up and complaining that she wants Marlin arrested for assault and battery. When asked if she has a witness, her neighbors turn their backs and walk into their homes.

Someone yells out, "I think she fell on a Guinness bottle."

Fitzroy want to walk to the ambulance, but no one is allowing it. He is carried on a stretcher to the road, where the ambulance with its bright red light and blaring siren is getting everyone's attention, including Lisa, who is driving up Jacob's Ladder with her little girls. Lisa spots Fitzroy on the stretcher being loaded into the ambulance.

"Oh my God! Oh my God! Is he okay?" she hollers out of the window to Roy, who is about to climb into the ambulance.

"Yes! And please don't upset Faith! Just tell her to come to the clinic," Roy says as the ambulance pulls away.

Marlin gets into the police cruiser as they haul Chee-Chee away to the police station.

Lisa is so nervous she has to pull over to the side of the road to get to her cellphone. Kamari is crying.

"What's wrong with Uncle, Mommy!" Kamari cries.

"He's going to be all right, honey," Lisa tries to comfort her as she dumps her purse out on the front seat of the car and retrieves her phone, calling Faith.

"Faith, you need to come to the clinic now! Fitzroy has been shot! Tell Mother Gloria to come too so she can take the kids. I need to be in that room when they dress his wounds. I don't trust these people to stitch up an iguana, let alone my brother-in-law."

The phone is quiet.

"Faith are you there? Faith! Girl, give Mother Gloria the phone!"

Faith collapses down on the couch in tears. Gloria takes the phone from her and listens as Lisa repeats herself; Gloria yells for Dot, Debbie, Byron and the girls to come and sit with fragile Faith while she goes to the clinic.

Byron can see his mother-in-law is nervous, so he insists on going and driving. Gloria kisses her daughter and tells her to fret not. God has Fitzroy in the palm of His hands.

# Chapter 22
## It's Hard Saying Good-Bye

Fitzroy's van pulls up to the airport. Behind him, Lisa and Billy park, followed by Cathy and Jean Paul, Hope and Dominique and behind them Dot and Marlin. Faith gets out and opens the passenger's door for Fitzroy, whose shoulder is heavily bandaged and his arm is in a sling. This doesn't stop him from getting out of the van and passing out 'Official Business' laminated signs for everyone to put in their car window.

"You sure this is legal, son?" Roy laughs.

"Don't you know he's the man around here?" Khalid fist pounds Fitzroy.

"Hey, not so hard! Can't you see the man is wounded?" Faith teases.

"Besides, the man is taking a leave of absence and we are going to Nevis until this baby is born," Faith says, beaming.

"Aw, man! Then how are we going to see you when we come back for winter camp?" Dante says as he pulls several bags of luggage out of the van and places them on the curb. Billy helps him with the heavy ones.

"I guess I'll just have to fly you guys to Nevis!" Billy says smiling.

"No way! No way! You're kidding, right!" Dante screams.

"He looks pretty serious to me," Byron says as he helps his daughters take their luggage out of Dot's truck. "Honey, you want to go and check in while I help the others?" Byron says to smiling Debbie.

"Did I hear someone say we're going to Nevis?" Hope inquires.

"No. Just the guys!" Dante quickly chimes his response.

"Yeah, right! Then I certainly won't be going with a bunch of guys. I need this beautiful lady with me," Dominique says, smiling at Hope, who smiles back.

"All right, all right, it's like that! Then when I come back, I'm going to bring my woman with me!" Dante brags.

Everyone pauses and looks at him.

"Got you! I'm talking about my momma! Now!"

"You better be!" Fitzroy warns.

Rochelle walks over to Fitzroy and Faith and hugs Faith.

"Now this hug is for you and your husband; being in the condition he's in, I don't want to hurt him with this giant, thank you for everything hug!" The women embrace as smiling Fitzroy watches.

"No, thank you, Rochelle. I hope you know how much you have blessed us. Remember we are just a phone call away if you need us." Faith takes an extra hug as tearful Rochelle steps into the ticket area.

Tourists, locals and taxi drivers watch as hugs are passed around by everyone, causing them to smile. Several locals who heard about Fitzroy's incident on the radio and television stop by to wish him a speedy recovery.

Cathy and Kesha bid everyone a farewell as they enter the airport to the El Shaddai ticket counter. Sean kisses his mom and departing Mookie hugs her.

"Mom, we'll meet you guys in customs," Dante says as he and Khalid race into the terminal to take care of some unfinished business.

"Where are you going? The flight is going to leave soon?" Rochelle asks them.

"To take care of some unfinished business. It won't take long." Both reply in concert.

Fitzroy follows the boys inside the terminal and see them stick their heads into Red's duty-free store.

Red comes to the door of the shop. "If you want trouble, I can provide you with some, now move away from me shop!" Red accosts.

"Sir, we just wanted to say we're sorry for disrespecting you and your business and would be happy if you would accept our apology." Dante and Khalid extend a hand for a shake.

Red spots Fitzroy in the background, who nods his head. Red shakes the boys' hands, pulling them into him for a hug.

"All right! Now go on and catch your flight and you better be good or you gon have to answer to me! Go on!" Red says, trying to sound tough with a smile on his face.

Red gives Fitzroy a thumbs up as the boys walk toward Fitzroy.

"Hey, you following us! I thought you were out of the business!" Dante teases.

"Who me? Follow you guys? Never! I just wanted to give you this before you boarded." Fitzroy reaches into his pocket and pulls out two envelopes. One for each of the boys. They rip the envelope open, dropping the paper to the floor.

"Hey! It's a money order for one thousand dollars!" Khalid screams.

"We can't take this!" Dante tries to hand it back.

"Speak for yourself, dude!" Khalid pushes his friend as he studies the money order.

"We made a bet, and I told you I would hold true to my end of the bargain!" Fitzroy says, smiling.

"No, man, we said we wouldn't cuss and we did," Dante says.

"A few times here and there, but I made the bet with you, hoping you would become men and not those hoodlums I met when you got off the plane… and look at you. You boys have become men and that's why you are winners. Now the money does come with a caveat," Fitzroy says.

"Is that something you eat!" Khalid asks.

"No, man, it means it comes with stipulations," Dante explains.

"It means that you are allowed to spend fifty percent of the money and the rest is for the first month tuition to your new school," Fitzroy says.

"New school? What new school?" Khalid is confused.

"Pastor Byron is going to look into putting you boys in a private school where you'll have a better chance of survival," Fitzroy says, smiling.

"I'm in, as long as they have some chicks in that school," Khalid says.

"Yeah, man, we ain't up for them all-boys' schools. We have to be around some honeys!" Dante adds.

"I'll make sure Byron knows that! Come on, watch the arm and give the old man a hug!" Fitzroy embraces the boys and watches them walk into the customs area, waving back to him with giant smiles on their faces.

"We love you, dude!" Dante yells.

# The End

www.ingramcontent.com/pod-product-compliance
Lightning Source LLC
Chambersburg PA
CBHW071851290426
44110CB00013B/1106